I0876850

Also from Veloce Publishing –

Speedpro Series
- Jaguar XK Engines, How to Power Tune – Revised & Updated Colour Edition (Hammill)

Essential Buyer's Guide Series
- Jaguar E-Type 3.8 & 4.2-litre (Crespin)
- Jaguar E-type V12 5.3-litre (Crespin)
- Jaguar Mark 1 & 2 (All models including Daimler 2.5-litre V8) 1955 to 1969 (Thorley)
- Jaguar S-Type – 1999 to 2007 (Thorley)
- Jaguar X-Type – 2001 to 2009 (Thorley)
- Jaguar XJ-S (Crespin)
- Jaguar XJ6, XJ8 & XJR (Thorley)
- Jaguar XK 120, 140 & 150 (Thorley)
- Jaguar XK8 & XKR (1996-2005) (Thorley)
- Jaguar/Daimler XJ 1994-2003 (Crespin)
- Jaguar/Daimler XJ40 (Crespin)
- Jaguar/Daimler XJ6, XJ12 & Sovereign (Crespin)

Great Cars
- Austin-Healey – A celebration of the fabulous 'Big' Healey (Piggott)
- Jaguar E-type (Thorley)
- Jaguar Mark 1 & 2 (Thorley)
- Triumph TR – TR2 to 6: The last of the traditional sports cars (Piggott)

General
- 1½-litre GP Racing 1961-1965 (Whitelock)
- AC Two-litre Saloons & Buckland Sportscars (Archibald)
- Alfa Romeo 155/156/147 Competition Touring Cars (Collins)
- Alfa Romeo Giulia Coupé GT & GTA (Tipler)
- Alfa Romeo Montreal – The dream car that came true (Taylor)
- Alfa Romeo Montreal – The Essential Companion (Classic Reprint of 500 copies) (Taylor)
- Alfa Tipo 33 (McDonough & Collins)
- Alpine & Renault – The Development of the Revolutionary Turbo F1 Car 1968 to 1979 (Smith)
- Alpine & Renault – The Sports Prototypes 1963 to 1969 (Smith)
- Alpine & Renault – The Sports Prototypes 1973 to 1978 (Smith)
- An Austin Anthology (Stringer)
- An Incredible Journey (Falls & Reisch)
- Anatomy of the Classic Mini (Huthert & Ely)
- Anatomy of the Works Minis (Moylan)
- Armstrong-Siddeley (Smith)
- Art Deco and British Car Design (Down)
- Austin Cars 1948 to 1990 – a pictorial history (Rowe)
- Autodrome (Collins & Ireland)
- Automotive A-Z, Lane's Dictionary of Automotive Terms (Lane)
- Automotive Mascots (Kay & Springate)
- Bahamas Speed Weeks, The (O'Neil)
- Bentley Continental, Corniche and Azure (Bennett)
- Bentley MkVI, Rolls-Royce Silver Wraith, Dawn & Cloud/Bentley R & S-Series (Nutland)
- Bluebird CN7 (Stevens)
- BMC Competitions Department Secrets (Turner, Chambers & Browning)
- BMW 5-Series (Cranswick)
- BMW Z-Cars (Taylor)
- BMW Boxer Twins 1970-1995 Bible, The (Falloon)
- BMW Cafe Racers (Cloesen)
- BMW Classic 5 Series 1972 to 2003 (Cranswick)
- BMW Custom Motorcycles – Choppers, Cruisers, Bobbers, Trikes & Quads (Cloesen)
- BMW – The Power of M (Vivian)
- Bonjour – Is this Italy? (Turner)
- British 250cc Racing Motorcycles (Pereira)
- British at Indianapolis, The (Wagstaff)
- British Café Racers (Cloesen)
- British Cars, The Complete Catalogue of, 1895-1975 (Culshaw & Horrobin)
- British Custom Motorcycles – The Brit Chop – choppers, cruisers, bobbers & trikes (Cloesen)
- BRM – A Mechanic's Tale (Salmon)
- BRM V16 (Ludvigsen)
- BSA Bantam Bible, The (Henshaw)
- BSA Motorcycles – the final evolution (Jones)
- Bugatti – The eight-cylinder Touring Cars 1920-34 (Price & Arbey)
- Bugatti Type 40 (Price)
- Bugatti 46/50 Updated Edition (Price & Arbey)
- Bugatti T44 & T49 (Price & Arbey)
- Bugatti 57 2nd Edition (Price)
- Bugatti Type 57 Grand Prix – A Celebration (Tomlinson)
- Caravan, Improve & Modify Your (Porter)
- Caravans, The Illustrated History 1919-1959 (Jenkinson)
- Caravans, The Illustrated History From 1960 (Jenkinson)
- Carrera Panamericana, La (Tipler)
- Car-tastrophes – 80 automotive atrocities from the past 20 years (Honest John, Fowler)
- Chrysler 300 – America's Most Powerful Car 2nd Edition (Ackerson)
- Chrysler PT Cruiser (Ackerson)
- Citroën DS (Bobbitt)
- Classic British Car Electrical Systems (Astley)
- Cobra – The Real Thing! (Legate)
- Competition Car Aerodynamics 3rd Edition (McBeath)
- Competition Car Composites A Practical Handbook (Revised 2nd Edition) (McBeath)
- Concept Cars, How to illustrate and design – New 2nd Edition (Dewey)
- Cortina – Ford's Bestseller (Robson)
- Cosworth – The Search for Power (6th edition) (Robson)
- Coventry Climax Racing Engines (Hammill)
- Daily Mirror 1970 World Cup Rally 40, The (Robson)
- Daimler SP250 New Edition (Long)
- Datsun Fairlady Roadster to 280ZX – The Z-Car Story (Long)
- Dino – The V6 Ferrari (Long)
- Dodge Challenger & Plymouth Barracuda (Grist)
- Dodge Charger – Enduring Thunder (Ackerson)
- Dodge Dynamite! (Grist)
- Dorset from the Sea – The Jurassic Coast from Lyme Regis to Old Harry Rocks photographed from its best viewpoint (also Souvenir Edition) (Belasco)
- Draw & Paint Cars – How to (Gardiner)
- Drive on the Wild Side, A – 20 Extreme Driving Adventures From Around the World (Weaver)
- Ducati 750 Bible, The (Falloon)
- Ducati 750 SS 'round-case' 1974, The Book of the (Falloon)
- Ducati 860, 900 and Mille Bible, The (Falloon)
- Ducati Monster Bible (New Updated & Revised Edition), The (Falloon)
- Ducati Story, The - 6th Edition (Falloon)
- Ducati 916 (updated edition) (Falloon)
- Dune Buggy, Building A – The Essential Manual (Shakespeare)
- Dune Buggy Files (Hale)
- Dune Buggy Handbook (Hale)
- East German Motor Vehicles in Pictures (Suhr/Weinreich)
- Fast Ladies – Female Racing Drivers 1888 to 1970 (Bouzanquet)
- Fate of the Sleeping Beauties, The (op de Weegh/Hottendorff/op de Weegh)
- Ferrari 288 GTO, The Book of the (Sackey)
- Ferrari 333 SP (O'Neil)
- Fiat & Abarth 124 Spider & Coupé (Tipler)
- Fiat & Abarth 500 & 600 – 2nd Edition (Bobbitt)
- Fiats, Great Small (Ward)
- Fine Art of the Motorcycle Engine, The (Peirce)
- Ford Cleveland 335-Series V8 engine 1970 to 1982 – The Essential Source Book (Hammill)
- Ford F100/F150 Pick-up 1948-1996 (Ackerson)
- Ford F150 Pick-up 1997-2005 (Ackerson)
- Ford Focus WRC (Robson)
- Ford GT – Then, and Now (Streather)
- Ford GT40 (Legate)
- Ford Midsize Muscle – Fairlane, Torino & Ranchero (Cranswick)
- Ford Model Y (Roberts)
- Ford Small Block V8 Racing Engines 1962-1970 – The Essential Source Book (Hammill)
- Ford Thunderbird From 1954, The Book of the (Long)
- Formula One - The Real Score? (Harvey)
- Formula 5000 Motor Racing, Back then … and back now (Lawson)
- Forza Minardi! (Vigar)
- France: the essential guide for car enthusiasts – 200 things for the car enthusiast to see and do (Parish)
- Franklin's Indians (Sucher/Pickering/Diamond/Havelin)
- From Crystal Palace to Red Square – A Hapless Biker's Road to Russia (Turner)
- Funky Mopeds (Skelton)
- The Good, the Mad and the Ugly … not to mention Jeremy Clarkson (Dron)
- Grand Prix Ferrari – The Years of Enzo Ferrari's Power, 1948-1980 (Pritchard)
- Grand Prix Ford – DFV-powered Formula 1 Cars (Robson)
- GT – The World's Best GT Cars 1953-73 (Dawson)
- Hillclimbing & Sprinting – The Essential Manual (Short & Wilkinson)
- Honda NSX (Long)
- How to Restore & Improve Classic Car Suspension, Steering & Wheels (Parish, translator)
- Immortal Austin Seven (Morgan)
- Inside the Rolls-Royce & Bentley Styling Department – 1971 to 2001 (Hull)
- Intermeccanica – The Story of the Prancing Bull (McCredie & Reisner)
- Italian Cafe Racers (Cloesen)
- Italian Custom Motorcycles (Cloesen)
- Jaguar E-type Racing Cars (Griffiths)
- Jaguar, The Rise of (Price)
- Jaguar XJ 220 – The Inside Story (Moreton)
- Jaguar XJ-S, The Book of the (Long)
- Japanese Custom Motorcycles – The Nippon Chop – Chopper, Cruiser, Bobber, Trikes and Quads (Cloesen)
- Jeep CJ (Ackerson)
- Jeep Wrangler (Ackerson)
- The Jowett Jupiter – The car that leaped to fame (Nankivell)
- Karmann-Ghia Coupé & Convertible (Bobbitt)
- Kawasaki Triples Bible, The (Walker)
- Kawasaki Z1 Story, The (Sheehan)
- Kris Meeke – Intercontinental Rally Challenge Champion (McBride)
- Lamborghini Miura Bible, The (Sackey)
- Lamborghini Urraco, The Book of the (Landsem)
- Lambretta Bible, The (Davies)
- Lancia 037 (Collins)
- Lancia Delta HF Integrale (Blaettel & Wagner)
- Lancia Delta Integrale (Collins)
- Land Rover Series III Reborn (Porter)
- Land Rover, The Half-ton Military (Cook)
- Laverda Twins & Triples Bible 1968-1986 (Falloon)
- Lea-Francis Story, The (Price)
- Le Mans Panoramic (Ireland)
- Lexus Story, The (Long)
- Little book of microcars, the (Quellin)
- Little book of smart, the – New Edition (Jackson)
- Little book of trikes, the (Quellin)
- Lola – The Illustrated History (1957-1977) (Starkey)
- Lola – All the Sports Racing & Single-seater Racing Cars 1978-1997 (Starkey)
- Lola T70 – The Racing History & Individual Chassis Record – 4th Edition (Starkey)
- Lotus 18 Colin Chapman's U-turn (Whitelock)
- Lotus 49 (Oliver)
- Marketingmobiles, The Wonderful Wacky World of (Hale)
- Maserati 250F In Focus (Pritchard)
- Mazda MX-5/Miata 1.6 Enthusiast's Workshop Manual (Grainger & Shoemark)
- Mazda MX-5/Miata 1.8 Enthusiast's Workshop Manual (Grainger & Shoemark)
- Mazda MX-5 Miata, The book of the – The 'Mk1' NA-series 1988 to 1997 (Long)
- Mazda MX-5 Miata Roadster (Long)
- Mazda Rotary-engined Cars (Cranswick)
- Maximum Mini (Booij)
- Meet the English (Bowie)
- Mercedes-Benz SL – R230 series 2001 to 2011 (Long)
- Mercedes-Benz SL – W113-series 1963-1971 (Long)
- Mercedes-Benz SL & SLC – 107-series 1971-1989 (Long)
- Mercedes-Benz SLK – R170 series 1996-2004 (Long)
- Mercedes-Benz SLK – R171 series 2004-2011 (Long)
- Mercedes-Benz W123-series – All models 1976 to 1986 (Long)
- Mercedes G-Wagen (Long)
- MGA (Price Williams)
- MGB & MGB GT– Expert Guide (Auto-doc Series) (Williams)
- MGB Electrical Systems Updated & Revised Edition (Astley)
- Micro Caravans (Jenkinson)
- Micro Trucks (Mort)
- Microcars at Large! (Quellin)
- Mini Cooper – The Real Thing! (Tipler)
- Mini Minor to Asia Minor (West)
- Mitsubishi Lancer Evo, The Road Car & WRC Story (Long)
- Montlhéry, The Story of the Paris Autodrome (Boddy)
- MOPAR Muscle - Barracuda, Dart & Valiant 1960-1980 (Cranswick)
- Morgan Maverick (Lawrence)
- Morgan 3 Wheeler – back to the future!, The (Dron)
- Morris Minor, 60 Years on the Road (Newell)
- Moto Guzzi Sport & Le Mans Bible, The (Falloon)
- The Moto Guzzi Story - 3rd Edition (Falloon)
- Motor Movies – The Posters! (Veysey)
- Motor Racing – Reflections of a Lost Era (Carter)
- Motor Racing – The Pursuit of Victory 1930-1962 (Carter)
- Motor Racing – The Pursuit of Victory 1963-1972 (Wyatt/Sears)
- Motor Racing Heroes – The Stories of 100 Greats (Newman)
- Motorcycle Apprentice (Cakebread)
- Motorcycle GP Racing in the 1960s (Pereira)
- Motorcycle Road & Racing Chassis Designs (Noakes)
- Motorcycling in the '50s (Clew)
- Motorhomes, The Illustrated History (Jenkinson)
- Motorsport In colour, 1950s (Wainwright)
- MV Agusta Fours, The book of the classic (Falloon)
- N.A.R.T. – A concise history of the North American Racing Team 1957 to 1983 (O'Neil)
- Nissan 300ZX & 350Z – The Z-Car Story (Long)
- Nissan GT-R Supercar: Born to race (Gorodji)
- Northeast American Sports Car Races 1950-1959 (O'Neil)
- Norton Commando Bible – All models 1968 to 1978 (Henshaw)
- Nothing Runs – Misadventures in the Classic, Collectable & Exotic Car Biz (Slutsky)
- Off-Road Giants! (Volume 1) – Heroes of 1960s Motorcycle Sport (Westlake)
- Off-Road Giants! (Volume 2) – Heroes of 1960s Motorcycle Sport (Westlake)
- Off-Road Giants! (Volume 3) – Heroes of 1960s Motorcycle Sport (Westlake)
- Pass the Theory and Practical Driving Tests (Gibson & Hoole)
- Peking to Paris 2007 (Young)
- Pontiac Firebird – New 3rd Edition (Cranswick)
- Porsche 356 (2nd Edition) (Long)
- Porsche 908 (Födisch, Neßhöver, Roßbach, Schwarz & Roßbach)
- Porsche 911 Carrera – The Last of the Evolution (Corlett)
- Porsche 911R, RS & RSR, 4th Edition (Starkey)
- Porsche 911, The Book of the (Long)
- Porsche 911 – The Definitive History 2004-2012 (Long)
- Porsche – The Racing 914s (Smith)
- Porsche 911SC 'Super Carrera' – The Essential Companion (Streather)
- Porsche 914 & 914-6: The Definitive History of the Road & Competition Cars (Long)
- Porsche 924 (Long)
- The Porsche 924 Carreras – evolution to excellence (Smith)
- Porsche 928 (Long)
- Porsche 944 (Long)
- Porsche 964, 993 & 996 Data Plate Code Breaker (Streather)
- Porsche 993 'King Of Porsche' – The Essential Companion (Streather)
- Porsche 996 'Supreme Porsche' – The Essential Companion (Streather)
- Porsche 997 2004-2012 – Porsche Excellence (Streather)
- Porsche Boxster – The 986 series 1996-2004 (Long)
- Porsche Boxster & Cayman – The 987 series (2004-2013) (Long)
- Porsche Racing Cars – 1953 to 1975 (Long)
- Porsche Racing Cars – 1976 to 2005 (Long)
- Porsche – The Rally Story (Meredith)
- Porsche: Three Generations of Genius (Meredith)
- Powered by Porsche (Smith)
- Preston Tucker & Others (Linde)
- RAC Rally Action! (Gardiner)
- Racing Colours – Motor Racing Compositions 1908-2009 (Newman)
- Racing Line – British motorcycle racing in the golden age of the big single (Guntrip)
- Rallye Sport Fords: The Inside Story (Moreton)
- Renewable Energy Home Handbook, The (Porter)
- Roads with a View – England's greatest views and how to find them by road (Corfield)
- Rolls-Royce Silver Shadow/Bentley T Series Corniche & Camargue – Revised & Enlarged Edition (Bobbitt)
- Rolls-Royce Silver Spirit, Silver Spur & Bentley Mulsanne 2nd Edition (Bobbitt)
- Rootes Cars of the 50s, 60s & 70s – Hillman, Humber, Singer, Sunbeam & Talbot (Rowe)
- Rover P4 (Bobbitt)
- Runways & Racers (O'Neil)
- Russian Motor Vehicles – Soviet Limousines 1930-2003 (Kelly)
- Russian Motor Vehicles – The Czarist Period 1784 to 1917 (Kelly)
- RX-7 – Mazda's Rotary Engine Sports car (Updated & Revised New Edition) (Long)
- Scooters & Microcars, The A-Z of Popular (Dan)
- Scooter Lifestyle (Grainger)
- Scooter Mania! – Recollections of the Isle of Man International Scooter Rally (Jackson)
- Singer Story: Cars, Commercial Vehicles, Bicycles & Motorcycle (Atkinson)
- Sleeping Beauties USA – abandoned classic cars & trucks (Marek)
- SM – Citroën's Maserati-engined Supercar (Long & Claverol)
- Speedway – Auto racing's ghost tracks (Collins & Ireland)
- Sprite Caravans, The Story of (Jenkinson)
- Standard Motor Company, The Book of the (Robson)
- Steve Hole's Kit Car Cornucopia – Cars, Companies, Stories, Facts & Figures: the UK's kit car scene since 1949 (Hole)
- Subaru Impreza: The Road Car And WRC Story (Long)
- Supercar, How to Build your own (Thompson)
- Tales from the Toolbox (Oliver)
- Tatra – The Legacy of Hans Ledwinka, Updated & Enlarged Collector's Edition of 1500 copies (Margolius & Henry)
- Taxi! The Story of the 'London' Taxicab (Bobbitt)
- This Day in Automotive History (Corey)
- To Boldly Go – twenty six vehicle designs that dared to be different (Hull)
- Toleman Story, The (Hilton)
- Toyota Celica & Supra, The Book of Toyota's Sports Coupés (Long)
- Toyota MR2 Coupés & Spyders (Long)
- Triumph & Standard Cars 1945 to 1984 (Warrington)
- Triumph Bonneville Bible (59-83) (Henshaw)
- Triumph Bonneville!, Save the – The inside story of the Meriden Workers' Co-op (Rosamond)
- Triumph Motorcycles & the Meriden Factory (Hancox)
- Triumph Speed Twin & Thunderbird Bible (Woolridge)
- Triumph Tiger Cub Bible (Estall)
- Triumph Trophy Bible (Woolridge)
- Triumph TR6 (Kimberley)
- TT Talking – The TT's most exciting era – As seen by Manx Radio TT's lead commentator 2004-2012 (Lambert)
- Two Summers – The Mercedes-Benz W196R Racing Car (Ackerson)
- TWR Story, The – Group A (Hughes & Scott)
- Unraced (Collins)
- Velocette Motorcycles – MSS to Thruxton – New Third Edition (Burris)
- Vespa – The Story of a Cult Classic in Pictures (Uhlig)
- Vincent Motorcycles: The Untold Story since 1946 (Guyony & Parker)
- Volkswagen Bus Book, The (Bobbitt)
- Volkswagen Bus or Van to Camper, How to Convert (Porter)
- Volkswagens of the World (Glen)
- VW Beetle Cabriolet – The full story of the convertible Beetle (Bobbitt)
- VW Beetle – The Car of the 20th Century (Copping)
- VW Bus – 40 Years of Splitties, Bays & Wedges (Copping)
- VW Bus Book, The (Bobbitt)
- VW Golf: Five Generations of Fun (Copping & Cservenka)
- VW – The Air-cooled Era (Copping)
- VW T5 Camper Conversion Manual (Porter)
- VW Campers (Copping)
- Volkswagen Type 3, The book of the – Concept, Design, International Production Models & Development (Glen)
- Volvo Estate, The (Hollebone)
- You & Your Jaguar XK8/XKR – Buying, Enjoying, Maintaining, Modifying – New Edition (Thorley)
- Which Oil? – Choosing the right oils & greases for your antique, vintage, veteran, classic or collector car (Michell)
- Wolseley Cars 1948 to 1975 (Rowe)
- Works Minis, The Last (Purves & Brenchley)
- Works Rally Mechanic (Moylan)

www.veloce.co.uk

First published in May 2018 by Veloce Publishing Limited, Veloce House, Parkway Farm Business Park, Middle Farm Way, Poundbury, Dorchester DT1 3AR, England. Tel 01305 260068 / Fax 01305 250479 / e-mail info@veloce.co.uk / web www.veloce.co.uk or www.velocebooks.com. ISBN: 978-1-787111-86-8 UPC: 6-36847-01186-4.
© 2018 Peter Griffiths and Veloce Publishing. All rights reserved. With the exception of quoting brief passages for the purpose of review, no part of this publication may be recorded, reproduced or transmitted by any means, including photocopying, without the written permission of Veloce Publishing Ltd. Throughout this book logos, model names and designations, etc, have been used for the purposes of identification, illustration and decoration. Such names are the property of the trademark holder as this is not an official publication. Readers with ideas for automotive books, or books on other transport or related hobby subjects, are invited to write to the editorial director of Veloce Publishing at the above address. British Library Cataloguing in Publication Data – A catalogue record for this book is available from the British Library. Typesetting, design and page make-up all by Veloce Publishing Ltd on Apple Mac. Printed in India by Parksons Graphics.

JAGUAR

E TYPE

FACTORY AND PRIVATE COMPETITION CARS

PETER GRIFFITHS
FOREWORD BY PAUL SKILLETER

VELOCE

Contents

Foreword

by Paul Skilleter

This is a book on E-Types unlike any other! Plenty of books on Jaguar's most famous sports car have been published, a number exceptionally detailed and well-researched. But they have all followed an orthodox approach and you know almost before you turn a page what you are going to get.

Not so here, as Peter Griffiths takes up the theme of the Jaguar E-Type in competition in a very different manner. The usual emphasis on just a few well-known cars driven by famous drivers is discarded and instead, Peter concentrates on, as he rightly says, the hundreds of E-Types which are not 'Lightweights,' were not driven by the likes of Graham Hill or Roy Salvadori and did not compete at Le Mans. Yet within their chosen branches of motor sport these cars and their amateur drivers were far more successful than any Lightweight against their contemporary opposition.

Because the hey-day of the E-Type in motor racing was not in fact the early 1960s, but from the middle of that decade into the early 1970s, I expect that many reading this book will not be old enough to have seen E-Types racing back then, but I can assure you that the drama and spectacle of three or four low, wide-wheeled E-Types contesting the lead at Brands Hatch, Thruxton or Silverstone during the Modsport era represented some of the most exciting sports car racing I have ever seen. And with just a few notable exceptions, for those few years it was invariably some sort of E-Type which won.

You may rightly detect that this period of Jaguars in motor racing is my personal favourite, and I knew some of the leading contestants well. I first met Warren Pearce at Brands Hatch in 1969, then circa 1972 I carried out a track test of 7 CXW, when it was being raced with great success by John Harper for Anthony Hutton's Forward Enterprises. John Quick and I were both on the board of the Jaguar Driver's Club around this time, as indeed was Peter Griffiths, while John Lewis became a good friend in more recent times (quite recently he drove me round Silverstone in 4 GXO, where in the early 1970s I had track-tested one of the ex-Cunningham Lightweights).

So when I conceived a book on the E-Type in competition, it was the Prodsports/Modsports eras that I wanted it to concentrate on – and Peter Griffiths, with his encyclopaedic knowledge of this period, was the obvious choice as the author. As you will find out, Peter has gone to enormous lengths to record and identify as many of the racing E-Types and their varied careers as he could, especially evident in the car-by-car and driver listings in the appendices. I am extremely grateful to Rod Grainger (my old commissioning editor when he was at JH Haynes) for taking on this major work when circumstances conspired against my publishing it, and I am delighted with the end result. I think you will be, too.

Paul Skilleter
Barton-on-Sea

Introduction

There are dozens, if not hundreds of books covering the Jaguar marque, some are specific to individual models while others are more general. Several fine books have been produced on the E-Type, perhaps the definitive sports car of the swinging '60s, or even the 20th century. Although the 12 Lightweights have been extensively covered, it is my view that all of the other racing E-Types have been overlooked, and definitely underestimated. This book encompasses the continuing racing exploits of the E-Type from 1961.

In this book I trace the development of the racing E-Type from the original '60s cars, including the Factory Lightweights, through the Modsports era and finally back to the 'replica Lightweight racing phenomena' of the present day.

A current trend in motorsport is to try and reproduce the racing of the early '60s, which has spawned an ever growing population of Lightweight replicas. Some claim spurious links to original cars, and mirror the contentious debates that arose about the originality of many of the Lister Jaguars, and even the Le Mans winning D-Types.

As well as covering the lengthy and colourful world of the Modsports era, it is necessary to put on record the whole racing E-Type story, warts and all, in order to give a clear picture of this iconic car, which is still winning races more than 50 years after it was conceived. The E-Type has appeared not only as a pure racing car, but also in sprints, hill climbs, rallying, autocross and even drag racing.

I have recorded every race E-Type that I have come across, some of which have been written off, some lost without trace, some 'reborn' as Lightweights and some even returned to their original road use. I want to acknowledge the minor and lesser known cars and drivers, not just the famous. This book is dedicated to the competition history of the Jaguar E-Type.

Naturally, with the ever increasing prices of E-Types, this book will be out of date the moment it is published. More race E-Types will have been prepared, more 'historic Lightweights' will have been 'discovered,' and more number plate changes will have been made, which can confuse the true identity of the cars. With virtually every part of the E-Type available to buy today as a new spare part, there is almost no end to the number of E-Types that will be 'found' to have had some sort of 'competition' history. It seems almost too ridiculous to record, but some cars even claim 'race history' when the nearest they got to the track was when they parked in the paddock next to a 'real' racer!

Although some of the better known cars warranted more pages, I hope the reader will appreciate that space is limited and there is a lot to include. So the book has become more of a photographic record of the E-Type's racing exploits rather than a detailed history of all the cars, which, no doubt, would cover dozens of volumes. (Philip Porter's excellent book *Jaguar Lightweight E-type – The Autobiography of 4 WPD*, is over 300 pages on just the one car, and his book on all the Lightweights/Factory Competition Cars, *Ultimate E-Type*, comprises over 500 pages on just 16 cars).

As you can see in the appendices, I have identified hundreds of E-Types with 'competition' history. The E-Type was always a very special sports car, and with over 70,000 cars made, it is inevitable that a large number of owners would have tried some form of competition at least once, as well as those who attended Jaguar Club 'test days' etc. This is the main reason that I have concentrated predominately on UK race cars, although more well known 'foreign' ones such as the Briggs Cunningham cars are included.

Numerous friends and colleagues involved in the Jaguar world have suggested to me that the information I provide here could well be used as a guide to recreate 'lost' cars, which concerns me. I believe it is incumbent upon me, therefore, to discourage any such ideas, and with that in mind, I have deliberately excluded certain information. For various reasons such as protection of privacy, controversiality, it is also appropriate for me to withhold specific details in some cases. In addition, having archived the history of the cars for over 40 years, I have far too much material to include in any one book!

The photographs have come from various collections, the main sources being my own, those of Ted Walker of Ferret Fotographic, Paul Skilleter, and Tony Bailey.

In particular I would like to acknowledge the continued assistance of Paul Skilleter, whose invaluable help in all aspects has made this book possible. I would also like to thank Tony Bancroft (a prolific collector of racing E-Type histories), Stuart Davey (mechanic to John Quick's WOO 11), Les Hughes (Editor of *Jaguar* magazine in Australia and racing E-Type driver), Michael Scott (CUT 7 and others), Glenn Watson (outstanding modsports mechanic) and Pat Wells (mechanic to Dick Protheroe and avid CUT 7 collector), all of whom are enthusiasts and have been generous with their time and contributions.

There is also Laurie Abbott, Rob Beere, Stuart Davey, Marc Devis, Les Hughes, Ian Hunt, Pablo Raybould, Graham Ravensdale and Paul Stanton to thank for allowing me to use their photos.

Last, but not least, I would like to express my appreciation to my wife Joanne, for her sustained support and encouragement in this endeavour.

I hope the book will help stir good memories.

www.velocebooks.com / www.veloce.co.uk
Details of all current books • New book news • Special offers

Chapter 1

Originality, Traceability and Values

Originality

In order to set the overriding theme for this book, I believe it is important to discuss originality.

If the 'Old Blacksmith's Hammer' has had three new handles and three new heads, is it still the original hammer which has just been repaired?

Similarly (and unfortunately, in my opinion), too many race E-Types fall into this category where, following race accident damage, parts are replaced but, more importantly, are *not* disposed of and are then reused on another car. Obviously the identity of either car can then be called into question.

Is the repaired car the original car or is the car carrying the original, discarded but now repaired, parts more original than the original? Confusing, isn't it?! Certainly where large sums of money and valuations are concerned, consequential arguments and even court cases may well arise.

If 'continuous history' is the guideline to identify an original car then surely it becomes impossible to destroy that car as, even if every single part is replaced, the car remains the 'original.' If you can prove a continuous history of the chassis number then you can lay claim to the original car in whatever state it currently finds itself.

Regarding E-Types with road registration numbers, it is important to point out that DVLA has strict rules that encompass changes to chassis and/or body, and in this context would include altering, say, a 2+2 or FHC to a Lightweight replica.

I refer the reader to the DVLA website headings:

Old vehicles
Rebuilt vehicles
Radically altered vehicles
Reconstructed classic vehicles
Kit converted vehicles
'Q' registrations

The reader may wish to acquaint themselves with the DVLA definition of what changes are permissible for a car to retain its legal identity and registration number. For the sake of clarity, Jaguar designated the engine frame as the component that carries the E-Type's legal identity. After 50 years now, I expect a significant number have been replaced.

Many racing E-Types have been 'thrashed and crashed,' and it is surprising therefore that most of them still seem to exist. Maybe this is because they have such high values and are worth rebuilding from the one remaining wheel nut? As for many C-Types, D-Types and Listers, many of them over the years have been 'lost' and then later 'found' – several notable examples have been 'found' twice with different owners laying claim to the car's identity. With a separate body and chassis it is inevitable that two owners can lay claim to the 'original' car if one owns the body and one owns the chassis. As with many 'racing cars' they were not always road registered, and therefore continuous history is not always easily achievable.

A good example is the famous Lister Jaguar 'Flat Iron' (HCH 736) which was raced by Bruce Halford and Jim Clark. This Lister (chassis number BHL5) was originally a 1955 2-litre Bristol engined, Wakefield bodied car. This was written off in its first year and the same chassis number was transferred to the newly created BHL 5 (version 2), which was a 3.4-litre Jaguar powered car with a body by Maurice Gomm and was known as the 'Flat Iron' (this was the forerunner to the 'knobbly' days). This car had an extremely hard racing life and was regularly campaigned throughout the '50s and '60s. The tired old battle-scarred aluminium body was eventually discarded (but not destroyed) and a shiny new body made for the chassis – this car has the continuous history, however, back in the '90s I actually purchased the original discarded body to add to my memorabilia collection. After a few years a good friend of mine prised it from me. He painstakingly rebuilt the body and attached it to a brand new chassis (which he made himself), and using various mechanical parts from an XJ6 4.2 manual saloon, he turned it into a wonderful road car.

My question is, which one would you like to own? The original beautiful now repaired one-off body, or the original chassised car (assuming that it still has its original chassis ... albeit version 2!) with a brand new body? The original body you look at now becomes a fake car, and the new bodied car now becomes original! Rumours abound that there are more Listers now than Brian Lister ever built, so perhaps that is why.

Some years later and after a few change of hands, the 'new HCH 736' with the original body was involved in a French court case when it was sold as being the 'original HCH 736.' My understanding is that the 'new HCH 736' with the original body was deemed to be a fake, and subsequently impounded by the authorities. I believe it went to a French museum.

From my point of view, I prefer to look at the original body which Jim Clark (and others) sat in and touched rather than the chassis, which is not visible. Surely, the 'original' item full of patina must be better than a brand new shiny 2015 bodyshell? Seemingly I am in the minority.

So, in the historic/classic car context, you can replace every nut and bolt on a car and according to the Law, because of 'continuous history' it is still the original and therefore deemed more valuable. In contrast, in the antiques world, should you change *all the legs and the top* of, say, a Chippendale table, it would be deemed not original and consequently worthless.

Back to E-Types ...

While the E-Type and Lister both comprise a body and a chassis frame, the construction of the E-Type differs in one important respect from the Lister: the E-Type's body is load-bearing while the Lister's is not. However, like the Lister, the E-Type's chassis (engine) frame carries the car's official identity. The dangers inherent in retaining an old rusty chassis means that many E-Types now have replacement chassis (basically the engine support frames), but the body is more easily repaired with many firms now offering after market repair panels.

Another car I have trouble with is the original Lightweight 4868 WK (chassis number S850662), converted to a Low Drag Coupe (LDC) in 1964. Unfortunately, the car is probably best known for the 1964 crash at Montlhery, which tragically killed Peter Lindner. The remains of the car ended up in the Kaus collection in Germany. Lynx Engineering was then commissioned to recreate the car in the early 1980s. This recreated car (initially with an incorrect roof line which had to be rebuilt again), carried the original number plate, and presumably the 'continuous history' transferred with it, although I cannot confirm this. The Lynx recreation was widely accepted as the 'original' car, whilst the actual damaged remains stayed in the Kaus collection. Years later, both the damaged remains of the original car and the Lynx recreation changed hands, and in 2011, the damaged remains of the original car were fully restored by CMC Ltd for the new owner.

Now ... Which is the 'original' car? Which should carry the number plate 4868 WK? Don't forget, the 'original' car was a roadster! To complicate matters even further, the first rebuilt 4868 WK (Lynx recreation) was dismantled, and its bodyshell turned into a new 'Lightweight' 4 GXO! Continuous history can become a real nightmare. I think I will let the reader decide which car is original.

Another well known E-Type that was changed from a successful modsports FHC racer into an aluminium LDC lookalike is the 1962 FHC (chassis number 860182), which was successfully raced by Nick Crocker and Robin Cardwell in the '70s and '80s. Whilst at Fred Cliffe's workshop in the early '90s for yet another rebuild, it was purchased in partly restored modsports form to become the basis of a LDC project. Simon Dunford was commissioned to replace the fibreglass panels with aluminium ones and replace the FHC roof with the LDC version. The beautiful wide racing wheels and tyres were replaced with alloy LWE replicas, and the entire car was transformed into an immaculate, fast road going car. The original bodyshell and much of the mechanicals were used on the rebuild, obviously the car retains its history and it is now registered USL 828.

Further examples of how cars have evolved are given in a later chapter.

In the context of originality, renowned motorsports journalist Denis Jenkinson compiled his own terminology to describe the state of preservation of historic racing cars. The 'Glossary of terms' are listed in his book *Directory of Historic Racing Cars – The Survivors, Genuine, Authentic and Facsimile* published by Aston Publications Ltd, 1987.

The terms he uses are as follows:

Original
Genuine
Authentic
Resurrection
Reconstruction
Facsimile
Duplication
Special
Converted
Destroyed
Scrapped
Broken up

With the continually changing race cars of today, I find it very difficult to place the racing E-Type into the above categories, especially with regard to what has transpired with the popularity of Lightweight E-Type replicas.

My suggestion would be to include the term 'Continually developed cars' and I believe many E-Types would fall into this category. This could include all E-Types which have been continually upgraded, improved, enhanced, changed, call it what you like, but they can never be described as 'original.'

New descriptions continue to be concocted in an attempt to attract buyers: 'Continuation,' 'Reincarnation' and even 'Evocation.' Definitions welcome, please. Is an evocation something that evokes a good memory of the original? Could a 'Challenger' E-Type with white paintwork and blue stripes be a Lightweight evocation? How should we describe the new 'Lightweights' built by Jaguar itself?

To recap ... Resurrection, reconstruction, facsimile, copy, replica, reincarnation, continuation, evocation, clone ... where does one start and one end? Are they all 'fakes' trying to be something they are not? In my opinion, if you can put your car easily into Denis Jenkinson's list as either original, genuine or authentic, and continuous history is without question, you should be on firm ground. If you cannot put your car easily into those categories, then some serious research is essential. If your car has one part from an original car, are you certain that someone else does not have two parts from the same original car on his?

Traceability

When cars changed hands, it was often the case that the new owner wanted to be disassociated with the earlier car, particularly if it was not famous or fast. Rather than being associated with the earlier, maybe slower car, the new owner would invariably change the colour, wheel design, etc in order to stamp their own individuality on a car. For the historian, this has made documenting the continuing history of some cars extremely difficult and frustrating. This is exacerbated when some owners create spurious links to earlier cars no longer in existence.

I hope my photo gallery showing the same car in different guises will give an insight into this issue. (See chapter two.)

In several publications, I have found that many driver's names have been confused with others, which, like the cars, has often made tracing a car's history all the more difficult.

For example:

Alistair Cowen raced in the same period as Alistair Crawford.

Jack Lambert raced in the same period as Jack Le Fort.

Roy Standley raced in the same period as Richard Scantlebury ... RS 2 was the number carried on Richard's modsports car

Apparently, the name 'Brian' was prevalent amongst '70s modsports drivers: Brian Murphy, Brian Litherland, Brian Mills, Brian Russel, Brian Spicer, Brian Waddilove, and Brian Redman. ... and if they were in the same race, it can be impossible to follow.

I have also seen the following error ... The genuine Lightweight of Phil Scragg was PS 1175. I have seen this attributed to Peter Sutcliffe, presumably because of the same initials.

Many cars changed their number plates, especially during the Modsports era, when cars were not taxed or used on the road. Some plates were genuine private plates, whereas others were perhaps made up for fun. Examples of this are as follows: (I cannot confirm which are genuine and which are made up)

RS 2	Richard Scantlebury
ROB 2	Rob Schroeder on 7 CXW
FNC 1	Fred Cliffe
FNC 2	Fred Cliffe
FNC 2D	Fred Cliffe
PW 1	Paul Webb
PWM 1	Paul Webb Motors.
RV 7	Bob Vincent
PB 1	Phil Bennet
JL 24	Jack Lambert
RL 26	Jack Lambert
TES 1	Tom Sleigh
AH 600	Anthony Hopkins

As you will see from the registrations list, there are many cars with number plate changes, in particular the Lightweights!

Another big factor, or hindrance, in tracing a car's history is the constant change of colour scheme. Examples of this are:

The Warren Pearce car 310 WK, which started as dark blue, then bright yellow, then dark yellow, then light blue and then back to dark blue.

The Ken Baker car 7 CXW started as bronze with black hard top, then red with white stripe and white hard top, then red with white hard top and white nose (but no stripe), and then back to bronze with black hard top.

The Mike Adams FHC started as red, then BRG, and then white with blue stripes.

Simon Watney's dark blue FHC ended up bright red when owned by Paul Webb.

The Malcolm Hamilton V12 car started life as dark yellow, then white with red and blue stripes, then white with black and grey stripes, then light blue, then white with red and blue stripes, then plain white, then white with red stripe, then dark blue, then BRG, and finally white with blue stripes.

The list is endless, but hopefully you get the picture how difficult traceability can be, especially if owners want to purposefully hide a car's identity.

Even the genuine Lightweights were not adverse to the odd colour change or two!

The 'Scragg' Lightweight PS 1175 started as white with black hard top, then green, and now back to white but with red hard top.

Lightweight 4 WPD started as light grey, then red and now back to light grey.

Lightweight 49 FXN started as BRG, then white, then red, then blue, and now back to BRG.

When modsports became 'unfashionable,' those with established race histories were sometimes 'reborn' as Lightweight replicas. These were more shiny, but perhaps would not be so successful. I suggest that not everyone would race a £200,000 car as enthusiastically as a £1000 car ! One car above all that has remained faithful to its roots is the Rob Beere/Malcolm Hamilton V12 roadster, which earned itself the title of 'The World's Fastest E-Type.' Conceived by Fred Cliffe and later fully developed by Rob Beere and Malcolm Hamilton, it was continually altered with whatever Jaguar's latest technology was, ultimately, Group C specification. This car has not, and hopefully never will be, returned to the road.

Values

The age old question of 'what's it worth?' will naturally depend upon whether you are buying or selling, but as seen previously with E-Types, it is now perhaps more important than ever, to decide which category the car sits in. Is it genuine? Is it a resurrection? Or could it be a fake?

As far as I am aware, there were no direct 'Factory' entered E-Types in the early races of 1961, and none in the '62 or '63 Le Mans, but it would be foolish to think that 'Factory' help was withheld to any privateer who asked. Indeed, as we shall see, the initial batch of E-Types (FHC and DHC) were for prioritised customers who would 'probably' go racing. Many of the initial batch of roadsters were 'Factory' modified specifically for this purpose and some, seven in particular, were to become known as the ZP cars, although not all of them ended up racing.

The Factory obviously helped develop 4 WPD when owned by Coombs, and of course similar help was forthcoming with Peter Lindner for 4868 WK, as Peter was the Jaguar importer for Germany. Jaguar's Competition Department still existed into the late '60s and as told in Peter Wilson's book *Cat out of the Bag* it was the Competition Department that did all the work on 4 WPD during its serious racing days.

It seems to me then, that if any link whatsoever can be established between the Factory and the car, it has the potential for a much inflated price. Whether that car was successful or not seems to be totally irrelevant. In fact, it could be true to say that in most cases, the least successful racing E-Types have commanded the highest sales values. I recall that 5115 WK was the first E-Type to pass the £1m price tag. I question the reasons why. Other Lightweights were pulled up accordingly, and at today's values they can now demand several million. I cannot comprehend how the very successful D-Types can be on the same price levels as the unsuccessful Lightweights!

From the music industry we often hear the term 'one hit wonder.' I suggest that many of the high value E-Types could be called 'one race wonders,' including the Lightweights (perhaps excluding 4 WPD) and Semi-Lightweights along with ECD 400, E2A, 503 BBO, 898 BYR, 1337 VC etc ... try and find out how many races these cars actually entered, let alone won. You might be surprised.

5115 WK is nearly always photographed with race number 15.
503 BBO is nearly always photographed with race number 8.
898 BYR is nearly always photographed with race number 9.
1337 VC is nearly always photographed with race number 10.

I hope you get the point!

Not until the E-Type was continually developed and modified did it begin winning races on a regular basis. The more famous early cars being Jack Lambert (RL 26), Ken Baker (7 CXW), Dick Protheroe (CUT 7), John Filbee (4778 LJ) , John Cuff (8448 TJ), John Quick (WOO 11), and Warren Pearce (310 WK). Later cars included those of John Burbidge, Guy Bedington, Fred Cliffe, John Oxborough, Dave Moore, Tony Shaw and Malcolm Hamilton. All these cars were regular and consistent race winners, and in my opinion are much more worthy of higher values than the 'one race wonders.'

My own point of view is that any E-Type purchase should be thoroughly checked and re-checked as to the authenticity of what is for sale, including car, paperwork (history/provenance) etc. Although no epic battles have recently surfaced regarding duplicate cars, I consider it only a matter of time before this happens, as it did with 'duplicate' D-Types a few years ago. Where there is big money involved, there will always be scammers ready to dupe the unwary. If you want to buy an original car, you are out of luck. If you want to buy a genuine or authentic car, you will not only have to do an awful lot of research, but also have very deep pockets. So, you will probably have to settle for one with continuous history that now has no original parts whatsoever ... 'The Old Blacksmith's Hammer.'

Chapter 2

How Cars Have Evolved

In this chapter I have included photographs of several cars in different guises to show how they have progressed over the years. The big question is: if the number plate was not there, would you be able to recognise it as the same car?

Sometimes there is a natural progression in a car's development, as better brakes are fitted, engines enhanced, and even simple colour changes can make identification problematic.

Perhaps what makes most cars difficult to trace was the advent of the Modsports era. Bodywork was changed, colour constantly changed, wheels changed as they became increasingly larger. Then of course there was the simple truth that drivers damaged their fixed heads and decided to rebuild the car as a roadster! Such cars as 888 RYA, CUT 7 (second car), 9 WKJ and even the Leeson supercharged car fall into this category. Some roadsters developed into Low Drag Coupes ... 4868 WK, 898 BYR, 49 FXN are all examples. Some registration numbers were only garage 'trade plates,' and therefore numbers like 2 BBC appeared on two different cars, one a fixed head and one a roadster.

There are a few cars where the new owner did not want to be associated with the previous owner's exploits, and so identities were changed and cars disguised. I have lost track of a few cars, and there are some I know of but which are probably too controversial to include here. I have also heard rumours that the Modsports era was a great way to 'hide' stolen cars.

BUY 1 4 WPD

Roy Salvadori at the Aintree Grand Prix meeting in 1961 in the original BUY 1 E-Type, later to become 4 WPD, the prototype Lightweight. (Copyright Ted Walker Ferret Fotographics)

An early shot of 4 WPD taken at Oulton Park in 1962 at the International Trophy meeting. (Copyright Ted Walker Ferret Fotographics)

4 WPD photographed at the E-Type Challenge at Silverstone in July 2011. (Copyright Peter Griffiths)

4 WPD, the original Lightweight E-Type, in one of its many guises at Donington in June 1991. (Copyright Peter Griffiths)

4868 WK at the 1963 1000km race, driven by Peter Lindner. This is clearly in its original Lightweight specification before it was converted to a Low Drag Coupe. (Copyright Ted Walker Ferret Fotographics)

4868 WK seen here in 1964 at Le Mans, driven by Peter Lindner. (Copyright Ted Walker Ferret Fotographics)

49 FXN

49 FXN driven by Peter Lumsden in the 1000km race in 1963. (Copyright Ted Walker Ferret Fotographics)

49 FXN in its modified long nose version seen here at Brands Hatch in 1965. (Copyright Ted Walker Ferret Fotographics)

Leeson supercharged car

The supercharged E-Type campaigned by Alan Leeson shown here at the 1970 JDC Silverstone meeting. See article reprinted in Appendix E. (Copyright Paul Skilleter)

John Oxborough in his highly modified ex-Leeson modsports car at Mallory Park in March 1976. (Copyright Ted Walker Ferret Fotographics)

The latest rebuild of the Leeson car, photographed at the author's home. (Copyright Peter Griffiths)

7 CXW driven by Ken Baker at the 1964 BARC meeting at Silverstone. (Copyright Ted Walker Ferret Fotographics)

7 CXW one of the most successful E-Types from the Modsports era ... the Forward Engineering car campaigned by John Harper and Anthony Hutton. (Copyright Paul Skilleter)

Paul Webb standing next to his recently rebuilt ex-Ken Baker car 7 CXW. (Copyright Peter Griffiths)

An early colour shot of Ron Beaty and John Harper standing next to 7 CXW in its modsports form. (Paul Skilleter Collection)

256 DJU

256 DJU seen here at Silverstone in 1963 driven by Roger Mac. (Copyright Ted Walker Ferret Fotographics)

The same car with number SVJ 345 in its roadster form. See page 32, later in this chapter. (Copyright Peter Griffiths)

898 BYR

898 BYR driven by Peter Sargent at the 1961 Boxing Day meet at Brands Hatch. (Copyright Ted Walker Ferret Fotographics)

898 BYR driven by Peter Lumsden/Peter Sargent at the September 1962 meeting at Crystal Palace.
(Copyright Ted Walker Ferret Fotographics)

W9 WKJ

9 WKJ, driven by Tony Knight in 1965 at Brands Hatch, in its original FHC form. (Copyright Ted Walker Ferret Fotographics)

9 WKJ again driven by Tony Knight at Brands Hatch in August 1966 ... now in the DHC version of the car. (Copyright Ted Walker Ferret Fotographic)

Beddington V12

The ex-Guy Beddington V12 E-Type in its later stage of development, seen here at Donington in June 1991 as part of the E-Type birthday celebrations. (Copyright Peter Griffiths)

The ex-Guy Beddington V12 FHC now in its current home in Australia. (Copyright Les Hughes)

DUCKHAMS

Brian Murphy at Brands Hatch in May 1976, driving his modsports E-Type roadster, which was a development of the original Warren Pearce roadster 310 WK. (Copyright Ted Walker Ferret Fotographics)

310 WK driven by Warren Pearce at Brands Hatch in 1965. (Copyright Ted Walker Ferret Fotographics)

310 WK, the original Warren Pearce car, seen here in heavily modified form when it was owned by Ron Lea. (Copyright Peter Griffiths)

ABD 799A

ABD 799A FHC Le Mans replica photographed at the E-Type Challenge at Silverstone in July 2011. (Copyright Peter Griffiths)

ABD 799A, the FHC of Mike Adams, seen here halfway up the Stelvio Pass in Italy, allowing it to cool down after overheating. During this trip to the continent in 1994, I was taken round the Nürburgring circuit by Mike, and this seems to have ignited his racing enthusiasm, as he subsequently began racing in earnest. The car later became the 'sister' car to Malcolm Hamilton's V12 when both were sponsored by the JEC in the late 1990s. Mike later exchanged this car for a Lightweight replica, which he races today. (Copyright Peter Griffiths)

Mike Adams with his FHC. (Copyright Laurie Abbott)

Hamilton V12

This highly developed V12 roadster has gone through a great number of changes, and with no registration has been difficult to track for the casual observer. It started life as a yellow modified car before its colour was changed to white with red and blue stripes, then white with grey stripes, then all pale blue, then white with red and blue stripes, then dark green, and finally white with blue stripes..

Original appearance of the 'World's Fastest E-Type' photographed in the mid '80s. (Copyright Peter Griffiths)

The current version of the 'World's Fastest E-Type.' (Copyright Peter Griffiths)

Robin Cardwell/Nick Crocker FHC

The modsports FHC run by Cardwell and Crocker. (Copyright Laurie Abbott)

USL 828, the reincarnation of the Cardwell/Crocker modsports car. (Copyright Laurie Abbott)

Other notable changes in a car's appearance are as follows:

CUT 7

CUT 7, FHC (2nd car) built by Dick Protheroe: Gunmetal grey.
Registered 256 DJU, FHC, with Roger Mac.
Then raced by David Cunningham, FHC: white with blue stripes (no number).
Later raced by Vesty and Ward, crashed 1966, rebuilt as DHC, dark blue.
Later registered PMB 324H.
Later registered SVJ 345H.
Later seen as just SVJ 345.
Later registered 256 DJU again.
Rebuilt to original CUT 7 FHC spec again, gunmetal grey ... full circle!

CUT 8

CUT 8, dark grey, spent some time with bright yellow coachwork when raced by Peter Walker and registered 105 ENX.

2164 WK

The last of the Protheroe garage cars, a fast 'standard' looking FHC. Later a much modified modsports racer before converting back to its 'standard' looking appearance.

2164 WK at the JDC test day in March 1971, driven by John May. (Copyright Ted Walker Ferret Fotographics)

2164 WK following its total rebuild, seen here at the JDC Silverstone meeting in 1978, driven by John Simms. (Copyright Ted Walker Ferret Fotographics)

The Simon Watney car

This car started its life as a fixed head hill climb car in the hands of Fred Cliffe.

Simon, a stalwart of the JDC, purchased the car and turned it into a successful race track car in dark blue with a yellow nose, and later a red nose. When eventually bought by Paul Webb, it was further modified and painted bright red. It carried an assortment of registration numbers, including PW 1, PWM 1 and 6900 WK. In modsports trim it was sold to Paul Palmer who started to put it back into standard trim (cutting off the wide wings, etc). The project stalled and I bought it and started to put it back into modsports trim (new wide wings attached!). The car was then bought back by Paul Webb who decided to convert it once again back to a concours standard FHC in metallic silver and carrying the registration 6900 WK. Full circle ... what a journey.

The Paul Webb red FHC at a later JDC meeting at Silverstone. (Copyright Peter Griffiths)

The Simon Watney dark blue FHC at an early JDC meeting at Silverstone. (Copyright Peter Griffiths)

This chapter gives merely a few examples of how difficult it can be to keep track of all the old racers, especially those that went through the Modsports era.

The E-Type has continued to evolve, sometimes more gracefully than others, but it has always progressed. I think Sir William Lyons would be quite proud of his 1961 car still winning races today. What a machine!

Chapter 3

Early Racing

Many Jaguar books, and even more magazine articles have covered the early racing exploits of Jaguar's new sports car, the E-Type. Developed from the race winning Le Mans D-Types, the E-Type was born to race. Or was it?

Jaguar, in order to promote sales, decided to 'go racing,' the Factory's main involvement, directly or indirectly, being from 1949 to 1959, the golden years of the C-Type and D-Type at Le Mans. As beautiful and as successful as the D-Type was, it only sold in small numbers. Even the road going XKSS version did not increase sales for Jaguar, and as a result, the Factory decided not to return to Le Mans. The dreadful 1957 Factory fire probably did not help matters either. Thankfully, many characteristics from the race proven D-Type would find their way into the new E-Type model which would be introduced in 1961.

There were no plans for the 'Factory' E-Type to go racing. The Competition Department was concentrating on the V12 race engine, which would eventually power its mid-engined sports car in the late '60s, the XJ13. Jaguar was well aware that its customers would see things differently and may want to race the new E-Type.

The swinging sixties would see the E-Type capture the imagination of the public like no other car. Unit sales would more than double those of the earlier XK models. I was lucky enough to have a D-Type replica based on the Le Mans long

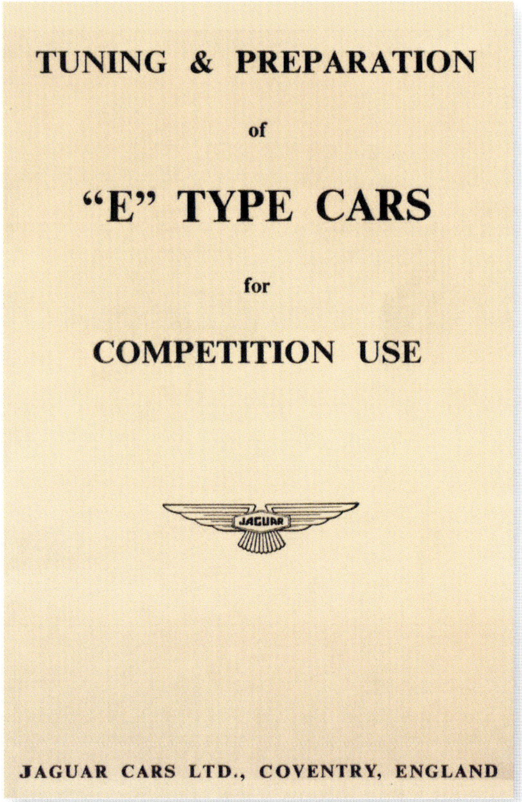
TUNING & PREPARATION

of

"E" TYPE CARS

for

COMPETITION USE

JAGUAR CARS LTD., COVENTRY, ENGLAND

The Factory produced booklet on preparing the E-Type for competition use.

Early colour photos of BUY 1 and ECD 400 at Brands Hatch on 3rd June 1961. (Lewin and Skilleter Collection)

nose version, and using all E-Type running gear. Driving the car was a wonderful experience, definitely the bee's knees; however, the dream was short lived when a member of the public enquired if it was a "new Batmobile!" I never had such a problem with the E-Type, which was recognisable by just about everyone, young or old the world over. I suppose 60 D-Types compared with 70,000 E-Types may have had something to do with it.

The E-Type, first and foremost, was a road car designed to make the driver feel like he had a race proven Le Mans winner under his control. In reality, it was a superb road car with racing styling that was years ahead of the game. As mentioned previously, Jaguar realised that customers would like to enter their new cars in competitive events, and if they were to hand-pick the first dozen or so owners who just might be interested in racing, the Factory would benefit from the free advertising!

To assist any potential racers, the Factory produced a booklet entitled *Tuning and Preparation of E-Type cars for Competition Use*. The introduction reads as follows: "This booklet is intended as a guide for owners of Jaguar E-Type models who, in addition to normal road use, may wish to use their cars on occasions for racing, it being understood that this model has not been designed as a competition car."

Out of the first 20 or so E-Types sold, the new owners list was a 'Who's who' of the racing world. Names like: Equipe Endeavour, Coombs, Sargent, Ecurie Ecosse, Sturgess, Lambert, Berry, McLaren, Wicken, Baille, to name but a few. The Factory had chosen wisely, and not many weeks went by before the E-Type was on the track and winning.

Two very rare colour photos of these early races are shown on p37, courtesy of the David Lewin/Paul Skilleter Collection.

At the time of the launch in early 1961, the Factory announced that seven of the early cars would be slightly modified for racing purposes, and these project ZP cars later became known as 'The Magnificent Seven.' They would have various engine modifications, different axle ratios, competition clutches, etc, just to help 'persuade' their new hand-picked owners to take them racing ... well, it would be rude not to! These cars are shown in chapter five, 'The Magnificent Seven.'

Did the standard E-Type go racing? Probably not. The era of 'modifying' the car for racing had begun in early 1961, and not in the '70s Modsports era as many would have you believe. The first race success came quickly at Oulton Park in April 1961 when the Equipe Endeavour car, ECD 400 – driven by none other than Graham Hil – came first, and Roy Salvadori in the Coombs car, BUY 1, came in third. Both cars were roadsters and both raced with soft tops and wire wheels. A very impressive debut for a new car.

The 1961 season saw further race victories for Salvadori, as well as Mike Parkes, Jack Lambert, George Wicken, Peter Sargent and Ken Baker, plus numerous second and third places. The E-Type race car had been born – no Factory involvement! Sales snowballed. Marketing genius perhaps?

Fixed head or roadster?

The 1962 season continued with more successes, and more owners joined the fray. Notable drivers, to name but a few, were Dick Protheroe, David Hobbs, Tony Davenport, Phil Scragg and Peter Lumsden. The 1962 season also saw private entries for the Le Mans 24 hour race, and I expect the Jaguar Factory couldn't believe its luck. The three Le Mans entries for 1962 were Briggs Cunningham and Roy Salvadori in the FHC, 1337 VC, Peter Lumsden and Peter Sargent in the roadster, 898 BYR, and Maurice Charles and John Coundley in the FHC, 503 BBO. Cunningham and Salvadori finished 4th and Lumsden and Sargent 5th. Charles and Coundley did not finish, but overall, still an outstanding result for a 'road car.'

Now, with two seasons down, which was the better car: the fixed head or the roadster? The roadster with soft top was a definite no, and all later races saw the cars with distinctive hard tops made of fibreglass. Jaguar had seen the potential, and the Coombs car (BUY 1) was being developed. It lost its soft top, wire wheels, bumpers, chrome headlight surrounds etc. It was being made lighter and more competitive, and of course, as is well documented, it became the development car for the 1963 'Lightweight' project.

The Cunningham/Salvadori FHC finished ahead of the Lumsden/Sargent roadster, but not all is as it seems. Their roadster had been converted to a fixed head style car for Le Mans. It retained its roadster windscreen, so had a slightly lower roof line, and in theory was more aerodynamic. The two Peters obviously liked this conversion, because when they acquired one of the genuine Lightweights for the 1963 season (49 FXN), they similarly turned it into a fixed head style, now referred to as a low drag style, but with the addition of a longer nose on the bonnet.

The fixed head car was also the preferred body style for Dick Protheroe and the CUT 7 dynasty. Dick's first car, FHC chassis number 4 (860004), was quickly followed by his second E-Type which was made from parts supplied by the Factory, starting with a fixed head bodyshell. His third CUT 7 was the Factory's experimental Low Drag Coupe chassis number EC1001 ... so, did Jaguar think the fixed head/low drag version was the better race car version?

The 11 Lightweights that followed BUY 1 were built as roadster bodied race cars, with all aluminium bodyshells, engine blocks etc, although it wasn't long before another one was turned into a Low Drag Coupe ... 4868 WK, the Lindner/Knocker car.

Other notable early fixed head successful racers are John Quick's WOO 11, John Cuff's 8448 TJ, as well as the cars of John Burbidge, Tony Shaw, Simon Watney, Alistair Cowin, and Peter Archer.

Was there any great weight advantage? Probably not. The early roadster weighed in at around 24cwt, and the fixed head around 24.1cwt. The difference in driver size and how much excess chrome, etc, you could get rid of would probably have made the cars fairly similar. Presumably, the fixed heads and low drag cars were preferred for Le Mans and the long distance events.

So, fixed head or roadster? I have been lucky enough to own both models, and even though I am vertically challenged, I found it far easier to get in and out of the fixed head, and therefore have always favoured that model. I also found the overall styling preferable and less claustrophobic.

3 BXV driven by Bruce McLaren on 7 April 1962, seen here at Druids Bend, Brands Hatch. (Copyright Ted Walker Ferret Fotographics)

3 BXV, driven by Hobbs, leads Protheroe in CUT 7 at the 1962 International Trophy meeting. (Copyright Ted Walker Ferret Fotographics)

Stirling Moss in the Ferrari leads Roy Salvadori in BUY 1 at the BEM Trophy meeting. (Copyright Ted Walker Ferret Fotographics)

4 WPD driven by Graham Hill in 1963 at the Goodwood Easter meeting. (Copyright Ted Walker Ferret Fotographics)

DOUBLE
RODO
30

Graham Hill in 4 WPD leads Masten Gregory in the 1962 International Trophy race. (Copyright Ted Walker Ferret Fotographics)

Roy Salvadori in BUY 1, just ahead of Graham Hill in ECD 400 at Brands Hatch, June 1961. (Copyright Ted Walker Ferret Fotographics)

The opening lap of the 1965 TT race at Oulton Park showing Dick Protheroe giving an early outing to the Factory prepared Low Drag Coupe CUT 7. (Copyright Ted Walker Ferret Fotographics)

A very early shot of the original CUT 7 taken at Prescott Hill Climb in 1961, driven by Dick Protheroe. (Copyright Ted Walker Ferret Fotographics)

John Wilson behind Warren Pearce (out of shot), and closely followed by John Filbee at Brands Hatch. (Copyright Ted Walker Ferret Fotographics)

Jack Lambert driving his 1961 roadster at the JDC Silverstone meeting in 1961. (Copyright Ted Walker Ferret Fotographics)

7 CXW, driven by Ken Baker, leads Robin Sturgess in 2 BBC at the 1962 BRSCC meeting at Silverstone. (Copyright Ted Walker Ferret Fotographics)

898 BYR, driven by Peter Sargent, leads Robin Sturgess in 2 BBC at the JDC Silverstone meeting in September 1961. (Copyright Ted Walker Ferret Fotographics)

Brian Spicer in E 141 at Brands Hatch, May 1966, leads Tony Knight in 9 WKJ. (Copyright Ted Walker Ferret Fotographics)

The 1963 season was to be all about the Lightweights. As in 1962, three E-Types entered Le Mans, but this time they were all Lightweights. All the Jaguar history books regularly report on the three 'Cunningham' entered cars in their white with blue stripes livery. Cars 5114 WK, 5115 WK and 5116 WK have together spawned an industry of Lightweight replicas and 'WK' registrations. Several low drag versions have been produced as well, but as these are no doubt more expensive to replicate, they are fewer in number.

1964 was the last time there were E-Type entries at Le Mans. These were the Lindner/ Knocker Lightweight, 4868 WK, and the Lumsden/Sargent Lightweight, 49 FXN, both cars sporting their own versions of the Low Drag Coupe bodywork. Neither managed to finish the race.

While all that high profile stuff was happening, in the real world, this prolific 'race car' was being campaigned all over the UK, and indeed worldwide. This 'standard' race car, which, as we have seen, has never really been standard, has continually been modified from day one. Dick Protheroe's CUT 7 for example, as early as 1962 had an aluminium bonnet, competition clutch and suspension, perspex rear door, and any excess weight removed. The natural development of this process, which began in the 1960s, came to be known as the Modsports era (modified sports cars). When it actually began depends upon your point of view ... some say the introduction of fibreglass (bonnet, doors etc), others say the wide wheels ... but how much fibreglass and how wide do the wheels need to be before a modsports car is born?

The Jaguar Factory produced the fibreglass hard top in 1961, and the Lightweights had wider wheels in 1963. Warren Pearce, driving 310 WK, possibly heralded the start of this era in 1966, when he introduced the one piece fibreglass rear end with wide wheels and everybody copied.

Respected author Doug Nye wrote a superb article in *Autosport* magazine in the 14th August 1975 issue. It was headed 'The End of an Era – 13 years of Jaguar E-Types in Competition.' He wrote a superb summary of the early racing years of the E-Type: not only E2A and the Lightweights, but recalling the foremost early privateers in 'standard' cars (such as Protheroe, Lumsden, Sargent, Baker, Waddilove, Sturgess, Lambert, Morrison, Earl of Denbigh, Delingpole as well as the American and German counterparts) and also the later Modsports era drivers (such as Schroeder, Quick, Lewis, Cowin, Shaw, Worswick, Beddington, Burbidge, Harper, Mills and Murphy).

I could list hundreds of race results – which E-Type won which race at what circuit, etc – but this would fill another book on its own. Philip Porter in his book *Jaguar E-Type The Definitive History*, lists a vast selection of race results for the E-Type from 1961 to 1970. By way of example, listed right are the lap records held by E-Types for the 1969 season, as recorded in *Autosport* magazine of 22nd January 1970.

The Modsports era that followed through the '70s and '80s produced some of the most spectacular races for these cars, and is by far my favourite period.

Aintree	Special GT cars over 2500cc	Brian Redman	3.8E
Aintree	Production sports cars over 3000cc	Ted Worswick	3.8E
Brands Hatch	"	John Quick/ Mike Franey	3.8E
Brands Hatch GP Circuit	"	Mike Franey	3.8E
Castle Combe	"	Tony Shaw	3.8E
Croft	"	Ted Worswick	3.8E
Crystal Palace	"	John Quick	3.8E
Llandow	"	Robin Darlington	3.8E
Lydden Hill	Special GT cars over 2500cc	Rob Schroeder/ Mike Loveday	3.8E
Lydden Hill	Production sports cars over 3000cc	John Quick	3.8E
Mallory Park (club)	"	John Filbee	3.8E
Mallory Park (full)	"	John Filbee	3.8E
Oulton Park	"	Mike Franey	3.8E
Silverstone (club)	"	Warren Pearce	3.8E
Snetterton	"	Warren Pearce	3.8E
Thruxton	"	John Quick	3.8E

Chapter 4

Lightweights, Semi-Lightweights and Specials

Although widely covered in just about every other Jaguar history book, it is necessary to mention the so-called 'Lightweights' in order to at least encompass all the racing E-Types that I can think of. The average Jaguar coffee table book will always include 'The 12 Lightweights,' but not the other Factory specials that were built for particular customers.

The 'Lightweights' were destined for proven race drivers chosen by the Factory. These cars have been extensively documented in many publications, and the list of drivers and owners gets longer with each passing year as these prized 'works of art' change hands at ever increasing prices. Their high value, however, does not always deter their owners from putting them on the track and using them for the purpose for which they were built. The E-Type 4 WPD, for example, seems to return to the track on a regular basis to try and destroy itself over and over again! In July 1994, it was very badly damaged at the Coys International Historic Festival at Silverstone, with substantial front, rear and side impacts, as well as the ensuing fire damage. Again at Goodwood in 2008 it suffered very substantial front and rear damage.

For those who want more detail than might be found in the average Jaguar book, Philip Porter has written extensively on these particular cars. His book, *Ultimate E-Type – The Competition Cars*, covers all the Lightweights and Specials. There is also his book on the first Lightweight, *Jaguar Lightweight E-Type – The Autobiography of 4 WPD*.

Would anyone, should anyone, dare to question anything about these cars? Well, perhaps it's worth a punt.

Let's take 4 WPD, the first 'Factory'-prepared race car. Even this standard roadster initially raced with its soft-top ... now, of course, it bears no resemblance at all to the original. This car was used for continuing Factory development work, and is also fully covered in the excellent book by Peter Wilson *Cat out of the Bag* ... he should know about it: he was there. So, how would you describe the original 4 WPD? I don't think I want to answer that particular question, probably because it is the most developed Lightweight of them all.

As you may know, the development of 4 WPD engendered the creation of a further 11 'Lightweight' cars. Unfortunately, only ten of these now exist, as 5116 WK was totally written off and later scrapped. Strange, therefore, that rumours persist about the return of 5116 WK as 'someone' has 'something' that they can build the original around. We await with bated breath the press coverage, if that recreation ever surfaces.

I think it is important to highlight here that there is no sales brochure for the Lightweight E-Type. This is because, for homologation purposes, these cars were simply modified standard cars: ie a production E-Type fitted with Factory optional extras – perhaps a little stretching of the rules is in evidence here, as nearly every part on the car was changed.

The Factory specials include 12 Lightweights, three Semi-Lightweights, one special roadster, one Low Drag Coupe, and one 'extra' Lightweight built from parts (but not by the Factory).

In my opinion, the terms Lightweight, Semi-Lightweight and Low Drag Coupe have become synonymous with the Factory cars, therefore, if you see a car described as a Lightweight or Semi-Lightweight and it is not included here, you might want to question it.

Lightweights and specials (all roadsters unless stated otherwise)

Chassis number	Registration number	First owner
1. S850006 (later S850658)	BUY 1 then 4 WPD	Coombs

4 WPD at a hill climb circa 1963. (Copyright Ted Walker Ferret Fotographics)

2. S850659 5115 WK Cunningham

Perhaps the most famous genuine Lightweight E-Type, 5115 WK at Donington Park in June 1991. (Copyright Peter Griffiths)

3. S850660 5113 WK? Qvale

The ex-Ed Leslie and Frank Morrill Lightweight E-Type at the Goodwood Revival in 2010. (Copyright Ian Hunt)

4. S850661 86 PJ Atkins

86 PJ at the Goodwood Revival in 2011. (Copyright Ian Hunt)

5. S850662** 4868 WK Lindner

4868 WK seen here in 1964 at Le Mans driven by Peter Lindner. (Copyright Ted Walker Ferret Fotographics)

4868 WK in its pre-low drag days. (Copyright Lothar Spurzem)

** As a point of interest, in Robert Berry's book *Jaguar – Motor Racing and the Manufacturer*, he states that the highest recorded brake horse power for a 3.8 E-Type was 344 in the Lightweight E-Type 4868 WK using an alloy block and fuel injection.

6.	S850663	49 FXN	Lumsden/ Sargent

49 FXN driven by Peter Lumsden in the 1000km race in 1963. (Copyright Ted Walker Ferret Fotographics)

7. S850664 5114 WK Cunningham

Genuine Lightweight 5114 WK. (Copyright Paul Skilleter)

8. S850665 5113 WK /5116 WK Cunningham

5116 WK at Le Mans in 1963. (Paul Skilleter Collection)

9. S850666 YVH 210 then SVM 740 Sutcliffe

Lightweight E-Type YVH 210 photographed at the E-Type Challenge at Silverstone in July 2011. (Copyright Peter Griffiths)

Lightweight E-Type SVM 740 owned by Brian Corser. (Copyright Peter Griffiths)

10. S850667 JAG 038 Jane

The Lightweight E-Type of Bob Jane.
(Copyright Les Hughes)

11. S850668 2 GXO Wilkins

Lightweight E-Type 2 GXO, seen at Donington in June 1991, when owned by Nigel Corner. (Copyright Peter Griffiths)

12. S850669 PS 1175 Scragg

Lightweight E-Type PS 1175, photographed at the Lynx test day at Goodwood. (Copyright Peter Griffiths)

13. EC 1001 LDC CUT 7 then 738 EUT Protheroe

738 EUT (formerly CUT 7) driven by M Wright at the Prescott Hill Climb in May 1967. (Copyright Ted Walker Ferret Fotographics)

14. 879401 5081 WK (13th LWE) Webb

Car no 31, the 13th Lightweight 5081 WK (Lynx Engineering), in company with 310 WK (Ron Lea). (Copyright Peter Griffiths)

15. S875027 9023 DU Cunningham

Semi-Lightweight 9023 DU. (Copyright Bryce Womeldurf)

The Cunningham roadster at the Le Mans test day in 1962, driven by Alfred Momo/Walt Hansgen. Although no registration number is present, it is believed to be 9023 DU. (Copyright Ted Walker Ferret Fotographics)

16. 860630 FHC 1337 VC, 931 PUU Cunningham

The Cunningham FHC at Le Mans in 1962. (Copyright Paul Skilleter)

17. S890193 FHC EYY 32B Bardinon

The special Semi-Lightweight FHC of Pierre Bardinon S890193. (Copyright Paul Skilleter)

18. S850817 1 WW, XAJ 1, CJX 672C Ropner

XAJ 1, one of the original Factory Semi-Lightweights, seen here at Silverstone in 1972. (Copyright Ted Walker Ferret Fotographics)

Another car that could be included (depending upon your point of view) is 4 GXO. This car is documented in the March 2013 issue of *Jaguar Enthusiast* magazine, when Paul Skilleter wrote a full article on the Lightweights. It seems to have acquired the status of the 14th Lightweight.

A nice shot of 4 GXO during its build, using the original tub employed on the rebuild of 4868 WK. (Copyright Paul Skilleter)

Author's note: Jaguar originally decided to build 18 Lightweights for competition use. Although 18 aluminium bodyshells were originally made, only 11 of those were fully built into Lightweights. One bodyshell was used to convert BUY 1 from a steel bodied car (one of the special ZP cars) after earlier attempts at using a lighter gauge steel. This resulted in the 12 Lightweights we know today. My understanding is that four of the six remaining bodies were used for 'in period' repairs – one on 4 WPD, one on 49 FXN, and two on the Peter Sutcliffe car YVH 210. One was used for the 13th Lightweight, and the last was used on the 4868 WK rebuild, which is now on 4 GXO. In 2014, Jaguar announced that it was going to build the six missing Lightweights from the original batch of 18 – or is that 17? So, if my maths is correct, there are now 20 Lightweights (14 + 6). If the original 18 bodies had already been made and chassis numbers allocated, then the six new bodies make a total of 24 Lightweights – or is that 26? My understanding is that the 'new' Lightweights do not conform to current standards to allow them to be road registered, so perhaps they can only be raced? The numbers remain confusing, despite these being the widely documented Factory cars.

Not even the individual Lightweights are free from controversy and some histories are far from simple. For example, 5113 WK: this was the registration number issued to S850665, but the number plate visible on the car was actually 5116 WK. However, a photograph in Philip Porter's book *Ultimate E-Type* shows 5113 WK on the Qvale Lightweight, chassis number S850660.

For a detailed look at all of these cars, it is well worth investing not only in the books previously referred to, but also *Jaguar C-Type, D-Type and Lightweight E-Type Register*.

With all the continual rebuilds of these and other racing E-Types, it seems that 5116 WK may well be resurrected soon. Many other E-Types have been totally destroyed, and yet still appear today. It may be worth looking at the website coventryracers.com to read about the continuing controversy surrounding this car. Even Porter's book highlights a potential claimant to the resurrection of 5116 WK ... Or perhaps that should be 5113 WK?

The age old question "When is a car written off?" will probably never be answered, the courts already having ruled that 'continuous history' is the yardstick, rather than originality of the car or its constituent parts.

Obvious examples of total rebuilds include:

4868 WK (version 2)
898 BYR
310 WK
7 CXW
CUT 7 (version 2)

The first version of CUT 7, for example, sold for around £350,000 in 2004, but of course looks very different to the car Dick Protheroe drove. When 4 WPD appeared at Goodwood in recent years, it looked quite different to the car Graham Hill drove. On the other hand, 7 CXW seems to have gone full circle: the car recreated by Paul Webb does look like the car raced by Ken Baker, but of course it went through many rebuilds in between, looking like several different cars. Ultimately, do many people really care? If you have paid for something and you are happy with it, does that spurious non-originality really matter? Perhaps it will only be an issue if two or more cars turn up claiming to be the original, as in the case of the D-Type Le Mans cars. Not forgetting Ferrari, of course. Thankfully, we have not heard of many duplicate

E-Types yet, but perhaps it is only a matter of time, as prices continue to rise – Lightweights currently reach anything up to £5 million.

In my opinion, there are hardly any 'true' Lightweight replicas, most simply being 'lookalikes.' The original Lightweight E-Types had aluminium tubs and aluminium engine blocks. How many of the so called 'replicas' can boast that?

Lynx Motors produced its fabulous D-Type replica, which was so good that people were proud to say that they owned a 'Lynx' and not a D-Type replica. From overall knowledge of working on original D-Types, Lynx did produce copies of the original, although I understand that the company hid a few tell-tale marks so that it could identify one of its cars should it ever be passed off as an original – this is very commendable, but not all companies are as honourable.

It is a shame to me that the ever increasing values of these cars means that they are treasured more for their financial value than their historical worth, and the all important part they played in the history of the Jaguar company.

The C- and D-Types helped create the Jaguar legend at Le Mans in the '50s. The E-Type did not continue this tradition, and Jaguar fans had to wait until 1988 when the mighty XJR 9-LM drove to victory once again.

Why then, has the Lightweight E-Type been coveted so much? What is so special about it? Did it win (m)any races? Was it built at the wrong time, when the competition was much better? I, for one, think the Lightweight E-Types are overrated.

I will finish this section with some descriptions taken from the programme of just one of the races at the 75th members meeting at Goodwood race circuit on the weekend of the 18th and 19th March 2017.

My comments are included in brackets after each entry.

Car	Drivers	Description given of car entered
14	Meins/Huff	Jaguar E-Type (This is the first CUT 7 E-Type ex-Dick Protheroe, correctly described)
29	Hancock/Rittweger	Jaguar E-Type Lightweight (This is a genuine Lightweight registration YVH 210)
17	Wakeman/Smith	Jaguar E-Type Semi-Lightweight spec (This is a roadster E-Type, registration number OWC 4 finished in silver to 'look like' a Semi-Lightweight.)
10	Gomm/Keith-Lucas	Jaguar E-Type (Correctly described E-Type in black, registration number KGJ 745A, although it does carry a lookalike Low Drag Coupe body.)
31	Lindsay/Lindemann	Jaguar E-Type Low Drag Coupe (Green with gold stripes, with a lookalike Low Drag Coupe body)
8	Breslow/Khan	Jaguar E-Type Lightweight (A blue roadster with Lightweight 'lookalike' body, not to be confused with number 29, the real thing.)
12	Blakeney-Edwards/Hunt	Jaguar E-Type Semi-Lightweight (A white roadster registration 49 FN built with certain Lightweight specs)

To recap, out of the seven cars entered in the race, only three were accurately described in my view. As someone who has spent years documenting the true history of Jaguar racing E-Types, it concerns me that, in years to come, these type of descriptions will lead to 'proof' about a car's provenance.

Chapter 5

The Magnificent Seven

These are the seven early E-Type roadsters produced under the direction of Claude Baily for project ZP 537/24. They have become known as the 'Magnificent Seven,' the 'ZP' cars, or simply the 'Factory Competition Cars.'

In order of chassis number, these seven cars are:

850005 This is the Equipe Endeavour car of Tommy Sopwith, ECD 400.

ECD 400 in the hands of Mike Parkes at Brands Hatch, October 1961. (Copyright Ted Walker Ferret Fotographics)

850006 This is the Coombs car BUY 1 (later 4 WPD), the Lightweight development car.

BUY 1 driven by Jackie Stewart at Brands Hatch in 1964. (Copyright Ted Walker Ferret Fotographics)

850007 This is 9 VPD, the second Coombs car used as a demonstrator. This has been rebuilt to full 'Lightweight' specification, and is now actively campaigned in historic racing.

850008 This is GB 8488, the car actively campaigned by Sir Gawaine Baillie.

9 VPD at the Goodwood Revival in 2011. (Copyright Ian Hunt)

GB 8488 – Sir Gawaine Baillie at Snetterton, 30 September 1961. (Copyright Ted Walker Ferret Fotographics)

850010 This is 3 BXV driven by Peter Berry (this car is quite often mistakenly identified in some articles as a genuine Lightweight, possibly because of its racing history, colour and Lightweight replica appearance).

3 BXV at the Goodwood Revival, 2009. (Copyright Ian Hunt)

850013 This is 4 BXV, the support car for 3 BXV, and now owned by George Missetzis, a true fan of these rare early cars, having meticulously restored this example to concours standard.

4 BXV, taken in July 2011. (Copyright Ian Hunt)

850018 This is the second Equipe Endeavour car, originally registered EE 400, now UPM 400.

A photo of UPM 400, seen at Goodwood in April 2013. (Copyright Paul Skilleter)

Only these seven cars are the true ZP cars.

Some articles have erroneously attributed other early race cars to this specification. Jaguar initially decided that 18 early cars should go to prospective customers who might race them, such as 898 BYR of Peter Sargent (chassis number 850009), 2 BBC of Robin Sturgess (chassis number 850012), 140 FPX of Briggs Cunningham (chassis number 850014), RL 26 of Jack Lambert (chassis number 850016), and YRP 999 (chassis number 850020), ie these are not ZP cars.

A photo of the original project specification is shown opposite.

The book *Jaguar – C-Type, D-Type and Lightweight E-Type Register* gives a detailed description of all 18 cars.

Paul Skilleter wrote a great article on the ZP cars in the February 2011 edition of *Jaguar World Monthly*.

Information on these cars is also available on the Jaguar Daimler Heritage Trust website, under the section on The Lightweight E-Type Collection – page 20 of 28.

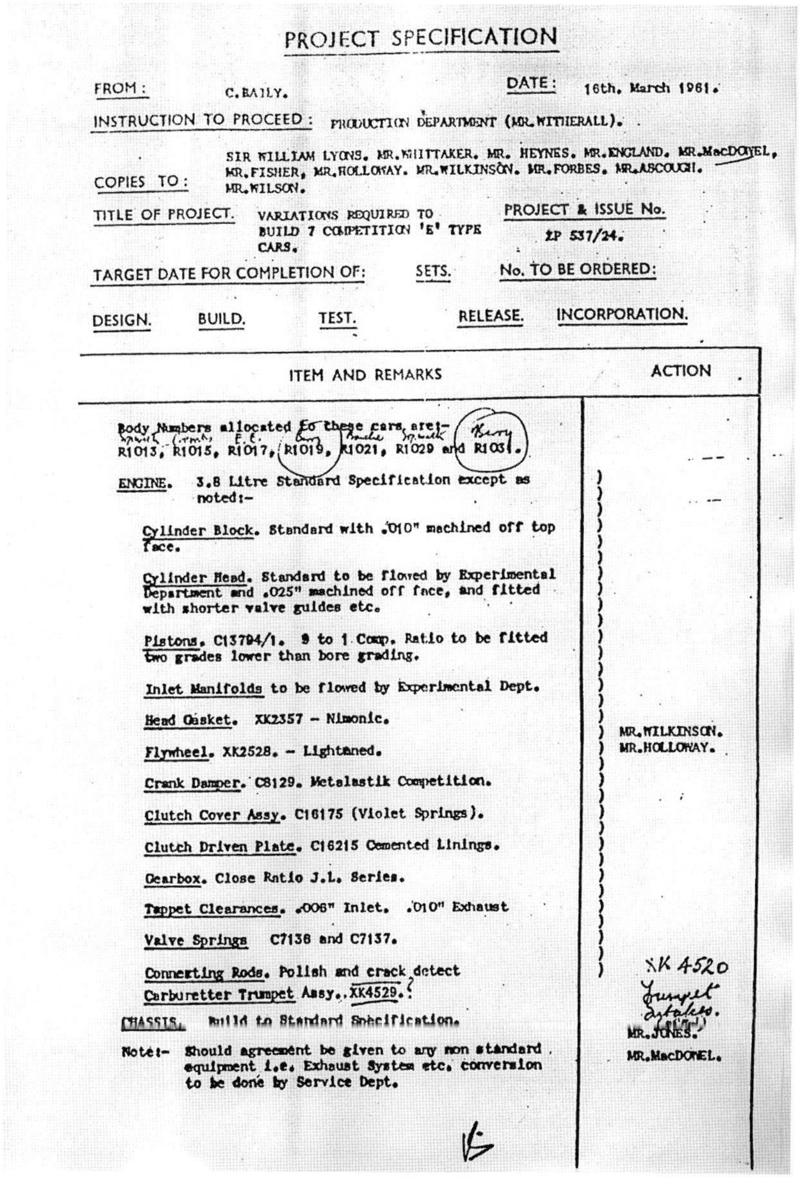

PROJECT SPECIFICATION

FROM: C. BAILY. DATE: 16th. March 1961.

INSTRUCTION TO PROCEED: PRODUCTION DEPARTMENT (MR. WITHERALL).

COPIES TO: SIR WILLIAM LYONS. MR. WHITTAKER. MR. HEYNES. MR. ENGLAND. MR. MacDOWEL, MR. FISHER, MR. HOLLOWAY. MR. WILKINSON. MR. FORBES. MR. ASCOUGH. MR. WILSON.

TITLE OF PROJECT. VARIATIONS REQUIRED TO BUILD 7 COMPETITION 'E' TYPE CARS.

PROJECT & ISSUE No. ZP 537/24.

TARGET DATE FOR COMPLETION OF: SETS. No. TO BE ORDERED:

DESIGN. BUILD. TEST. RELEASE. INCORPORATION.

ITEM AND REMARKS	ACTION
Body Numbers allocated to these cars are:- R1013, R1015, R1017, R1019, R1021, R1029 and R1031.	
ENGINE. 3.8 Litre Standard Specification except as noted:-	
Cylinder Block. Standard with .010" machined off top face.	
Cylinder Head. Standard to be flowed by Experimental Department and .025" machined off face, and fitted with shorter valve guides etc.	
Pistons. C13794/1. 9 to 1 Comp. Ratio to be fitted two grades lower than bore grading.	
Inlet Manifolds to be flowed by Experimental Dept.	
Head Gasket. XK2357 – Nimonic.	MR. WILKINSON. MR. HOLLOWAY.
Flywheel. XK2528. – Lightened.	
Crank Damper. C8129. Metalastik Competition.	
Clutch Cover Assy. C16175 (Violet Springs).	
Clutch Driven Plate. C16215 Cemented Linings.	
Gearbox. Close Ratio J.L. Series.	
Tappet Clearances. .006" Inlet. .010" Exhaust	
Valve Springs C7136 and C7137.	
Connecting Rods. Polish and crack detect	XK 4520
Carburetter Trumpet Assy.. XK4529.?	
CHASSIS. Build to Standard Specification.	MR. JONES.
Note:- Should agreement be given to any non standard equipment i.e. Exhaust System etc. conversion to be done by Service Dept.	MR. MacDONEL.

The project specification notice for the Factory ZP cars. (Paul Skilleter Collection)

Chapter 6

E-Types at Le Mans

Like the 12 Lightweights, the cars that raced at Le Mans are widely covered in most other Jaguar publications, but still need to be included here. The mere fact that a car raced at Le Mans seems to have pushed its value skywards, regardless of whether it even finished or not. An overall summary of the cars is shown in this chapter.

49 FXN at Le Mans in 1964 driven by Peter Lumsden. (Copyright Ted Walker Ferret Fotographics)

4868 WK (Low Drag Coupe form) driven by Peter Lindner and Peter Nocker leads 49 FXN (long nose form) driven by Peter Lumsden and Peter Sargent. (Copyright Ted Walker Ferret Fotographics)

Drivers	Chassis	Race no.	Reg	Finished
1960				
Gurney/Hansgen	E2A	6		DNF

VKV 752 (E2A) at Goodwood in 2012. (Copyright Ian Hunt)

1962				
Cunningham/Salvadori	860630	10	1337 VC	4th

The Cunningham FHC seen at Le Mans in 1962. (Copyright Paul Skilleter)

Lumsden/Sargent	850009	9	898 BYR	5th

898 BYR at Le Mans in 1962. (Copyright Ted Walker Ferret Fotographics)

Charles/Coundley	860458	8	503 BBO	DNF

A nice shot of the Maurice Charles car in the paddock at Le Mans in 1962. (Paul Skilleter Collection)

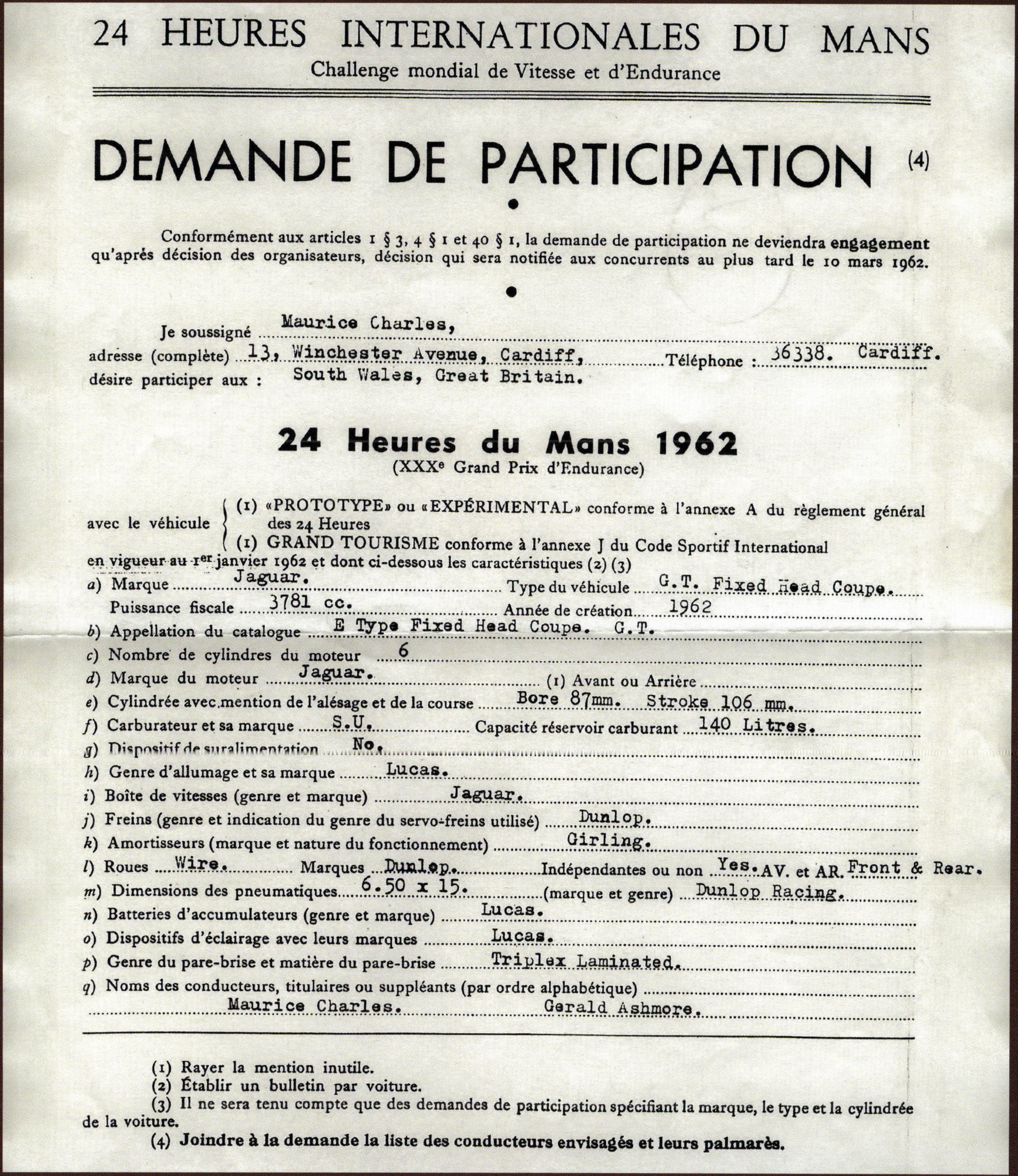

24 HEURES INTERNATIONALES DU MANS

Challenge mondial de Vitesse et d'Endurance

DEMANDE DE PARTICIPATION (4)

•

Conformément aux articles 1 § 3, 4 § 1 et 40 § 1, la demande de participation ne deviendra **engagement** qu'après décision des organisateurs, décision qui sera notifiée aux concurrents au plus tard le 10 mars 1962.

•

Je soussigné Maurice Charles,
adresse (complète) 13, Winchester Avenue, Cardiff, Téléphone : 36338. Cardiff.
désire participer aux : South Wales, Great Britain.

24 Heures du Mans 1962

(XXXe Grand Prix d'Endurance)

avec le véhicule (1) «PROTOTYPE» ou «EXPÉRIMENTAL» conforme à l'annexe A du règlement général des 24 Heures
(1) GRAND TOURISME conforme à l'annexe J du Code Sportif International
en vigueur au 1er janvier 1962 et dont ci-dessous les caractéristiques (2) (3)

a) Marque Jaguar. Type du véhicule G.T. Fixed Head Coupe.
Puissance fiscale 3781 cc. Année de création 1962
b) Appellation du catalogue E Type Fixed Head Coupe. G.T.
c) Nombre de cylindres du moteur 6
d) Marque du moteur Jaguar. (1) Avant ou Arrière
e) Cylindrée avec mention de l'alésage et de la course Bore 87mm. Stroke 106 mm.
f) Carburateur et sa marque S.U. Capacité réservoir carburant 140 Litres.
g) Dispositif de suralimentation No.
h) Genre d'allumage et sa marque Lucas.
i) Boîte de vitesses (genre et marque) Jaguar.
j) Freins (genre et indication du genre du servo-freins utilisé) Dunlop.
k) Amortisseurs (marque et nature du fonctionnement) Girling.
l) Roues Wire. Marques Dunlop. Indépendantes ou non Yes. AV. et AR. Front & Rear.
m) Dimensions des pneumatiques 6.50 x 15. (marque et genre) Dunlop Racing.
n) Batteries d'accumulateurs (genre et marque) Lucas.
o) Dispositifs d'éclairage avec leurs marques Lucas.
p) Genre du pare-brise et matière du pare-brise Triplex Laminated.
q) Noms des conducteurs, titulaires ou suppléants (par ordre alphabétique)
Maurice Charles. Gerald Ashmore.

(1) Rayer la mention inutile.
(2) Établir un bulletin par voiture.
(3) Il ne sera tenu compte que des demandes de participation spécifiant la marque, le type et la cylindrée de la voiture.
(4) **Joindre à la demande la liste des conducteurs envisagés et leurs palmarès.**

A rare photo of the 1962 Le Mans entry form for the Maurice Charles car. (Paul Skilleter Collection)

1963

Cunningham/Grossman	S850659	15	5115 WK	9th

Le Mans 1963. (Copyright Ted Walker Ferret Fotographics)

5115 WK at Le Mans in 1963, driven by Cunningham/Grossman. (Copyright Ted Walker Ferret Fotographics)

Bob Grossman. Seen here trying to pull out the damage! (Copyright Ted Walker Ferret Fotographics)

5115 WK at Le Mans in 1963, following its accident when driven by Bob Grossman. (Copyright Ted Walker Ferret Fotographics)

Salvadori/Richards	S850665	16	5116 WK **	DNF	** Apparently this car S850665 was originally registered 5113 WK, but at Le Mans it carried the registration number 5116 WK (perhaps to link with the race number?).

E-Type no 16 at Le Mans in 1963. (Copyright Paul Skilleter)

Hansgen/Pabst	S850664	14	5114 WK	DNF

Cunningham cars 5114 WK and 5115 WK seen here at Le Mans In 1963. (Copyright Ted Walker Ferret Fotographics)

1964

Lindner/Nocker	S850662	16	4868 WK	DNF

4868 WK, seen here in 1964 at Le Mans driven by Peter Lindner. (Copyright Ted Walker Ferret Fotographics)

Lumsden/Sargent	S850663	17	49 FXN	DNF

49 FXN at Le Mans in 1964, driven by Peter Lumsden, being chased by 4868 WK. (Copyright Ted Walker Ferret Fotographics)

A good article on the E-Types at Le Mans appeared in *Jaguar World Monthly* in July 2003. It stated: "Unlike the C-Type, the E-Type was never designed to win at Le Mans, but it put up a worthy fight!"

Is the E-Type, therefore, all we would like it to be? Nine cars entered Le Mans over a four year period, but only three managed to finish. The highest place attained was 4th by a privately entered fixed head coupe. Of the five Lightweights that entered, only one finished, and that only managed 9th. As questioned earlier, is the fixed-head E-Type a better car than the roadster? Prices achieved by E-Type roadsters, and in particular the Lightweights, are always far above that achieved for a fixed head. I think the fixed head is a far prettier car, and has certainly proved to be a better racing car. Dick Protheroe would only have fixed heads, Robin Sturgess changed from a roadster to a fixed head, and even the two Peters, Lumsden and Sargent, changed their roadster (898 BYR) into a fixed head, and later did the same on their Lightweight (49 FXN). Remember, the Low Drag Coupe 4868 WK started life as a roadster.

The high values commanded by the Le Mans E-Types seem to have no bearing on their race results:

E2A – Whilst not an actual E-Type, I have included it for the sake of completeness. The car retired after 89 laps because of a damaged fuel line.

1337 VC – The most successful Le Mans car having finished 4th in the 1962 race. This beautiful fixed head coupe 860630 (always seen carrying its race number 10) is pictured in most books, but sadly went into retirement in 1966 after only a few unsuccessful races.

898 BYR – Chassis 850009, the next most successful Le Mans car, having finished 5th behind the Cunningham car 1337 VC in 1962. This very early roadster was converted to its distinctive fixed head form for the race. It raced a further handful of times in 1962 before retiring and returning to the road. It was destroyed in 1970 only to be rebuilt in the '90s

503 BBO – Chassis 860458 was the third E-Type in the 1962 race. Unfortunately the engine broke with conrod failure after three hours. I cannot find evidence of any later races in period.

5115 WK – This is probably the best known and most widely photographed E-Type, let alone Lightweight. It did manage to finish 9th at Le Mans but only after the lengthy bonnet repair following brake loss and subsequent crash. A replacement bonnet was not allowed under the rules, so it was repaired with part of the bonnet from 5114 WK, which had already retired. At least this Lightweight was not retired after Le Mans, but continued to race in the UK and US for many years, with a reasonable amount of success. Perhaps notoriety came in 1990 when it sold for £1.2m, which was the first time an E-Type had made over a million pounds.

5116 WK (or should we say 5113 WK) – This car crashed and caught fire at Le Mans, and was totally written off. The remains were taken back to Jaguar at Coventry, some parts were salvaged and returned to Cunningham.

5114 WK – Following a gearbox failure, the car did not finish the 24 Hours ... but at least part of its bonnet did!

4868 WK – Despite not finishing the 24 Hours, this car has become famous, perhaps not for its racing history, but for the crash at Montlhéry later in 1964 when driver Peter Lindner and four others were killed. The car was then impounded for ten years before being 'rebuilt' twice. A Channel 4 TV program in

2015 on Jaguar's new Lightweights (*Inside Jaguar: making a million pound car*) featured this car, and whilst suggesting it was now worth in the order of £5m, the second rebuild, using the original damaged aluminium panels (now repaired), may render the car now unsuitable for serious racing because of the reduced inherent strength in the reworked aluminium.

49 FXN – Another beautiful Low Drag Coupe built on the original Lightweight roadster bodyshell. At Le Mans, as well as several other races over the next ten years or so, the race positions were recorded as DNF. In 1966 it was rolled at Oulton Park but later rebuilt.

To summarise, the Lightweights could have proved successful racing cars, but in my opinion they were not. They were dogged with unreliability issues, possibly due to the lighter weight parts. These cars were always expensive (maybe the reason why they didn't build, let alone sell, the last six of the original batch of 18). Towards the end of the 1960s you could have a very much cheaper, and probably more reliable modsports car. My view is that the fixed head is a better race car, and I think Jaguar should have made these the 'Lightweights,' rather than the roadsters

Chapter 7

The Modsports Era

The front row of the grid at Brands Hatch showing the impressive line-up of Warren Pearce (on pole closest to clock), John Quick and John Wilson. The best of modsports racing in the golden years. (Copyright Ted Walker Ferret Fotographics)

Believe it or not, there was a time when, like the D-Type before it, the E-Type could be bought for under £1000. I can even recall drooling over a genuine Lightweight being offered for £5000, probably the equivalent of five years' salary at the time – obviously a good investment, looking back! When, eventually, the next generation of models emerged, the E-Type, like all production cars, reached the end of the line, and by 1975 it was past its prime.

In the late '60s/early '70s, club racers saw great potential in being able to buy a 150mph E-Type sports car for around £1000, and modify it to go even quicker by lightening what was a fairly heavy car. Heavy steel panels were replaced with fibreglass, the car was lowered, the wheels widened, and all for very little cost. For those with a little spare cash the engine could be improved, Weber or Dellorto carbs could be fitted, a race exhaust could be added, and all again without breaking the bank.

Dozens of modsports cars popped up all over the country at just about every race circuit, and the E-Type was once again winning races. It seems to me that there were two main groups, which, because of the distances involved, rarely raced against each other. The 'southern' cars tended to concentrate on the circuits at Brands Hatch and Lydden whilst the 'northern' cars concentrated on the circuits at Croft, Donington, Oulton Park and Rufforth, with only the occasional meet ups at the central circuits of Silverstone, Mallory Park and Snetterton. Those were the days when the race cars were trailered behind the family saloon and circuits at the other end of the country meant too great an expense with extra petrol and hotel bills.

Drivers who did not wish to take part in full race meetings found an outlet for their race E-Types in sprint and hill climb events, at which the modsports car became extremely competitive. I will never forget experiencing the ground shaking V12 of Will Cole's monster at the start of the Wiscombe Hill Climb! On the internet there is also an example of a pink E-Type dragster 'Snoopy,' which in 1968 did achieve 170mph, but sadly it crashed killing the driver.

As modsports racing naturally progressed, the cars became wilder and consequently more expensive to build, run and maintain. One such example is Warren Pearce's car 310 WK, which started out as a virtually standard roadster that he continually developed. It was later progressed by Brian Murphy and subsequently Fred Cliffe. The car was damaged at Aintree in 1982 by its next owner, Ron Lea, who rebuilt it to the spec when last raced by Warren Pearce. This is documented in Ron's book *If at first you don't succeed.*

The modsports owner, often also the driver and the mechanic, had a genuine interest in development, and was prepared to try all manner of alterations to enhance the car's performance. In those days, the car was of more importance than its monetary value.

So, when did the 'modified' E-Type become the 'modsports' E-Type?

I cannot find any mention of a purely original 'standard' E-Type having competed in any race meeting with any success. Even the first racers, ECD 400 and BUY 1, had various Factory modifications, despite looking like standard cars with their soft tops and wire wheels. From as early as 1961 then, the E-Type had been modified for racing. Warren Pearce in 310 WK seems to have started the modsports E-Type trend in the mid to late '60s and others followed suit.

Many would suggest that the Modsports era began in the early '70s when fibreglass body panels and wide wheels became commonplace. Although some of the earlier cars did have wider wheel arches, the modsports E-Types were extended even further by a foot or more ... so, the distinction between modified and modsports is just a matter of degree. I think it is difficult, therefore, to pin down exactly when one might say the 'Modsports era' actually began.

The E-Type was a fabulous road car but was never sold as a racing car, neither did Jaguar itself enter it in any form of competition. However, for customers who wanted to race, in 1961 the Factory had supplied specially prepared cars with inbuilt modifications, such as the ZP roadsters. Those with standard models could refer to Jaguar's booklet *Tuning & Preparation of E-Type cars for competition use.* Certain enhancements were absolutely necessary for safety reasons, for example, brakes, suspension and roll cage. Other modifications were simply to make the car faster. These might be lighter body panels, improved engines and gearboxes.

Following the success of the modified E-Types, Jaguar seized the opportunity for publicity via the racing exploits of customers and consequently, the Factory began its own development program with the Coombs roadster BUY 1, later to become 4 WPD. Studying Philip Porter's excellent book *Jaguar Lightweight E-Type – The Autobiography of 4 WPD,* it seems this car underwent several changes from as early as July 1961. Wider steel wheel arches followed in 1962 and even larger ones were evident in 1964. Also, the Factory had chosen fibreglass for the production roadster's hard top as early as 1961.

Evidently, the only difference between the wide wheels

and fibreglass of the Factory cars versus those of the modsports cars, is the size of wheels and the amount of fibreglass used. In my opinion, modsports are far superior to the Lightweights; they were certainly more effective at winning races due to the improved setup. Possibly, drivers were prepared to risk higher speeds in a car with a £50 fibreglass bonnet rather than a £5000 aluminium one.

A very early example of a privateer modifiying his E-Type for racing is Dick Protheroe in his FHC, chassis number 4 – the original CUT 7. The car soon ran with an aluminium bonnet, perspex rear door and D-Type engine, as well as numerous other improvements. Dick's second CUT 7 was created from parts supplied by the Factory, having virtually no interior, no heater system, no radio, no bumpers or any other chromework ... really 'modsportish' perhaps! Other 'modified' 1960s era cars besides Dick Protheroe's included those of Warren Pearce, Harding Scott Wiseman, and Rhoddy Harvey Bailey.

The E-Type even in 'standard' form could get the better of most of its contemporaries, but with the emergence of modified Lotuses, Healeys, Corvettes and the like, it was not long before the E-Type needed further improvement in order to remain competitive. The RAC Blue Book rules permitted increased freedoms for modsports racing, which resulted in unprecedented developments. The E-Type lent itself to fairly easy modification, both in terms of mechanical enhancement and outlandish body styles to cover the ever increasing tyre sizes – 14in rears were common. Lowered suspension and other alterations often meant that the engine and ancillaries were too high, so holes were cut all over the bonnet to allow the radiator, throttle linkages, even cam covers to poke through. Cooling scoops were also added to the bonnet to help the over-stressed brakes.

It would be remiss of me if I were not to mention Fred Cliffe in this chapter; he was a highly successful racing driver during this era, as well as an expert in E-Type modifications, and many modsports cars have passed through his workshop at some stage. A few of the E-Types that Fred owned include; the Sir Robert Ropner Semi-Lightweight (XAJ 1), the ex-Lumsden/ Sargent Le Mans entered 898 BYR, John Quick's WOO 11, John Cuff's 8448 TJ, the Warren Pearce/Brian Murphy 310 WK, in addition to several of his own creations. Cars that he built include the Simon Watney FHC, later raced by Paul Webb, his own 4.2 roadster FNC 2, and, in my opinion, his best achievement, the V12 roadster destined to become 'The World's Fastest E-Type' when later owned by Rob Beere and Malcolm Hamilton.

The following are examples of typical modsports modifications:

Bodywork

Every panel would be altered in some way to either save weight or to cover the ever widening tyres or altered mechanicals. For the club racer of the '70s, fibreglass ruled – it was readily available, easily repaired in the event of an accident, cheap to buy or make, and extremely light.

The steel monocoque was lightened as much as possible in order to compensate for the addition of the roll over bar, and holes were drilled to let cold air in, and hot air out. The bonnet, doors, roof (FHC), bootlid (DHC), and rear wings were all made of fibreglass; even the roadster's heavy Factory hardtop was replaced with a much lighter fibreglass one, devoid of any chrome fittings. Although fibreglass bonnets were available for the road cars, these were too heavy for racing and special lighter ones were ordered from the manufacturers. The heavy steel boot floors were not really necessary, and were replaced with a Maserati birdcage type rear end, just to give a framework to hold the fibreglass panels. Doors, in a lot of cases, were just door skins in fibreglass, maybe with a steel bar for health and safety!

With the removal of all these steel panels, side and head lights, door furniture, the glass replaced with Perspex (even the windscreen), a smaller petrol tank fitted, and original seats replaced with a racing one, the overall weight could be reduced to under one ton.

With E-Types weighing in at around 24cwt for a series 1 3.8, up to around 29cwt for a V12 2+2, any weight saving was of tremendous help – these were modifications for the average club racer in the '60s and '70s. Nowadays aluminium or carbon fibre panels are used. I believe they are no lighter than the fibreglass ones, though they are very expensive and make the car more aesthetically pleasing to some!

Richard Scantlebury driving the Ziebart car at Brands Hatch in May 1976. (Copyright Ted Walker Ferret Fotographics)

John Oxborough at Brands Hatch in May 1976 driving his much modified roadster which, in fact, started life as an FHC originally driven by Alan Leeson. (Copyright Ted Walker Ferret Fotographics)

Brian Mills at the 1972 JDC meeting at Silverstone. (Copyright Ted Walker Ferret Fotographics)

Ron Lea driving the ex-Dave Moore modsports car at Snetterton in March 1978. (Copyright Ted Walker Ferret Fotographics)

The two Comet Delltune modsports E-Types of John Burbidge and Tony Shaw. (Copyright Graham Ravensdale)

John Burbidge at Snetterton in June 1966. (Copyright Ted Walker Ferret Fotographics)

John Burbidge at Snetteron in June 1970.
(Copyright Ted Walker Ferret Fotographics)

John Burbidge at Snetterton in June 1970. (Copyright Ted Walker Ferret Fotographics)

Brian Spicer seen here at Snetterton in May 1969. (Copyright Ted Walker Ferret Fotographics)

James Mayhew at Snetterton In March 1972. (Copyright Ted Walker Ferret Fotographics)

R Forbes at Snetterton in March 1972. (Copyright Ted Walker Ferret Fotographics)

590 DXR seen here at Castle Combe in September 1966. It was known as the Egal (E-Type with Galaxy V8 engine).
(Copyright Ted Walker Ferret Fotographics)

590 DXR at Castle Combe in September 1967.
(Copyright Ted Walker Ferret Fotographics)

This is 2164 WK at the JDC test day at Silverstone in March 1971 driven by John May. (Copyright Ted Walker Ferret Fotographics)

2164 WK after its horrific accident at the JDC test day in 1971 when driven by John May (thankfully, John survived intact). (Copyright Ted Walker Ferret Fotographics)

PBC 112 driven by John Wilson, with its later colour scheme at Silverstone in 1968. (Copyright Ted Walker Ferret Fotographics)

Brian Spicer in E 141 at Snetterton in April 1970. (Copyright Ted Walker Ferret Fotographics)

Mechanical modifications

Rear suspension

The four Metalastik brackets holding the rear cage to the underside of the monocoque would be welded up to give a firm ride with no movement, ie cheap worn out brackets would be used, so, no money being wasted here! The round 'doughnut' rubbers at the end of the radius arms were simply turned 90 degrees to stop any sideways movement. The wishbones were usually modified in order to lower the cars ride height; this was achieved by removing the shock absorber pickup points (mid point through the wishbone) and re-welding them under the wishbone. Shock absorbers were replaced with either Konis or Spax depending on your budget and preference. Spax could be adjusted on the car, and although not always liked as much as Konis by the perfectionists, they did give a more user friendly setup. Drive shafts were usually standard, as were the hub carriers, but there was always someone who thought they knew better than Jaguar! Rear discs were also standard for most, although as budgets increased and racing was taken more seriously, ventilated discs were fitted, along with appropriate callipers using racing brake fluid. The usual E-Type splined hubs were replaced with the standard Jaguar five-stud ones, usually from a Mark 2 or early XJ.

Of course, once the racing became more competitive, someone would have to try something different. Warren Pearce, for example, did away with the conventional wishbones and had them re-fabricated in box section tubing with rose-jointed ends. The anti-roll bar was also stiffened and rose-jointed. Most of the mods were done by home mechanics, the plethora of Jaguar specialists were not around in those days.

Differential

The standard ratio on most UK E-Types was 3.31:1, although depending upon whether you were sprinting, hill climbing or long distant racing (and then depending on the actual circuit), the other options of 3.54:1 or 3.77:1 could be chosen. I learnt from John Quick that he usually settled for 3.77:1 on WOO 11.

Front suspension

An area ripe for development! If you lowered the rear suspension, the front would require similar treatment. This was normally achieved by making the top pickup point for the front shock absorber higher, by removing the 'picture frame' and welding the pickup point higher, just like the D-Type arrangement. Alternatively, by cutting the frame and bending the ends upwards, then welding in a triangulated bracket. The front anti-roll bar was replaced with a stiffer one, and the torsion

A Warren Pearce trademark rear suspension modification, showing the lower wishbones refabricated and rose-jointed. (Copyright Peter Griffiths)

Front suspension detail on 310 WK when owned by Fred Cliffe. One of Fred's 'trademarks' was to drill into the top wishbone (weightsaving at every opportunity). (Copyright Peter Griffiths)

bars received similar treatment. Some drivers experimented with getting rid of the torsion bars altogether and replacing them with coil springs over the shockers. Again, Konis or Spax were the order of the day. Most bushes would be replaced with phosphor bronze rather than the normal Metalastik ones. Various treatments were given to the wishbones, including rose-jointed ones, but the Jaguar originals were hard to improve on. A typical Fred Cliffe modification was to drill holes in the top wishbone … it saved a few grams! I have also seen later Lightweight replicas with similar modifications. Stronger ball joints were fitted, standard uprights were usual, and the hubs were changed to Mark 2 or XJ like the rears. Early brake modifications were to use the larger Mark 9 discs until budgets increased and you could upgrade to ventilated ones. I recall the beautiful setup on Fred's E-Type, 310 WK, which had very large ventilated discs (possibly from a Porsche) with enormous alloy callipers as used on the XJ13.

Engine

It was all down to pounds, shillings and pence! It was the '60s!

The standard engine in the early days of club racing appears to have been adequate, perhaps with the inclusion of air trumpets on the SUs rather than the usual air filter. But then … you could use Weber or Dellorto carburettors, how about a 'bunch of bananas' exhaust manifold? Perhaps high-lift camshafts, big valves, a wide angle head, a dry sump system? Or why not have a D-Type engine?

As the cars had usually been lowered, it was normal and necessary for the exhaust to exit the car just after the front tyre, rather than at the rear. This meant little or no silencing, which was okay at some circuits, but not at all, and trouble with the sound police was common. On one car, I used rubber grommets up the exhaust to help solve the problem, reducing the noise to below the required decibel limit (easily removed just prior to the race!). Life seemed simpler back then.

Detailed shots of the author's modsports E-Type. (Copyright Peter Griffiths)

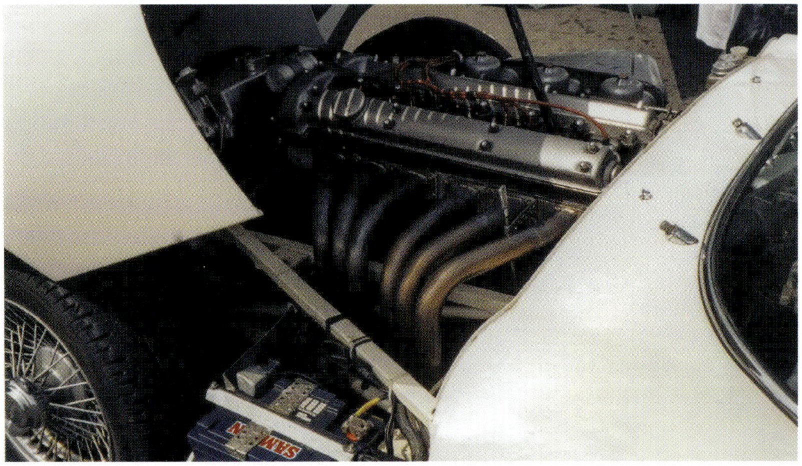

888 RYA, a Lightweight replica photographed at Donington in May 1992. (Copyright Peter Griffiths)

Engine photo of the rebuilt Leeson car showing 3 x 45DCOE Webers. (Copyright Peter Griffiths)

The engine bay of the modsports FHC owned by Bernie Breeze, seen here at Brands Hatch in 1990 – note the engine is set back further toward the middle of the car, and if you look closely you will see the double breather on the front of the engine. This is the original six-cylinder racer of Malcolm Hamilton before he progressed to the V12 'beast.' (Copyright Peter Griffiths)

Neville Robinson's E-Type at the JDC test day at Mallory Park. (Copyright Peter Griffiths)

Engine bay shots of the modsports FHC raced by Harry Phillips. (Copyright Peter Griffiths)

Engine bay shot of the extremely modified FHC driven by John Smith and Charlie Saunders. (Copyright Peter Griffiths)

Engine bay shots of the modsports FHC ALJ 92A raced by Jeff Hickson seen here at Brands Hatch in 1990. (Copyright Peter Griffiths)

Gearbox

The 3.8 and 4.2 standard gearbox was quite acceptable, perhaps with the addition of a competition clutch and stronger thrust race – no Getrag five-speeds here!

The ex-Simon Watney FHC modsports car photographed at the JDC Silverstone meet, the original colour being dark blue. (Copyright Peter Griffiths)

Interior

One racing seat, one full racing three or four point harness, a simplified dashboard: nothing else was needed. The trick was again all about saving weight.

In order to help cool the rear brakes, the upward sloping floor pan located just behind the driver's seat would usually have a large piece removed. Air was captured in large scoops behind the doors on the leading edge of the rear wings, and channelled via flexible ducting pipes to the above mentioned floor cut out, onto tubular fabricated brackets to hold them in place. Another benefit was that, as long as this floor panel was removable, it enabled easy access for changing the rear inboard brake pads. This 'modsports trick' was instigated by Dick Protheroe in 1962!

The massive air intakes typical of a modsports car. (Copyright Peter Griffiths)

The stark interior of the Leeson modsports car. Only items that were strictly necessary are present. (Copyright Peter Griffiths)

Wheels

The original wire wheels were soon dispensed with in order to run wider tyres. The cheaper option was to take Mark 2 or XJ steel wheels, and simply have them widened by welding in a steel band to your preferred width. Weller Wheels became the experts at this, and most racing Jaguars of all types would usually run them. Such wheels would, in time, fall foul of the scrutineers who considered a potential problem if some of the 'home' welds should fail. This led to bracing straps being welded in. Perhaps the most beautiful wheels of this era were those on 7 CXW when raced by Rob Shroeder and John Harper.

Drivers that had larger budgets opted for alloys from JA Pearce, Wolfrace, Minilites, or split rims from Mamba or Compomotive.

A selection of the various types of wheels used on modsports cars depending upon your budget, ranging from widened steel rims, to Minilites and Mambas, up to XJ220 race wheels. (Copyright Peter Griffiths)

Overall then, the name of the game seems to have been to jettison as much weight as possible, lower the centre of gravity, widen the tyres for better grip, increase the engine power, and then upgrade the brakes, clutch etc to take all this modification.

To what degree you got the balance right was usually manifested in the results. John Quick and WOO 11, Warren Pearce and 310 WK, Keith Holland and 9 WKJ, John Harper and 7 CXW, all bear witness to driver ability and well set up cars.

I remember with enormous affection the 'Intermarque' series of races where Jaguar battled with Astons, ACs, Porsches and Ferraris. One highlight of this series was in 1986 when the E-Type modsports team won the Championship outright. The six drivers were Malcolm Hamilton, Dave Moore, Ron Lea, Chris Shipton, Mike Tye, and Martin Wheatley.

The eventual decline of modsports was hastened by the lack of suitable races for these cars; when does a prodsports become a modsports? What mods are allowed? The arguments from the race scrutineers, judges and stewards, would inevitably take the fun out of club racing. The all important FIA Papers sounded the death knell for the modsports race series.

Many modsport cars have now disappeared forever because the current trend has been to take these old racers with their history, and possibly (but not likely) use their mechanicals to turn them into replica Lightweights.

There are still plenty of us around who have fond memories of the Modsports era, and I wanted to record this fabulous part of Jaguar history which, for the most part, has been overlooked by the regular Jaguar authors and purists.

Chapter 8

The Modern Racing Era

The Jaguar E-Type has gone through several phases in its long racing career, and has been very successful in competition, despite the fact that it was never intended as a racing car. From the 1960s, in the early years of racing, the cars were generally standard models which had been mildly modified. Simultaneously, the Factory was engaged in the Lightweight development programme, which saw several Le Mans entries.

Successive enhancements from the late '60s through to the '80s saw the Modsports era, E-Types with wide, often outrageous bodywork and increasing speeds. The modsports designs did not always find favour with the purists of the racing fraternity, but this was the period when most of the E-Type race histories were made.

Modsports racing declined towards the end of the '80s as fewer race series were available for these heavily modified cars. Racing for production looking cars was becoming increasingly popular – fibreglass was soon replaced by aluminium panels in order to give a more standard appearance. Although some had scorned the Modsports cars, it became acceptable to seek out these old racers in order to 'attach' their race history to the new cars – often Lightweight replicas. This trend would herald the next phase of the E-type race history which saw the return of the more standard looking cars on the racetrack.

By the '90s, technological advancements meant that, whilst the newer cars may look like regular road cars, they were far from standard in construction. One of the earlier race series was the HSCC Standard Road Sports Championship which attracted many of the new 'standard' E-Types. In 1992, *Jaguar Quarterly* magazine sponsored an historic race series just for E-Types. A full grid was achieved by allowing different classes to compete, from 'standard' to 'modified' cars, and a new era of E-Type racing had commenced. Several old cars came out of retirement, and, in addition, a profusion of newly prepared cars arrived 'from nowhere,' some with race histories, some with 'histories attached.'

Such was the interest in the return to the older style of 'standard' racing, the 'E-Type Experience' was created which enabled drivers to hire cars for track days, as well as the new race series. Several new specially built cars added to the ever growing number of Lightweight replicas.

More championships evolved to cater for the new wave of E-Types, and owners were eager to get race results under their belts. Such series included: The E-Type Experience – The JEC Challenge, the Cloth Cap European Race Series for Pre '66 Sportscars, the Sebring Salute European Historic Race Series for Pre '74 GTs, Sports and Touring Cars, the Masters Series, and perhaps the pinnacle, The E-Type Challenge.

Organised by Jaguar Heritage and the HSCC as part of the 50th anniversary of the E-Type in 2011, the E-Type Challenge launched at Brands Hatch, with subsequent races at Silverstone, Oulton Park and the Nürburgring. The Challenge ran with two classes: the FIA Appendix K specification cars prepared to period race trim, and the second class for just standard cars.

Almost 100 cars registered for the series, which attracted a host of notable drivers such as Jackie Oliver, Desiré Wilson, John Cleland, and Barrie 'Whizzo' Williams.

Although initially planned for the anniversary year only, in response to competitor demand, the series was extended into 2012, launching at the Donington Park Historic Festival. It continued for a third season into 2013.

In 2015 Jaguar, in partnership with the HSCC, expanded on the scope of the popular E-Type Challenge and announced a new single marque European series open to pre-'66 models. The newly named Jaguar Heritage Challenge Series ran at the same five circuits.

The success of these type of Championships has resulted in a whole new generation of replica Lightweights. These cars appear in race programmes as 'Semi-Lightweight' or just simply 'Lightweight'! This 'third' era of E-Type racing continues to thrive.

The E-Type has been racing in some guise or other continually since 1961, and although modern technology has helped, this 57 year old design is still winning races today. Personally, I find the individuality of the modsports cars more exciting, but seeing the E-Type still to the fore in the Challenge series and Goodwood Revival races only goes to prove that all those years ago, Jaguar did, in fact, build quite an exceptional sports car.

In 2014, Jaguar announced that it was to build the six 'missing' Lightweights from its 1963 project, when only 12 out of the 18 cars originally planned were completed. If these cars are not able to be road registered they may well be kept in private collections – optimistically we may see one on the track ... I haven't seen one yet!

Please see my notes on these cars in the chapter on Lightweights.

The 'missing' six Lightweights have been covered in numerous publications, and whilst it is necessary for completeness to mention them in this book, they are really outside the scope of the 'racing E-Type.'

An excellent article by Paul Skilleter on the new cars appeared in *Jaguar Enthusiast* magazine of January 2016. Channel 4 made an interesting documentary *Inside Jaguar: Making a Million Pound Car* which received extensive coverage.

Several cars from the modern race era are shown below.

KGJ 745A photographed at the E-Type Challenge at Silverstone in July 2011. (Copyright Peter Griffiths)

HJP 400 photographed at the E-Type Challenge at Silverstone in July 2011. (Copyright Peter Griffiths)

ANU 415A photographed at the E-Type Challenge at Silverstone in July 2011. (Copyright Peter Griffiths)

Several cars photographed at the E-Type Challenge at Silverstone in July 2011. (Copyright Peter Griffiths)

81 WPD Low Drag Coupe replica photographed at the E-Type Challenge at Silverstone in July 2011. (Copyright Peter Griffiths)

LNX 7 Low Drag Coupe replica photographed at the E-Type Challenge at Silverstone in July 2011. (Copyright Peter Griffiths)

Chapter 9

Jaguar E-Types in Rallying

I consider the term 'racing E-Type' to cover all competition cars, and not just those racers that go round a circuit for ten laps or so. The rally cars are usually overlooked and their achievements barely get a mention.

ECD 400 (chassis 850005), the early roadster driven by Graham Hill to win the marque's first race at Oulton Park in April 1961, became famous because of that one race. Some of the Le Mans cars never finished the race, yet all are famous and well documented. In contrast, the rally cars compete for hours, even days, demonstrating the E-Type's reliability and stamina, but they are often left out of the Jaguar history books altogether.

There are substantial differences between the rally cars vs the racing cars; all original equipment, such as windscreen wipers, bumpers, handbrake, alternator, etc, was required for rallying, whereas these would be absent in racing versions where weight saving was an aid to increased speed.

The E-Type has remained a favourite in rallying ever since 1961. Events like the Tulip Rally, Monte Carlo Rally, Tour Auto, Alpine Rally, Targa Florio, Historique Monte Carlo, Rallye Maroc, ADAC Mittelrhein Rallye, Baden Classic Rally, Nurnberg Classic, the Great Race Road Rally, Tour de Bretagne Rally, Saxony Classic Rallye, and even the Rallye des Princesses, always manage to field an E-Type.

John Quick's series 1 FHC racer, registered WOO 11 began its early competition career as a rally car, taking part in the Tulip Rally in 1964 and the Alpine rally in 1965. Coincidentally, John Cuff also entered his FHC E-Type (8448 TJ) in the 1964 Tulip rally in Holland, alongside John Quick. Although it appears John enjoyed rallying, he seemed to prefer circuit racing, and was soon asking his local Jaguar dealer, Playford's garage, to turn WOO 11 into a race car.

A 1967 4.2 roadster (NKT 237F) driven by Henry Pearman (owner of Eagle E-Types) and Gordon Cruickshank took 1st place in the 1989 Pirelli Classic Marathon, and once again brought the E-Type to the notice of the motoring press.

A small selection of other E-Type rally participants I have come across:

1962, Dutch driver Steunebrink in his S1 FHC took part in the Tulip Rally. (see *Thoroughbred and Classic Cars* March 1992)

1963, the widely photographed red FHC of Baggio and Ravetto, registered 880 EXK, numbered 122 ran in the Targa Florio.

1963, The S1 roadster 7004 WD of Ray and Michael Merrick entered the Monte Carlo Rally. (See *Autosport* 25 January 1963)

1965, the S1 FHC registered CTV 55B, number 104 entered the Monte Carlo Rally – distinctive because of its roof rack which held the spare wheel. (See *Thoroughbred and Classic Cars* April 1990.)

Taken at the Monte Carlo Rally in 1964. (Copyright Ted Walker Ferret Fotographics)

1969, two Bolivian drivers, Oscar Crespo and Walter Ovando entered the 1750 mile Gran Premo of Peru in their S1 roadster. (See *Autosport* 2 October 1969.)

1986, Targa Florio an Italian green FHC came seventh.

1990, Targa Florio fielded a blue FHC.

1992, Sigi Huber in his silver S1 FHC took part in the Historic Vltava Rallye.

1992, Dave Bennett and David Astle in their S1 roadster took part in the Mitsubishi Classic Marathon. (See *Auto Classic Weekly* 12 August 1992.)

HWD 669D driven by Gordon Whiting at the 1967 Tulip Rally. (Copyright Ted Walker Ferret Fotographics)

E-Type NKT 237F at Silverstone 2011. (Copyright Peter Griffiths)

1992, Eugenio Renna won the Targa Florio in his S1 FHC (blue with red stripes). (See *Classic and Sportscar* January 1993.)

1993, Pirelli Classic marathon a red S1 FHC (BFW 559B) achieved fourth overall and first in class. (See *Jaguar Driver* April 1994.)

1993, Alex Van Tienhoven and Hans Rieters from Holland, took part in the Liège-Rome-Liège rally with their S1 FHC, achieving 1st in class. (See *Thoroughbred and Classic Cars* December 1993.)

Each year in Malta they hold the GP of Valletta, a four day festival of historic motoring including hill climb and street racing events and rallying on closed roads. In 2012 Richard Burton competed in his blue S1 roadster. (See *Jaguar Enthusiast* March 2013.)

The Ennstal Classic rally of 2012, Christian Mitterdorfer and Isobel Barth came third in their red S1 roadster. (See *Jaguar Enthusiast* October 2012.)

2012, Marc Milosevic and Vagelis Perperas competed in the Historic Acropolis rally in their S1 FHC. (See *Classic and Sportscar* October 2013.)

NKT 237F
C16 XJS
5 VPH
J47 UAP

A regular in the Tour Auto (a rally from Paris to the Riviera) is Alain Figare in his S1 FHC, silver with white stripes. (See *Octane* July 2010.)

In addition to the more serious rallies there are of course numerous reliability trials and classic car tours which always attract E-Types.

One major event that regularly draws large numbers of E-Types is the annual Norwich Union Classic Run. This 'rally' for road cars adheres to road traffic laws, and is more of a fun day out visiting places of interest on route. It has multiple start points converging on one central location for an end of rally get together. By way of example, the 1990 run fielded 37 E-Types, starting from seven locations around the country and finishing at Donington Park circuit.

For those who might be more adventurous (and possibly more competitive?!), the Historic Endurance Rallying Organisation (HERO) promotes several events each year including reliability trials and tours.

The 'Rallye Monte Carlo Historique' has inspired new interest in the sport and attracted more E-Types, notably VS 70, VS 71, and VS 1966: a team of three red FHC E-Types from Latvia which are regular competitors and make for a great spectacle. Also in the 2014 rally was the FHC 450-XB-69 of the French Sapet brothers, their white E-Type on Minilites and wider arches looking a brute of a machine. Photographs of all these cars are widely available on the internet but not often reported in the UK press – perhaps because most of the rallies are held in Europe.

The Jaguar Driver's Club magazine, *Jaguar Driver*, ran a series of articles on the exploits of Debbie Edwards with her dark blue S2 FHC registered TEU 82C, then VHT 195H and later 2 HAO. Debbie was a regular competitor in the UK and in the Rallye Villa de Bilbao, Spain, where she finished first in class twice. *Classic Cars* magazine also featured a great article on Debbie, 'Me and my E-Type rally car' in March 2008.

It seems to me that the E-Type will continue its success in competition, both on and off the track.

2 HAO photographed just before leaving for the RAC Historic Rally in 1991. (Copyright Peter Griffiths)

Appendix A

The cars

A list of the racing E-Types by registration number
Designed to emulate or confuse?

Many racing E-Types still carry their original registration numbers as a sign of authenticity and provenance. In several instances, number plates have been changed – this could be in order to increase value by elevating the perceived status. This practice is not new, but does seem to have become more prolific with regard to E-Type replicas.

Unfortunately, not all race E-Types, even if registered, carried number plates. As soon as they entered the 'Modsports' era many lost their plates, as fibreglass bonnets were added and every effort was being made to save weight. It was some time later when these fine old workhorses were reincarnated as 'Lightweight replicas' with race history attached, that the need to find the original registration numbers took hold and the price of E-Type log books rocketed.

Some cars, on the other hand, never had a registration number at all. In the Modsports era it was not necessary to own a 'complete' E-Type, as an awful lot of the car was discarded anyway, meaning a competitive race car could be built out of parts without the need for all the 'expensive' road going items such as interiors (door trims, carpets, headlinings, heaters, radios and even the leather seats replaced by a cheaper race seat), lights, glass, steel panels, etc. This practice, however, was not new. Dick Protheroe did exactly the same when building the second CUT 7 back in 1962! Not only did Dick not have to buy unnecessary parts but also he probably did not have to pay purchase tax as the car did not need to be road registered.

When turned into Lightweights, any unregistered cars needed log books, and hence the price of these continued to rise. Even 2+2 log books had a price, given that you could show a body change to convert these to a roadster and then on to a Lightweight replica.

Several cars in the following lists may of course be duplicated, as in they have more than one registration number. Early 1963/1964 cars carrying a standard A or B suffix may well have acquired a WK registration by now!

The reader should therefore be very aware that all that glistens is not necessarily gold! Registration numbers come and go, and as the history of legal decisions has taught us, only the chassis number and continual history can be relied upon to prove provenance.

Here are a few examples of the confusion that can occur with more often seen numbers:

9023 DU – Original Cunningham roadster
9032 DU – Original Cunningham roadster

I have photos of both these numbers, on what appears to be the same car. I am unsure of the correct numbers for the

Cunningham roadsters. Other plates used included 612-669 and 606-984.

CUT 6	Dick Protheroe's XK120 registration.
CUT 7	Dick Protheroe's E-Type registration, used on three different E-Types that he raced.
CUT 7A	Rebuilt second CUT 7 bodyshell into new car.
CUT 8	Protheroe garage (not Dick) E-Type registration. Registered RAC 100 and later 105 ENX. Uncertain as to when it was registered CUT 8, the DVLA shows September 1991, although the number was shown on the car in the '60s.
290 CUT	Dark blue FHC racer.
256 DJU **PMB 324H** **SVJ 345 H** **SVJ 345**	Follow on numbers used on the second CUT 7.
636 CJU	The follow on number used on the first CUT 7.
738 EUT	The follow on number used on 3rd CUT 7.
671 EUT	Mike Miles roadster racer/modsports.
BUY 1	Coombs garage number used on the first E-Type Lightweight and several other Jaguars.
BUY 12	Another Coombs garage number.
2 BBC	Sturgess garage number used on E-Type roadster and FHC racers.
4 WPD	The number allocated after BUY 1 on the first Lightweight E-Type
5 WPD	Lightweight replica.
81 WPD	Lightweight replica LDC.
4 KPD	Series 1 FHC racer.
13 WPF	Lightweight replica LDC.
XAJ 1 **1 WW** **LMD 24B** **CJX 672C**	Genuine Factory Semi-Lightweight roadster with original and subsequent registrations.
LMD 24B	Above, but LID 24B seen on Lightweight replica ex-Jack Lambert (originally RL 26).
86 PJ	Original Lightweight.
95 PJ	Lightweight replica.
26 PJ	Lightweight replica.
49 FXN	Original Lightweight, long nose.
924 FXC	Replica Lightweight, long nose.
13 FXN	Replica Lightweight.
ECD 400	Original roadster racer chassis no 5.
E 141	Original roadster racer.
EE 400	Original roadster chassis no 18 Equipe Endeavour.
E 400	Lightweight replica.
18 EE	Eagle E-Type LDC Lightweight replica.
E 1500	Early outside bonnet-lock roadster seen at Merchiston Mews as Ecurie Ecosse support car.
77 RW	Original roadster test car chassis no 3.

1600 RW	Original Lofty England car chassis no 4.
6162 RW	Early FHC chassis no 10.
6182 RW	Later FHC race car.
140 FPX	Roadster, chassis number 14 ... now Lightweight replica.
170 FPX	Modified 1962 FHC.
TUF 3	FHC Lightweight.
TUF 4	Lightweight replica.
TUF 6	Lightweight replica.
2 GXO	Genuine Lightweight.
4 GXO	Replica Lightweight, but has acquired the status of the 14th Lightweight, as it was built with a genuine bodyshell.
888 RYA	Original FHC race damaged, now Lightweight replica.
9600 HP	Pre-production first FHC, initially LHD, now RHD.
6900 WK	FHC modsports car of Paul Webb ... was PWM 1 (Paul Webb Motors).
PS 1175, RV 7	Both numbers for same original Lightweight.
YVH 210, SVM 740	Both numbers for same original Lightweight.
1 VHP	Chassis no 1, the first FHC.
VPL 9	Lightweight replica.
936 VPL	Lightweight replica.
9 VPD	Original chassis number 7, one of the special ZP cars.
4 WPD	Compare previous.
2152 WK	FHC racer of Bob Jane.
2164 WK	Protheroe garage last E-Type.
4868 WK	Original Lightweight converted to LDC.
5081 WK	13th Lightweight.
5114 WK	Original Lightweight.
5115 WK	Original Lightweight.
5116 WK	Original Lightweight.
5497 WK	Dunford replica LDC.
5916 WK	Lynx replica LDC.
9999 WK	Replica Lightweight LDC.

The list of 'new' WK registrations would fill another book. A few examples are shown here (all Lightweight replicas).

1480 WK
3553 WK
3613 WK
3857 WK
4264 WK
4875 WK
5104 WK
5497 WK
5916 WK

Some non-racing registrations are included in the following list where they are 'famous cars' and race cars have used 'similar' numbers.

When looking at a photograph of a car, don't just assume you know which one it is because of the number plate. For example:

CUT 7 appeared on three different E-Types.

WOO 11 (when sold abroad) lost its number and

ended up on John Quick's road car. At Donington in 1991, I photographed WOO 11 on John's Honda! Later the number appeared on another standard FHC, although it has now been reunited with the owner of the original WOO 11.

2 BBC was the Sturgess garage number and appeared on the race FHC and the DHC.

BUY 1 was the Coombs garage number, which appeared on the first Lightweight but also on many other Jaguars.

9 WKJ appeared on Tony Knights FHC and his DHC.

888 RYA was on the race damaged FHC, and later on a Lightweight replica.

Some cars kept changing their number plates, which makes recognition all the more difficult. For example, 8448 TJ, the John Cuff car, later changed to 126 FLY, then to WAK 1, then FNC 1 (also FNC 2) before reverting to 8448 TJ.

Numerical list

I have listed here by registration number all the E-Type race cars I have come across during my years of research. Some information is more detailed than others mainly because it would take many volumes to do justice to all of them.

1 ACB Lightweight LDC replica, built by Brian Wingfield.

1 EMN Lightweight replica in silver. Raced by Stirling Moss in the 1991 Manx Rally. A full report appears in *Jaguar Quarterly* magazine in Jan/Feb 1992.

1 EMN seen at Donington 25 May 1992. (Copyright Peter Griffiths)

1 EMN seen at Donington 25 May 1992. (Copyright Peter Griffiths)

1 FUE Penny Woodley's modsports FHC, also registered UWD 645G. This was built using the original FHC body from Dick Protheroe's second CUT 7, after it was written-off and rebuilt as a roadster. The bodyshell was later rebuilt to the original CUT 7 (version 2), although for a while it was registered CUT 7A.

E-Type UWD 645G of Penny Woodley here chatting with Geoff Protheroe (Dick's son), Tony Ward and Pat and Jan Wells. (Copyright Paul Skilleter)

1 PKL Early racer ex-George Wicken. Chassis number 850011 was an early racer driven by George Wicken, whose early career was in Cooper F2 cars, and later a Jaguar XK120. The car crashed in 1962, which sadly brought an abrupt end to its racing career. It has also carried the number 823 DCR and currently I have seen it noted as being 16 XKE, although it has been seen racing in recent years with the 1 PKL registration. I am, however, unsure as to the correct registration/ chassis number as 16 XKE and 1 PKL have appeared together at the same race meeting!

1 PKL photographed at the E-Type Challenge at Silverstone in July 2011. (Copyright Peter Griffiths)

1 TDF Lightweight replica.

1 VHP This is chassis number 860001, the first FHC produced. Also registered 480 HYT and XVE 1.

E-Type 1 VHP seen at Silverstone in 2011. (Copyright Peter Griffiths)

1 WW The original Semi-Lightweight of Sir Robert Ropner. Chassis number S850817. Later registrations include 166 YHN, XAJ 1, BXG 326B and currently CJX 672C. See photo under XAJ 1.

2 BBC A Sturgess garage number. Initially this number was allocated to E-Type roadster chassis number 850012. Driven by Robin Sturgess during 1961, when he successfully raced against Jack Lambert and others. Later registered 848 CRY, it became much more famous in subsequent years in the fateful scene from *The Italian Job*, when the Mafia crushed it. In 1962, 2 BBC was put onto Sturgess' red FHC E-Type, and at Mallory Park achieved 1st place in the GT category, quickly followed by Jack Lambert in his E-Type roadster.

Very early shot of 2 BBC (DHC) driven by Robin Sturgess at the 1961 JDC meeting at Silverstone. (Copyright Ted Walker Ferret Fotographics)

2 BBC as an FHC driven by Robin Sturgess at the 1962 International Trophy meeting. (Copyright Ted Walker Ferret Fotographics)

2 GXO Original Lightweight E-Type, which is still raced today and a regular at Goodwood. The 'Wilkins' Lightweight, chassis number S850668.

Lightweight E-Type 2 GXO seen at Donington in June 1991 when owned by Nigel Corner. (Copyright Peter Griffiths)

2 HAO The series 2 FHC rally car made famous by Debbie Edwards. A regular rally entrant in the 1990s, Debbie won the Bilbao rally in 1996, one of many awards achieved with this well known car. Also, Debbie wrote the 'Rally News' section of *Jaguar Driver* magazine, and appeared on the front cover of *Jaguar Driver* at least three times in February 1991 (car registered VHT 195H), May 1992 (2 HAO), and July 1998 (2 HAO), with great photos appearing in the May 1992, October 1992 (TEU 82C), October 1993, May 1994, June 1994, August 1994, November 1995, June 1996, July 1996, October 1996, May 1997, July 1998, and December 1998 issues. See rally section also.

2 HAO photographed just before leaving for the RAC Historic Rally in 1991. (Copyright Peter Griffiths)

2 XKE Black Lightweight replica.

2 XKE seen at Silverstone in 2010. (Copyright Ian Hunt)

3 BXV Chassis number 850010 is one of the original seven Factory competition ZP cars delivered to Peter Berry Racing, but which gained instant fame when driven by Bruce McLaren. Its first outing at Silverstone in 1961 resulted in McLaren achieving 2nd place. This 'standard car' had the usual wire wheels, bumpers and soft top, but later owners, acknowledging its provenance, soon turned it into a Lightweight replica, and as such it has often been misquoted as being one of the original Lightweights. David Hobbs also drove for Peter Berry, and *Road and Track* magazine in May 1962 stated that he drove a good 2 seconds per lap quicker than Walt Hansgen in the Cunningham E-Type. Other articles on the car appear in *Motor Racing* magazine in October 1961, and *Thoroughbred and Classic Car* magazine in October 1990, when a lengthy article was produced with the then owner Tony Kember. This particular Lightweight replica has been modified to appear slightly wider at the rear and is still campaigned to this day.

So why has this car often been called a Lightweight when it is not? In the early to mid '80s the car was owned by Paul Palmer, and by this time it had been extensively modified and was beginning its metamorphosis into a Lightweight replica. It was silver with a Lightweight style boot lid, but carried a standard hard top. When put up for sale in 1985, the advert read: "The ex McLaren-Hobbs preproduction Semi-Lightweight E-Type Jaguar." It cannot be denied that this was a successful and heavily modified racing E-Type, but, in my opinion, a Semi-Lightweight it is not. By preproduction I presume this was a reference to the very early cars which were allocated to certain customers before the 'mass' production for the general public. The myth was continued in later years when the car was up for sale again. The advert read: "1961 Jaguar E-Type Semi-Lightweight, ex Bruce McLaren ... 3 BXV, one of the seven Semi-Lightweight competition roadsters prepared by the factory" ... stretching the truth here a little, perhaps? Again, in my opinion, an extremely misleading advert. The seven ZP cars were nothing like the Factory 'Semi-Lightweight.' The seven ZP cars in 1961 were 'mechanically' modified and nothing 'Lightweight' bodywise. A 1961 car can not be anything like a Factory 'Lightweight,' as the Factory did not make them until two years later!

Because the number 3 BXV is similar to the number 2 GXO, and the car made to look the same, even down to the silver colour, perhaps it is no surprise that 3 BXV has been described as a Lightweight.

After Peter Berry (with drivers Bruce McLaren and David Hobbs), the car passed to the following E-Type race drivers, Paul Palmer, John Young and Tony Kember, all of whom continued with the cars race successes and further development. A good article appears in the *Jaguar Driver* magazine of April 1989 when it was owned by John Young. The car was originally light green, although this was soon changed to silver with black hard top and later completely silver. Internet photos also show the car with bright yellow livery and the car continues to be regularly campaigned.

In my archives I have a copy of the four-page detailed specification prepared for Paul Palmer in the early 1980s. The main highlights (abbreviated) in alphabetical order are as follows:

Anti-roll bars: Aluminium bearings and rose jointed links.

Block: 3.8-litre bored to +.04in with Cosworth pistons.

Brakes: Can-am callipers, 4 pot front and 2 pot rear.

Camshafts: Piper JR2

Cam followers: Lightened.

Carburettors: Three Weber 45DCOE.

Clutch: AP Racing triple plate, sintered linings.

Con rods: XJ6 balanced and shot peened.

Crankshaft: Balanced and polished.

Chassis: Rear cradle mountings made solid and fitted higher into body to lower the car.

Differential: E-Type 3.54:1 modified power lock.

Fuel: 100 octane minimum.

Fuel pump: Facet

Flywheel: Lightened and modified

Lubrication: Wet sump, extra baffles, remote oil filter, oil cooler fitted.

Suspension: Front. Top wishbones fulcrums lowered. Steering arms raised. Rack solid mounted and raised. Coil springs fitted over dampers. Spax shock absorbers.

Rear. Mountings made solid and lowered. Increased spring rate.

Valves: Terry's valves, inlet 2in, exhaust 1⅝in.

JDC Silverstone meeting 1984 showing 3 BXV. (Copyright Paul Skilleter)

E-Type 3 BXV. (Copyright Laurie Abbott)

3 OKV FHC Lightweight (note – OKV 3 was on an original D-Type)

3 XKK Hill climb car. S1 FHC.

4 BXV Factory competition car. Another of the 'Magnificent Seven' Factory competition ZP cars. Chassis number 850013 was the sister car to 3 BXV being also delivered to Peter Berry. The car was later owned by John Burton, chairman of the E-Type register, and has now been fully restored by its present owner George Missetzis. The car has been frequently photographed in various issues of *Jaguar Driver,* and a superb article on the car appeared in *Jaguar World* magazine in February 2011. Also registered 39 PE and 24 BXV.

E-Type 4 BXV fully restored. (Copyright Paul Skilleter)

4 GXO 'New' Lightweight built around the spare aluminium tub originally used in the rebuild of 4868 WK, after that car was rebuilt again with its original tub. A comprehensive article on this car appeared in *Jaguar Enthusiast* magazine in March 2013, written by Paul Skilleter. When put up for sale in 2012, the car was referred to as the 14th Lightweight. See also *Octane* magazine, August 2012.

4 KPD Pale blue FHC S1 racer.

4 KPD photographed at the E-Type Challenge at Silverstone in July 2011. (Copyright Peter Griffiths)

4 RH Later number on Lightweight PS 1175.

4 WPD The original Lightweight development car, initially registered BUY 1, is probably the most famous of all the Lightweights, and is extensively covered in most Jaguar books and magazines. Chassis number S850006.

E-Type 4 WPD seen at Silverstone. (Copyright Peter Griffiths)

5 RPP Lightweight replica in green with silver nose.

5 RPP photographed at the E-Type Challenge at Silverstone in July 2011. (Copyright Peter Griffiths)

5 WPD A 1962 3.8-litre DHC competition Lightweight replica.

An advert for 5 WPD in 2012 reads as follows: "… one of the most successful Jaguar E-Type historic competition racing cars of the modern era … 860392 was built to works Lightweight specification … using a combination of original and post production Lightweight parts. The original parts including the front suspension, torsion bars, front anti-roll bar, header tank and radiator, exhaust manifolds and complete rear suspension cage that were sourced from the Lightweight E-Type racer 503 BBO that competed at Le Mans in 1962 driven by John Coundley and Maurice Charles. The engine was acquired from another important historic race car as it was reportedly fitted to the E-Type belonging to John Lewis that won the 1987 historic Racing Championship driven by Roger Mac. An accomplished racing unit, it has a wet sump, triple Weber carburettors and an aluminium cylinder head …"

My observations on this advert:

1. Chassis number 860392 relates to an FHC, not a roadster.

2. The Le Mans car, 503 BBO, was *not a Lightweight*. Chassis number 860458 was an original standard 1962 FHC, so it could not possibly have had original Lightweight parts from a 1963 Lightweight car. If anything, the car was modified using D-Type parts, not Lightweight E parts.

3. Regarding "built to works Lightweight specification" … It may have an aluminium bonnet, but does it have an aluminium bodyshell? That would be a first!

4. There is nothing special about a wet sump. I wonder whether it should say dry sump?

5. The advert states "aluminium cylinder head," but it does not say the block is aluminium. Hardly built, then, to "works Lightweight specification."

I have included this as an example (and by no means a one-off) of an inaccurate sales advert.

6 SKD FHC racer. White with green stripe.

7 CXW This early car, chassis number 850096, was a very successful racer piloted by

Ken Baker. An article on this car entitled '7 CXW: The Ken Baker Car' appeared in *Jaguar Quarterly* magazine in April 1991. The car is recorded in almost every Jaguar book and other magazine articles, including the *Jaguar Quarterly* March 1992 and *Autosport* 14 December 1962. Following its sale in the late 1960s, it entered the modsports, world and became one of the most successful modsports E-Types of its era. It appeared on the front cover of *Hot Car* magazine in January 1969, when owned by Rob Schroeder. Later it was owned by Alan Minshaw, before being picked up by Forward Engineering, and driven with great success by John Harper. The subsequent owner was Stephen Sharp. In the early 1990s the car was converted back to virtually Lightweight E-Type specification by its current owner, Paul Webb. Also registered GKP 631D and ROB 2.

7 CXW now with hard top competing at Brands Hatch in 1966 still in the capable hands of Ken Baker. (Copyright Ted Walker Ferret Fotographics)

8 COW 1964 Lightweight replica.

8 HYP 1965 4.2 FHC race car built in 2001 for the E-Type Experience Race Series.

8 WXL Early 3.8 Series 1 FHC. Modified road car.

9 VPD Factory competition car. Chassis number 850007 was one of the seven Factory prepared competition cars known as 'Project Specification ZP 537/24.' These were delivered to special Jaguar customers who were thought to be able to promote the cars' racing potential. Along with BUY 1, this was delivered to John Coombe's garage in 1961. After an early racing career it seems to have languished quietly until 2002, when it was purchased at auction and restored to Lightweight specification. It is now a regular competitor at Goodwood, and even the Le Mans Classic. Also registered 532 FS.

9 VPD seen in the paddock at Goodwood Revival 2009. (Copyright Ian Hunt)

9 WKJ This very early FHC was owned and driven by Tony Knight. It was written-off after only a few races, and 9 WKJ then appeared on a DHC, also raced by Tony Knight. In 1966 it was driven for a short while by Alistair Crawford, before passing into the hands of Keith Holland. Another E-Type race car has been linked with Keith Holland during this period, but I cannot find any evidence of this. During 1966 and 1967 Keith Holland became probably the most successful E-Type racer, finishing 1st in just about every race he entered. In 1968 the car passed to Mike Loveday, who raced it successfully for a further two years. A few years ago, and not entirely unexpectedly, the car was listed on the XKE Data website as being in the process of being rebuilt. I know for certain that it was spurious claim, and contacted the administrator to have it removed.

11 XK Lightweight replica.

11 XK Lightweight replica photographed at the E-Type Challenge at Silverstone in July 2011. (Copyright Peter Griffiths)

12 MY Early roadster racer. Red with matching hardtop. I believe that this is the ex-Jack Lambert car in its later Lightweight guise.

E-Type 12 MY seen at Silverstone. (Copyright Laurie Abbott)

13 FXN Longnose Lightweight replica, metallic green and later silver.

13 FXN long nosed replica photographed at the E-Type Challenge at Silverstone in July 2011. (Copyright Peter Griffiths)

13 WPF Lightweight LDC replica.

16 XKE Chassis 850011, the ex-George Wicken racer, now rebuilt as a Lightweight replica. See 1 PKL. The DVLA website has the date of first registration as 24th August 2002.

16 XKE photographed at the E-Type Challenge at Silverstone in July 2011. (Copyright Peter Griffiths)

18 EE Lightweight LDC replica built by Eagle E-Types.

18 HYO An early 3.8 DHC racer driven by J Woodbridge.

18 HYO at Snetterton in September 1967 driven by J Woodbridge. (Copyright Ted Walker Ferret Fotographics)

20 DWV Series 1 FHC hill climb car driven by Gary Dickens.

22 EHR Wingfield Lightweight replica.

22 EHR Lightweight replica photographed at Donington in June 1991. (Copyright Peter Griffiths)

24 BXV Current registration allocated to 4 BXV, chassis 850013.

26 PJ Lightweight replica.

27 DEC Lightweight replica. White with two red stripes.

31 EM Race prepared dark blue RHD FHC.

38 BYB Early 3.8 FHC, Lightweight specification.

39 PE See 4 BXV.

40 FKT Lightweight replica.

40 FN Car raced by Jon Minshaw in the current E-Type Challenge series, which seems to be winning just about everything it enters. Although this is quite a standard-looking roadster, anyone who has seen it race must assume that it is far from standard underneath the bonnet!

49 FXN Original Lightweight E-Type converted to longnose specification for Peter Lumsden and Peter Sargent. This E-Type was entered at Le Mans, and has chassis number S850663.

Lightweight 49 FXN. (Copyright Brian Snelson)

Lightweight 49 FXN.
(Copyright Brian Snelson)

61 E Green Lightweight replica in E-Type Challenge.

77 RW Chassis number 850003. As chassis 1 and 2 were prototypes, this is, in effect, the first E-Type roadster. Used as the Jaguar road test car.

E-Type 77 RW seen at Silverstone 2011.
(Copyright Peter Griffiths)

77 WK LDC replica in silver.

80 FOE Tony Griffiths 3.8 FHC hill climb car.

81 WPD Lightweight LDC replica dark blue.

82 EXE Wingfield Lightweight replica built in 1994 by Bryan Wingfield for its first owner Sir Anthony Bamford.

86 PJ Original Lightweight initially driven by Roy Salvadori for owner Tommy Atkins, later by Roger Mac. Chassis number S850661.

Lightweight E-Type 86 PJ seen at Goodwood Festival of Speed in 2011.
(Copyright Ian Hunt)

87 GXM E Minihan, early racer.

91 XBH S1 FHC racer.

95 PJ Lightweight replica, Silver blue colour, seen at Isle of Man sprint.

103 AMY 44 Roadster rally car.

105 ENX Later number on CUT 8, the Ed Nelson car from the Protheroe garage.

Edward Nelson in 105 ENX at Castle Combe in March 1966. (Copyright Ted Walker Ferret Fotographics)

111 EK FHC silver with Lightweight features.

111 EK FHC photographed at the E-Type Challenge at Silverstone in July 2011. (Copyright Peter Griffiths)

128 MAL The original registration on the Tony Shaw FHC racer, now registered BGC 22B. See details under BGC 22B.

129 KVA Early FHC driven by Eric Stansfield, Fred Cliffe, James Blackhall and Dave Bye.

E-Type 129 KVA seen at Silverstone July 2011. (Copyright Peter Griffiths)

130 HPO Series 1 3.8 FHC silver hill climb car, driven by Andrew Fordyce.

138 FLY The ex-John Cuff car 8448 TJ carried this number when owned by Ted Worswick in 1968/69.

138 XKE Sprint car driven by Derek Green.

140 FPX Early chassis no 850014, now Lightweight replica, Goodwood competitor, gunmetal grey.

Mike Parkes' victory lap at the Brands Hatch International meeting in August 1962, being driven round in 140 FPX. (Copyright Ted Walker Ferret Fotographics)

140 HPO A modified FHC in red, a regular competitor at the Brighton Speed Trials, driven by Robert Oram.

151 FRT 92 LHD S1 FHC racer, dark blue with white nose.

159 XKK This is the early DHC racer of Eric Falce. In his first ten races he achieved three 1sts, three 2nds, and four 3rds. The car gained notoriety, however, when it rolled and caught fire at Brands Hatch in 1965 in front of the main grandstand, and was virtually destroyed. A photograph in the December 1991 issue of *Jaguar Driver* shows Eric Falce running away from the damaged car. The remains were later to become a modsports car with a Cadillac engine.

A photograph appears in the February 1992 issue of *Jaguar Driver* magazine. In 2008, the highly modified bodyshell (without mechanicals) came up for sale on French website Forum Auto. This E-Type 'speciale,' sporting a Lola type bodyshell, claims to be the reincarnation of 159 XKK.

166 YHN Later number used on Semi-Lightweight Ropner car, S850817.

168 XUU Yellow, series 1 FHC, LHD rally car.

170 FPX Heavily modified 1962 FHC racer, chassis no 860545.

170 FPX seen at Snetterton in April 1963 driven by Malcolm Fruitnight. (Copyright Ted Walker Ferret Fotographics)

179 WK DHC Lightweight replica.

179 WK photographed at the E-Type Challenge at Silverstone in July 2011. (Copyright Peter Griffiths)

188 HYT Series 1 roadster autocross car of Andrew Smith.

207 YPP Black series 1 roadster rally car.

214 BWK S1 FHC Lightweight spec in copper coloured livery with two centre white stripes.

244 YUS LDC replica.

245 YUB Lightweight replica of Mike Adams.

245 YUB the beautiful Lightweight replica of Mike Adams photographed at the E-Type Challenge at Silverstone in July 2011. (Copyright Peter Griffiths)

256 DJU Second CUT 7.

283 XPG Lightweight replica, metallic silver bronze coachwork, green check hard top.

290 CUT FHC racer, dark blue.

300 DOU Lightweight replica in green, built new by Valley Motorsport as a 'Semi-Lightweight competition roadster.'

300 DOU at the Silverstone Classic 2011. (Copyright David Merrett)

300 DOU photographed at the E-Type Challenge at Silverstone in July 2011. (Copyright Peter Griffiths)

310 WK

The 'Warren Pearce' E-Type is probably one of the better known modsports cars from the '60s and '70s. The continual development of this particular car made it one of the fastest and most outrageous from this period. Unless you have followed its career, you will hardly be able to recognise it from one year to the next. Ever-changing body design, colour schemes, and many owner changes have made it extremely difficult to keep up with.

The dark blue, standard looking roadster of Warren Pearce is the same car as the bright yellow/blue stripe car of Brian Murphy, which is the same car as the yellow ochre highly developed car of Fred Cliffe, which is the same car as the pale blue/dark blue car of Ron Lea, which, after its last accident, was rebuilt in the style of the original Warren Pearce car with its dark blue paintwork! Clearly a case of full circle!

Warren Pearce Motors of Cadogan Lane, London, SW1, specialised in Jaguar performance conversions. Their adverts read: "gas flowed cylinder heads, triple carburettor manifold conversions for all Jaguar models, brake and suspension modifications for competition work."

The complete one-piece fibreglass rear end of most modsports roadsters has become known as the 'Warren Pearce' back end. The original modsports styling can, in most cases, be traced back to Warren for the roadsters, and to John Quick for the fixed heads. These two were amongst the most successful drivers of this period.

Warren's successful escapades are well documented in *Autosport* issues of the mid-sixties. The dark blue 310 WK originally ran on wire wheels, with bumpers and even a soft top!

Paul Skilleter's book *The Jaguar E-Type – A collector's guide*, has a great picture of Warren chasing 86 PJ (the ex-Tommy Atkins Lightweight E) during the Guards 1000 miles race at Brands Hatch in May 1965. A very 'standard' looking roadster.

A 29th April 1966 *Autosport* article shows that the car had acquired a Factory hard top, although the body still looked standard and still showed front quarter bumpers. This report on the Mallory Park meeting gives Warren 1st place in the marque sportscars over 3000cc, as well as fastest lap.

A photo from the end of the 1966 season of the Snetterton meeting (*Autosport* 21 October 1966), clearly shows how 310 WK had 'grown.' The wide rear end had appeared, and was accompanied by a vented boot lid, similar to the Lightweights ... the Modsports era had begun.

In *Motorsport* magazine January 1967 there is an excellent article in which Warren's car is track tested. It reports on the superb 1966 season, recording 17 outright victories in 35 starts, six further class wins, and four 2nd places. The article gives an insight into Warren's racing history, beginning in 1952 and progressing to Jaguars in 1955 with an XK120, after which he became a confirmed "Jaguar man." Car number 310 WK came along in 1964, "a secondhand E-Type which had been badly repaired after an accident."

A synopsis of the initial mods reads as follows:

• Dunlop R6 racing tyres, on 6in rims at the front, and 6.5in rims at the rear (later changed to splined Minilites with Goodyear tyres).

• Substituting a 3.54 axle ratio for 2.9 (later changed to 3.77).

• Koni shockers fitted, rear suspension lowered.

• Special anti-roll bars.

• Large disc brakes from a Mark 9 Jaguar.

• Engine bored to 3.9 litres, gas-flowed head with larger valves.

• D-Type camshafts and triple Webers.

• Special inlet and exhaust manifold.

• Aluminium bonnet fitted, works fibreglass hardtop, and Perspex windows fitted. Full roll cage added.

The car was briefly owned by Frank Wright in the early '70s with limited development, and in 1974, having competed for several more years, the car ended up with Brian Murphy.

The 1975 season saw Brian winning the 3000cc class of the BRSCC modsports championship.

The car was featured on the cover of *Cars and Car Conversions* magazine in August 1976 in bright yellow with blue stripes and revised bodywork, it looked nothing like the original 310 WK. Brian pays tribute to the Warren Pearce rear suspension setup; part of the whole package that gave him the edge over other racing Jags. According to the article, the car "was built for the 1975 season using a brand new, un-used monocoque straight from the factory." The car as now modified began to show the full extent of modsports styling during the 1970s with beautiful Gotti split rims, 10"x15 on the front and 12"x15 on the rear. Wider wheels and corresponding wheel arches made for truly mean looking cars.

A synopsis of the car reads as follows:

• Body-fibreglass bonnet, ultra thin, this was moulded from John Quick's aluminium bonnet, with air dam, fibreglass aftermarket (Lenham) light weight hardtop, fibreglass doors with perspex windows and one piece fibreglass rear end, even a fibreglass seat.

• Brakes – CanAm ventilated discs, four pot callipers on the front. Standard rears.

• Suspension – Front: standard with rose jointed anti-roll bar (this actual one was fitted to the rebuilt Leeson car) Spax shock absorbers. Rear: Modified Warren Pearce setup. Fully rose jointed and fabricated rear wishbones. Koni shock absorbers with modified coil springs.

• Engine – 4.3-litre using +60 pistons. Triple Webers. D-Type inlet manifold, home fabricated exhaust.

The magazine article gives the power at this stage as 340bhp.

The 310 WK number plate is missing, and no hint of the heritage is shown, that is, until the number plate reappeared in the early '90s on Ron Lea's rebuilt car.

The car was then campaigned by Roy Standley until it was eventually sold during the late '70s to Fred Cliffe, who rebuilt it with further extensive developments.

The most obvious modification was the decision to put the water radiator in the boot to aid weight distribution ... I think that was the theory. This involved the addition of huge air intakes just behind the doors which added to the cars already outrageous styling. The wheels were now split rim Solar Mambas, 12s and 14s, making the appearance of the widest E-Type ever. The extra water needed to fill the pipework to the rear radiator did unfortunately add weight but the overall balance of the car was improved. Fred's preparation included chromed front frames, highly polished wishbones and suspension components, polished brass header tank etc, all giving a more concours appearance than a '70s racer. The car was painted in deep yellow ochre, with no sponsorship decals, unlike earlier or later recreations.

Fred campaigned the car extensively, and even entered the very last race at Rufforth in 1977, in which he won his class and achieved fastest lap.

In 1982, 310 WK passed into the hands of club stalwart Ron Lea. The car was repainted light blue/dark blue, Ron's company colours. Unfortunately, after only two races Ron crashed the car at Aintree in June 1982, and the car was locked away while he concentrated on racing his V12 E-Type and replica D-Type.

After ten years, Ron decided on a rebuild of the car back to the original Warren Pearce specification of the 1960s. John Oxborough was commissioned to carry it out. A short story of the car along with the rebuilt car was shown in *Jaguar Driver* magazine in June 1992.

The car was exhibited at the Jaguar meeting at Donington that year, alongside Fred Cliffe's latest project, the aluminium fixed head (8448 TJ).

Since 1996 the car has resided in a sports car museum in Lany Czechoslovakia. The car can be seen with current photos on the museums website; auto-muzeum.cz. If the car were to return to the track, further modifications would be required in order to comply with current European standards.

As you can see, 310 WK has had a long racing career with continual development, and body and mechanical changes galore. With reference to my comments on E-Type recreations, despite its several rebuilds, I consider this car to have a continuous history. Probably the only original parts are the rebuilt Warren Pearce modified suspension parts, which give an important link to the car's heritage.

Warren Pearce in 310 WK at the Brands Hatch International meeting in August 1965. (Copyright Ted Walker Ferret Fotographics)

310 WK seen at a JDC test day at Mallory Park when owned by Ron Lea. (Copyright Peter Griffiths)

See article reprint in Appendix E.
More photos of the car are in the book *The Jaguar E-Type – A Collectors guide*, by Paul Skilleter, pages 64 and 71.

318 XUN 3.8 LDC replica built by R S Panels, bodystyle to CUT 7 specification

336 PAR The early FHC racer driven by Peter Archer, later modified to FIA historic specification by Lynx Motors. Bright yellow coachwork with Lightweight style roof vent.

Peter Archer in his modsports FHC at the Cadwell Park meeting in 1971. (Copyright Ted Walker Ferret Fotographics)

Modsports FHC of Peter Archer. (Copyright Ted Walker Ferret Fotographics)

363 DLD Early FHC race car.

395 AAY Lightweight replica in pale metallic blue, of Michael and Kallum Gray.

406 VPC Chassis number 850015, originally belonged to Bruce McLaren, who used it to travel between his home in Surbiton to the various Grand Prix circuits at which he raced.

414 VHY FHC track car

433 QMM Silver LHD S1 FHC rally car.

437 YUJ Lightweight replica , black.

450 XB 69 FHC Rally car, LHD. Monte Carlo historic entrant. White with red stripe and black/ white checks.

459 BVK 92 Series 1 FHC , LHD rally car. White/blue stripes, Cunningham style.

475 TOD Lightweight replica.

480 HYT See 1 VHP.

Brian Corser's Lightweight E-Type and FHC 480 HYT – the first right-hand drive FHC – at the JDC meeting at Donington. (Copyright Peter Griffiths)

490 ABB 67 LHD FHC racer.

492 YUF LHD Series 1 Roadster of James Cottingham. Red coachwork with silver hard top.

499 WK Lightweight replica painted in Cunningham colours, white with blue stripes.

A Lightweight replica 499 WK pictured in 2012 at Wilton House, Wiltshire. (Copyright Ian Hunt)

503 BBO This 1962 FHC was driven at Le Mans by Charles and Coundley. Chassis number 860458.

503 BBO. (Copyright Bill Abbott)

504 FOF Early FHC racer of Harding Scott-Wiseman. A regular competitor in the 1960s. A nice shot of this car features in *Autosport* magazine of July 28th 1967. This successful Carmen red FHC was meticulously maintained, and when advertised for sale in 1968 it boasted 100 per cent reliability, and had been placed 17 times out of 19 races during the 1967 season.

504 FOF seen here at Snetterton in July 1967 driven by Harding Scott-Wiseman. (Copyright Ted Walker Ferret Fotographics)

529 FN Series 1 Lightweight replica. Dark EE blue with two white nose stripes, driven by Jon Minshaw.

532 FS See 9 VPD.

590 DXR V8 'Egal.' This well known roadster fitted with a Ford Galaxy V8 engine was a regular competitor in the 1960s and 1970s. Driven originally by Rob Beck and later by Barry Williams, Chris Summers and Bob Kerr. Well covered in many magazines and good photos in *Jaguar Sports Cars* by Paul Skilleter, page 259, and also Paul's *Jaguar Drivers' Yearbook* of 1979/80, page 62.

590 DXR, known as the Egal (E-Type with Galaxy V8 engine), seen here at Castle Combe in September 1966. (Copyright Ted Walker Ferret Fotographics)

600 FBP Early FHC sprint and race car.

600 FBP parked alongside 1 EMN in the paddock for the historic races on the Isle of Man in 1992. (Copyright Peter Griffiths)

613 DYX Series 1 FHC used in Firestones advert.

616 AUF See EE 400.

636 CJU Later registration of first CUT 7.

636 CJU. This photograph shows the original CUT 7 converted to more conventional road usage with the addition of a sunshine roof. (Copyright Ted Walker Ferret Fotographics)

638 BLN 31 French rally car, a series 2 FHC in black.

666 DUL Chassis number 860136 from January 1962 is an early 3.8 FHC driven by A C LeFort (Jack), a well known racing member of the JDC. The car was later modified to modsports specification, including a supercharger by Alan Leeson. See detailed article *Jaguar Enthusiast's Club* magazine, December 2008. See also JNU 399C. Raced by Jack Le Fort, Alan Leeson, John Oxborough and Dave Moore. Later owned by myself before its sale to Petra in Czechoslovakia. See article reprinted in Appendix E.

667 YUL 1961 3.8 FHC Lightweight spec sprint car.

671 EUT Early modified roadster driven by Mike Miles and sometimes by his wife, Liz.

696 CWN Blue Lightweight replica.

700 FVN Orange FHC Lightweight, circuit and hill climb car campaigned by Grahame Bull.

700 FVN photographed at the E-Type Challenge at Silverstone in July 2011. (Copyright Peter Griffiths)

703 YUH RHD Series 1 FHC racer in Briggs Cunningham colours. Pre 66 GT racer series.

716 WPB Series 1 DHC light grey racer, Goodwood car.

738 EUT Number used on the LDC, chassis number EC1001, formerly the CUT 7 Protheroe car.

738 EUT (formerly CUT 7) driven by M Wright at the Prescott Hill Cimb in May 1967. (Copyright Ted Walker Ferret Fotographics)

796 NRR DHC trials car.

805 NMJ Zealia Lightweight replica.

815 FYK Early FHC racer, 1963 chassis number 861107. Raced in late '60s by Frank Riches.

823 DCR See 1 PKL.

824 FBX S1 FHC grey racer.

828 WFM Racer driven by Roberto Giordanelli.

835 XUD 1961 3.8 FHC FIA race car.

846 FDN LDC replica, dark blue.

848 CRY Sturgess, also 2 BBC. Now rebuilt by Philip Porter. Famous as the E-Type that got crushed in the film *The Italian Job*.

E-Type 848 CRY (the famous *Italian Job* car) seen at Silverstone, 2011. (Copyright Peter Griffiths)

851 UXL Silver roadster with black stripes, Lightweight replica.

854 UXE FHC Lightweight series 1 3.8-litre, built to FIA specification.

858 MY George Humble early racer.

870 EXV S1 roadster Brighton speed trials.

880 EXK 1963 Targa Florio FHC rally car.

888 RYA Chassis number 860747 denoted this car as a 1962 3.8-litre RHD FHC coupe. This

888 RYA, a Lightweight replica photographed at Donington in May 1992. (Copyright Peter Griffiths)

888 RYA photographed at the E-Type Challenge at Silverstone in July 2011. (Copyright Peter Griffiths)

early car was a regular competitor in its FHC form until its rather tragic accident at Brands Hatch in 1982. It was later totally rebuilt as a replica Lightweight with various period race upgrades, including Weber carburettors, tubular racing manifolds, lowered and stiffened suspension, and a choice of competition wire wheels or J A Pearce alloys. The car is now painted as a replica of the Bob Jane Lightweight in white with red stripes.

898 BYR

This is a very early 1961 roadster, chassis number 850009. It was not one of the ZP batch of Factory competition cars, but it was fitted from new with a competition clutch, and was one of the initial priority list cars available to specific owners who were likely to race them. Peter Sargent certainly fell into this category.

The car's first outing was in August 1961 at the Nürburgring, where Peter finished seventh, racing with wire wheels and a soft top. 898 BYR raced a further seven times that year, with Peter Lumsden also driving the car. The two Peters achieved one 1st, one 2nd, one 3rd, three 4ths, and one 5th.

Looking towards 1962 the two Peters decided on an attempt at Le Mans and the first three months of the New year were spent modifying the car ready for testing at the French circuit in April, in preparation for the main event in June. The 'standard' car was fitted with an aluminium bonnet and the one off distinctive fastback style coupe body. As mentioned elsewhere in this book, it is my opinion that the only successful early racers appear to have been the coupes and not the roadsters. I could never understand why the Factory chose the DHC for its Lightweights.

The *Autosport* report of 13th April 1962 on the Le Mans practice stated the following:

"The Peters, Lumsden and Sargent, put in a lot of lappery (sic) in their E-Type, which now appears to have a complete alloy body. This car was slightly bent in practice when Sargent went off at Indianapolis (the article shows the NSR wing seriously crushed). Ingenious cold air ducts feed the front brakes and carburettors and roof mounted vents feed cold air ducts blowing on the inboard rear disc brakes. The bodywork was vented for under bonnet hot air release and cooling slots had been cut for the rear wheels. This car was one of the first to fit 12.5in Dunlop Mark 9 brakes. A side exhaust system and 6.50x15 tyres were other features of this car." (Note: a lot of modsports stuff going on here!)

Modifications included D-Type enhancements (I smile when the best E-Type modifications seem to be a 'backward' step to the good ol' D-Type days). A wide angle head and dry sump lubrication was fitted, along with D gearbox and triple plate clutch. The rear axle for Le Mans was changed to 2.93:1 and incorporated an oil cooler. One modification which was necessary, but perhaps later regretted, was the fitting of a 140-litre fuel tank.

Following the Le Mans testing, the car was entered into the 1000km race at the Nürburgring in May, but did not finish. It did, however, complete the 24 Hour race, and despite a broken gearbox managed a very respectable 5th place. The 6th July 1962 *Autosport* report by John Bolster included a photo of 898 BYR as the lead picture.

The car competed a further eight times in 1962, achieving three 1st, two 2nd, one 7th, and also two DNFs.

In the last quarter of 1962 the car was sold, and ended up with E-Type racer Fred Cliffe. Fred, whilst using it as a road car in 1970, was involved in an accident which virtually incinerated the car with its full Le Mans long range fuel tank. It was reported in *The Yorkshire Evening Press* of Monday June 15 1970: "Crashed car inferno ... Driver escapes as villager fights petrol blaze ... an E-Type Jaguar with 40 gallons of petrol in the tank caught fire after a three car collision. York fire brigade arrived in time to put out the flames before they spread to the highly inflammable tank of the ex-Le Mans car which was being driven by Mr Frederick Cliffe ... A fire brigade spokesman said three-quarters of the car and its contents were completely destroyed."

The *Jaguar Driver* magazines of February and March 1974 give full details of the car in the 'E-Type of the month' articles, recollections of Fred Cliffe. The remains were retained by Fred until it was purchased by Allen Lloyd, who commissioned a rebuild by Renascence Cars. The excellent article in *Jaguar World* magazine of July 1993 reunited Le Mans driver Peter Sargent with the newly created car at Goodwood.

898 BYR driven by Peter Sargent at the 1961 Boxing Day meet at Brands Hatch. (Copyright Ted Walker Ferret Fotographics)

898 BYR driven by Peter Lumsden/ Peter Sargent at the September 1962 meeting at Crystal Palace. (Copyright Ted Walker Ferret Fotographics)

898 CVN S1 Grey FHC Goodwood standard racer.

898 BYR driven by Peter Lumsden in the 1962 1000km race at the Nürburgring. (Copyright Ted Walker Ferret Fotographics)

905 TKN Lynx Lightweight LDC replica.

The Low Drag Coupe replica 905 TKN taken at Goodwood during the Lynx test day. (Copyright Peter Griffiths)

924 FXC The beautiful Lightweight copy of the longnose car (49 FXN) built by Paul Castaldini.

931 PUU Alternate number for the Cunningham Le Mans FHC, 1337 VC.

936 VPL Lightweight replica. Dark blue with orange nose. Chassis noted as 887223 and also could be road registered as GSL 156.

936 VPL at the Oldtimer Grand Prix in 2011. (Copyright Marco Verch)

962 38 E This is a 1962 3.8 FHC built to FIA spec, and won the European FIA GT Championship in 1989-91. A for sale advert in 2005 stated the following: "FIA papers 5033, Ligier built, torsionally rigid chassis, aluminium bonnet and doors, D-Type wheels. Snetterton 1min 20.79sec. Rob Beere 3.8, 348bhp engine. Great history." Interestingly, the bodyshell including both doors and rear hatch appeared on eBay in August 2009 for under £1000.

964 EOP 'Standard' S1 FHC chassis number 860037. Competed in Spa 6hr Endurance 2009.

964 EOP photographed at the E-Type Challenge at Silverstone in July 2011. (Copyright Peter Griffiths)

964 FPJ 92 Lightweight replica, dark metallic grey/silver.

968 UXY Lightweight replica in green, regularly raced by Chris Scragg

977 DRY FHC racer.

995 FOO An early FHC racer initially driven by John Dean and later by Jack Hayden. The distinctive colour scheme of blue with a red nose and stripe made it suitable for period photographs and even as an advertising vehicle for Ilford Films, an example can be seen in

Autosport magazine 29 April 1966. On a very wet weekend at Phoenix Park in September 1967 the car left the track and hit a tree, but thankfully Jack was unhurt. Further photographs of the car appear in *Autosport* 3 April 1964 and 22 September 1967.

A nice colour shot of 995 FOO. (Copyright Ted Walker Ferret Fotographics)

1196 WK Light green Lightweight replica in E-Type Challenge.

1302 WK FHC raced extensively by Paul Castaldini, a full history of the car was featured over 2 issues of the *Jaguar Enthusiasts* magazine in October and November 2006. Paul's growing stable also included 924 FXC the replica low drag long nose car.

1337 VC Cunningham's Le Mans FHC later 931 PUU and BUO 505. Chassis number 860630.

1423 KY Dark green FHC Lightweight spec race car

1480 WK Lightweight replica raced by Andy Dee-Crowne. A well prepared red, 1962 3.8.

1600 RW This is chassis number 850004, and the first owner was none other than Jaguar's Works Competition Manager 'Lofty' England. It was later owned by Tommy Sopwith of Equipe Endeavour, and then Mike Parkes. A nice article appeared in the December 2002 issue of *Classic Cars* magazine.

E-Type 1600 RW at Silverstone 2011. (Copyright Peter Griffiths)

1913 W 91 Low drag coupe replica in silver.

1967 XKE American S1 DHC red rally car.

1991 WK 1967 Low Drag Coupe recreation by Bryan Wingfield.

1993 AC Lightweight replica built by Alan Collins

2014 HZ Series 1 FHC raced by Tony Quinn in New Zealand.

2065 DF FHC Racer driven by Paddy McNally.

2101 WK LDC replica.

2152 WK Series 1 FHC, chassis number 860621, raced by Bob Jane before he went on to purchase the Lightweight.

Bob Jane's E-Type. (Copyright Les Hughes)

2164 WK Last 'Protheroe' FHC.

2747 WK Light green Lightweight replica.

3142 BH Early 1962, 3.8 FHC racer driven by Ronald Wren.

3550 WK Lightweight replica, race winner of the John Coombs trophy 2013.

3553 WK Lightweight replica race car.

3613 WK Lightweight replica driven by Roy Hatfield.

The beautiful Lightweight replica 3613 WK belonging to Roy Hatfield, seen here at Donington Park in June 1991. (Copyright Peter Griffiths)

3857 WK Early Lightweight replica built by LWR Ltd run by Paul Webb and Mike Harris. LWR 001. More of a concours car than a racer.

4190 NE Lightweight FHC/E-Type experience.

4264 WK A Lightweight replica built from an early FHC.

4270 WK Joseph and Jeff Hickson's FHC modsports car, originally registered ALJ 92A. When advertised for sale in 1995 it stated the following: Carillo rods, Cosworth pistons, triple Dellortos, M3 sport gearbox, AP brakes, full cage and fire system. Holder of 1994 JDC Roger Joyce Memorial Trophy. Originally white but later silver.

4270 WK photographed at Donington on 25 May 1992, sporting its revised air dam. (Copyright Peter Griffiths)

4444 RK Lightweight replica.

4778 LJ John Filbee's red and gold modsports roadster has had a long and eventful life from its very early racing days in the 1960s right through to its eventual rebuild to virtually concours specification by Vicarage. An excellent article appears in *Jaguar E-Type, Celebrating the world's most famous classic sports car* published by *Jaguar World Monthly*. The car, chassis number 850031, achieved over 20 race/class wins in its first 6 years of racing, as well as numerous 2nds and 3rds. A regular competitor against the likes of John Quick, Warren Pearce, Rhoddy Harvey-Bailey, Ed Nelson and J Woodbridge. There is a race report of the Prodsports event at Silverstone in *Autosport* magazine 11 April 1969 which features a photograph of the car.

4861 KX Lightweight FHC RHD in pale green. Tom Harris.

4868 WK Original Lightweight converted to Low Drag Coupe in 1964. Unfortunately, the car is probably best known for the 1964 crash at Montlhéry which tragically killed Peter Lindner. The remains of the car were bought by Peter Kaus for his collection in Germany. Lynx Engineering was commissioned to recreate the car for him in the early 1980s. In 2011 the remains of the original car were fully restored for its new owner. Chassis number S850662.

The Lightweight E-Type 4868 WK receiving rear axle maintenance at the April 1982 JDC meeting at Silverstone. (Copyright Paul Skilleter)

4875 WK Dunford Lightweight replica.

4915 NE Lightweight replica/E-Type experience.

4920 WK Lightweight replica.

4990 VM Silver Lightweight replica.

5081 WK Known as the 13th Lightweight, this was built with genuine Lightweight spares after the initial 12 were produced. It was raced and owned by Paul Webb. A detailed article on this car appeared in *Thoroughbred and Classic Cars* magazine in May 1982.

Car number 31, the 13th Lightweight 5081 WK (Lynx Engineering) in company with 310 WK (Ron Lea). (Copyright Peter Griffiths)

Paul Webb's E-Type at Silverstone in 1984. (Copyright Paul Skilleter)

5104 WK Lightweight Cunningham replica campaigned by Andy Dee-Crowne and Andy Morris. This was one of the early Lightweight replicas built by LWR Ltd, run by Paul Webb and Mike Harris.

5113 WK Number seen on the 'Qvale' Lightweight, chassis no S850660. Shown on the DVLA website as first registered on 20 January 1999.

5114 WK 5114, 5115, 5116 were the three Lightweight E-Types entered by Briggs Cunningham in the 1963 Le Mans race. All three cars are widely covered in most Jaguar books and magazines. 5114 WK is chassis number S850664.

Cunningham cars 5114 WK and 5115 WK seen here at Le Mans in 1963. (Copyright Ted Walker Ferret Fotographics)

5115 WK Briggs Cunningham Le Mans. Chassis number S850659

5115 WK at Le Mans in 1963 driven by Richards/Grossman. (Copyright Ted Walker Ferret Fotographics)

5116 WK Briggs Cunningham Le Mans. Chassis number S850665.

5145 WK LDC replica.

5167 KV A 1962 Series 1 FHC that has been campaigned in the Masters Gentleman Series, HSCC Guards Trophy, E-Type Challenge Series, and others. Yellow coachwork with large white centre stripe. Drivers were Justin Rockett and later Mark Russell.

E-Type 5167 KV raced by Justin Rockett. (Copyright Albert Mensinga)

5292 UR Early racer Bill De Selincourt.

5292 UR seen here at Goodwood driven by Bill De Selincourt. (Copyright Ted Walker Ferret Fotographics)

5303 VB LDC Lightweight replica, silver. 2016 Jaguar Classic Challenge winner. Pictured on front cover of *Historic Racing Technology* magazine Autumn 2016.

5350 VU Lightweight replica, Allen Lloyd.

5350 VU the Lightweight replica of Allen Lloyd at Brands Hatch. (Copyright Peter Griffiths)

5350 VU, the excellent Lightweight replica of Allen Lloyd taken in the paddock in 1992 during the Isle of Man race meeting. (Copyright Peter Griffiths)

5497 WK Lightweight LDC replica Dunsford driven by Michael O'Shea, Mark Gibbon and David Hall at Spa in the 2007 6-hour race . Silver coachwork. Masters Historic Racing series.

5658 WD White Lightweight replica.

5777 OF Lightweight replica.

5916 WK Lynx Lightweight LDC replica.

5949 JL 78 LHD series 1 roadster rally car in dark blue.

6162 RW Jaguar press car. A full and interesting road test was done on the 4 May 1962, by the magazine *Sporting Motorist*.

6182 RW FHC race car.

Peter Lanfranchi driving 6182 RW at Castle Combe in 2007. (Copyright Tony Harrison)

6182 RW and Barry Williams photographed at Silverstone in July 2011. (Copyright Peter Griffiths)

6230 KV Autocross car.

6321 WK Lightweight replica dark green with white stripes.

6900 WK This early FHC was converted to racing specification in the early 1970s by Fred Cliffe, who used it as a hill climb car. It was then sold to Simon Watney, who regularly raced it during the 1970s. His account of the car appeared in *Jaguar Driver* magazine in July 1975. Simon would later manage the E-Type team in the intermarque 6 hour relay races. The racing career of the car continued well into the 1980s, when it was owned and driven by Paul Webb. During this time it carried the number plate PWM 1 (presumably standing for Paul Webb Motors), and later 6900 WK. After a successful, but somewhat hard life, it passed into the hands of Paul Palmer and then to me. I started a rebuild, but part way through sold it back to Paul Webb, who decided to rebuild the car to a standard FHC Lightweight with a completely new body and mechanics.

Paul Webb driving his modsports E-Type 6900 WK at the 1984 JDC Silverstone meeting. (Copyright Paul Skilleter)

7004 WD Monte Carlo Rally entrant, early S1 DHC. Perhaps just as famous because a Burago 1/18th scale model was made, albeit registered 004 WD.

7266 WK Lightweight replica, green with white stripes.

7597 PE 'Standard' DHC racer built from a somewhat derelict roadster. Chassis 850148 beautifully restored in red with black hardtop to pre-'63 GT race specification.

7597 PE photographed at the E-Type Challenge at Silverstone in July 2011. (Copyright Peter Griffiths)

8448 TJ An early FHC, chassis number 861227, successfully raced by John Cuff during 1963-1967. The car's racing history continued with great success in the hands of Ted Worswick from 1968-1971 and then later with John Walker until 1974. The car, when run by John Walker in the early 1970s, carried the registration number WAK 1. During the 1980s and early 1990s it was campaigned by Fred Cliffe using registration number FNC 1.

Fred completely rebuilt the car with aluminium bonnet, roof, doors and wings. The car was exported to the USA in 1993 and in 2003 was transferred into the hands of its current owner Jaime I Del Valle, who has extensively researched its history, and a full article on the car appeared in *Jaguar Enthusiast* magazine in May 2012. A brief race history is shown here:

13/10/63 Scarborough hill climb 3rd
20/4/64 Tulip rally 2nd
21/3/64 Oulton Park 1st
29/3/64 Rufforth 2nd
30/3/64 Woodvale 1st
3/8/64 Croft 3rd
5/9/64 Oulton Park 3rd
11/10/64 Scarborough
5/6/65 Rufforth 3rd
7/6/65 Woodvale 1st
12/6/65 Oulton Park
3/7/65 Crystal Palace 3rd
24/7/65 Aintree 2nd
1/8/65 Oulton Park
15/8/65 Croft 1st
21/8/65 Oulton Park 1st
30/8/65 Croft no 41 1st & 2nd
25/9/65 Oulton Park 1st
26/9/65 Woodvale 1st
2/10/65 Aintree 1st & 2nd
9/4/66 Oulton Park
6/9/66 Oulton Park
26/8/67 Silverstone no 56 3rd

The rebuilt ex-Cuff car at Donington in May 1992. (Copyright Peter Griffiths)

The engine of Fred Cliffe's ex-John Cuff car. (Copyright Peter Griffiths)

8888 WK Lightweight replica.

9000 WK Lightweight replica racer. White with blue hard top. Also seen in white with green stripe/hard top.

9009 UR Early FHC rally/hill climb car.

9022 DU Cunningham roadster. Chassis number 875015.

9023 DU Cunningham roadster. A full and detailed article on 'the' Cunningham roadster appeared in *Jaguar World* magazine in March 1993. In that article, the photograph showed the car with the registration plate 9032 DU, however, in *Jaguar Driver* magazine in May 1998, the car is shown with registration number 9023 DU. Chassis number 875027.

I understand that Briggs Cunningham ordered three roadsters (before the three Lightweights that came later) and 9023DU was tested at Le Mans, but he chose to drive the FHC (1337 VC instead). 9023 DU was, however, successfully raced in the States, and these races are recorded in the *Jaguar Driver* article.

According to the DVLA website, 9023 DU was first registered in February 1993, and 9022, 9024 and 9032 are not registered at all. I can only guess that the cars were never registered in 1961 as they were exported to the States and only when 9023 came back to the UK it was registered in 1993, the year when the article was written. I can also only guess that 9032 was an error, but I am uncertain.

9024 DU Cunningham roadster. Chassis number 875026.

9032 DU Cunningham roadster see above.

9100 RC 24 Left-hand drive roadster rally car.

9600 HP 1st FHC

E-Type 9600 HP seen at Silverstone 2011. (Copyright Peter Griffiths)

9999 WK Lightweight LDC replica

123202 TR Red LHD series 1 roadster rally car.

Alphabetical list

AAH 210B FHC Lightweight … silver grey with blue nose.

AAN 389C 4.2 FHC hill climb car driven by Jim Thomson

ABD 799A The FHC racer of Mike Adams. Initially with red coachwork, (see article *Jaguar Driver* October 1994), but later changed to green when it was part of the JEC race team with Malcolm Hamilton's V12 'Beast.' Also see *Jaguar World* magazine March/ April 1996 when Jim Patten wrote an article on Mike's car. I was lucky enough (aka frightened to death!) when on a European holiday with Mike, to be driven around the Nürburgring at full speed, something I shall never forget. I think that is where Mike caught the racing bug! A further colour change to white with blue stripes came with the next owner Nick McCaffrey.

Mike Adams in the paddock at Silverstone with ABD 799A. (Copyright Peter Griffiths)

ACK 241A Series 1 FHC racer.

ACK 241A photographed at the E-Type Challenge at Silverstone in July 2011. (Copyright Peter Griffiths)

AE 06 15 Lightweight replica.

AFD 250 Early racer Davenport. This is chassis number 860002, the second FHC produced. This was the personal number of Anthony Frederick Davenport, who had previously raced his XK150. Articles on the car appeared in *Jaguar Driver* issues of June 1996, July 1996, February 1997, and September 1997. The car also is shown in *Jaguar World Monthly* February 2011 issue at the Prescott Hill Climb, driven by John Burton of the E-Type Register.

E-Type AFD 250 seen at Silverstone 2011. (Copyright Peter Griffiths)

AFK 659B Possible later number used on 898 BYR for a while.

AFW 165A Lightweight replica built and raced by Mike Wilkinson.

AGS 858D Lightweight replica, white with red stripes owned by Jools Holland.

AH 255 VD Silver S1 rally car.

AH 600 Antony Hopkins private number used on the 'Scragg' Lightweight PS 1175, chassis number S850669.

AJN 985A Series 1 FHC race car driven by Tim Wander.

ALJ 92A The modsports car of Jeff and Joseph Hickson, later registered 4270 WK. The pure white FHC was sponsored by Hilltop Motors. The car featured on the front cover of *Jaguar Enthusiasts Magazine* in July 1990, and regularly appeared in Jaguar magazines of the 1990s. Later painted silver.

ALJ 92A, the modified FHC of Jeff Hickson seen here at Brands Hatch in 1990. (Copyright Peter Griffiths)

AlJ 92A seen at Brands Hatch in 1990 before it upgraded to its 4270 WK registration. (Copyright Peter Griffiths)

ALS 430B Classic Marathon car.

ANU 415A Phil Stott Lightweight replica/E-Type experience.

AP-017-ZP FHC rally car, LHD, silver with white stripes, Tour Auto 2013 entrant. Alain Figaret. A Ninco model was made of the car.

AVT 575A Speed trial FHC car of Phil Judd.

AVT 579A Lightweight replica.

AYM 182B Lightweight replica. Painted in Cunningham colours; white with blue stripes.

B1 AS19H S1 FHC German 'Lightweight racer.'

B 131 Early 'standard looking' metallic blue FHC racer.

E-Type B131 seen here at Brands Hatch in 1963 in a standard production sports car race. (Copyright Ted Walker Ferret Fotographics)

BB 111 Early DHC Monte Carlo rally car.

BB JE 43 H Early DHC classic rally car in Germany.

BF 791 ZG Series 1 RHD FHC rally car. White with green stripes.

BFW 559B Pirelli Classic Marathon S1 FHC in red.

BGC 6B 1963 3.8 FHC FIA race car.

BGC 22B The well known Comet Delltune FHC of Tony Shaw, the sister car to the similar FHC of John Burbidge. No number was shown on the car during its racing days, but I am informed it was 128 MAL originally.
Tony and his 3.8 FHC modsports regularly raced with John Burbidge in the late 1960s, both cars successfully competing under the sponsorship of Comet-DellTune, with their distinctive blue-green livery combination. The car continued its racing career in the hands of Pino Scarpino, Warren Pearce, Jon Waterman (Maidstone Commercials) and Paul Webb. I photographed the car at Mallory Park when owned by Paul; it was painted white with three top stripes (red/grey/black) and carried the number plate '4D GROUP.' The car then passed to Roger Cook, who painted it dark blue and used it for sprints and hill climbs. After a couple of years the rear wheel arches were extended, and the car was painted bright red. It was put up for sale in the mid 1990s, and again in early 2015, bright red, with virtual standard bodywork and, per the advert: "the Ex-Tony Shaw Comet-DellTune 1964 3.8-litre FHC E-Type. Continuous race history in Modsports Era from 1966 to 1996. Over 52 victories and podiums to its credit. This all steel car has undergone total professional body and mechanical restoration to Historic Road Sport specification including many period Lightweight parts."

The 2 Comet Delltune modsports E-Types of John Burbidge and Tony Shaw. (Copyright Graham Ravensdale)

The ex-Tony Shaw FHC at the JDC Mallory Park test day driven by Paul Webb. (Copyright Peter Griffiths)

BHG 1 Lightweight replica.

Lightweight replica BHG 1 photographed at the E-Type Challenge at Silverstone in July 2011. (Copyright Peter Griffiths)

BHK 267A LHD S1 FHC 'fast road use' painted in Cunningham colours of white with blue stripes.

BHK 278A Lightweight replica in silver.

BL 367 CK LHD Series 1 FHC White with blue stripes (Cunningham colours) Targa Florio entrant.

BMP 331 USA registration allocated to the Qvale Lightweight S850660, later to be given 5113 WK.

BMT 606H Hill climb DHC driven by John Harding.

BNE 438B 3.8 DHC modified race/rally car driven by Per Jonsson in several European events LHD.

BNE 438B photographed at the E-Type Challenge at Silverstone in July 2011. (Copyright Peter Griffiths)

BRW 26 This is a 1962 FHC driven by Brian Waddilove, who achieved great success during 1962 and 1963, gaining over 40 awards including several lap records. It boasted a full D-Type engine, Weber carburettors, Lightweight flywheel and full Le Mans brake modifications. Regular competitor at Rufforth and Harewood. Colour: metallic silver/blue.

BTB 640A Interim number used on the 'Sutcliffe' Lightweight (S850666). Also, RV 7, SVM 740 and YVH 210.

BUL 3H 4.2 series 2 roadster.

BUL 452C Standard 4.2 FHC hill climb car.

BUO 505 Cunningham FHC later number.

BUY 1 Coombes garage number, which became 4 WPD, the first Lightweight.

BUY 1 at the Aintree Grand Prix meeting in 1961. (Copyright Ted Walker Ferret Fotographics)

BUY 1 at Brands Hatch in June 1961 again driven by Roy Salvadori. (Copyright Ted Walker Ferret Fotographics)

A nice shot of the engine bay of BUY 1 photographed at Crystal Palace in May 1961, showing its original SU carburettors before transformation to Lightweight specification. (Copyright Ted Walker Ferret Fotographics)

BUY 12 Coombes garage number used on several cars.

BV 664 BV LHD FHC Tour Auto rally car series 1 in pale blue.

BW-543-QM Series 1 FHC rally car. Yellow with green stripes.

BXG 326B Later number on the Ropner Semi-Lightweight S850817.

BYN 950B Early fairly standard roadster with early race modifications.

BYN 950B photographed at Silverstone. (Copyright Peter Griffiths)

CJX 672C Original Semi-Lightweight, ex-Sir Robert Ropner supplied by the Factory in 1964. Chassis number S850817. Also registered XAJ 1 and 1 WW.

The Bonhams sale catalogue for CJX 672C in September 2011. (Copyright Peter Griffiths)

CK 613 AF Cream with white stripe LHD FHC Tour Auto rally car

C MT 2 H Pale blue LHD V12 FHC. German rally car.

A 1972 series 3 V12 FHC enjoying the Saxony Classic Rallye in 2010. (Copyright Andre Karwath)

CR 505 JJ LHD dark blue with white stripe FHC rally car.

CTV 55B 1965 Monte Carlo Rally entrant. Seen numbered CTV 552 by mistake .

CUT 7 Used by racer Dick Protheroe on 3 of his E-Type race cars. Shown on the DVLA website as first registered 16th January 1992.

Dick Protheroe seen here in the original CUT 7 in September 1961 at Crystal Palace. (Copyright Ted Walker Ferret Fotographics)

Lightweight E-Type 86 PJ leads Dick Protheroe in the Low Drag Coupe CUT 7 at the Silverstone meeting in May 1964. (Copyright Ted Walker Ferret Fotographics)

See article reprint in Appendix E.

CUT 7A Number once used on the rebuilt FHC using the bodyshell of Dick Protheroe's second race E-Type, which was later raced as a DHC registered 256 DJU.

CUT 8 Protheroe garage car. Shown on the DVLA website as first registered on 18th September 1991. Also 105 ENX

CUT 8 photographed at the E-Type Challenge at Silverstone in July 2011. (Copyright Peter Griffiths)

CVY 10C 4.2 FHC Racer driven by Alan Mountain.

CWA 740B S1 FHC driven by Paul Slade. Red with Minilites.

CZ 985 GR Silver with black stripes. S1 FHC LHD Tour Auto rally car. 2014 Rallye des Princesses.

An LHD series 1 FHC enjoying the Rallye des Princesses in 2014. (Copyright 'Blood Destructor')

DDY 375D Series 1 FHC standard racer

DEA 615C Green S1 FHC modified for fast road.

DF 358 Series 1 DHC Racer driven by D Plumstead

DF 358 driven by D Plumstead at Ilford in 1966. (Copyright Ted Walker Ferret Fotographics)

DJ 44E Made up number plate ... Don and John (Oxborough's) 4.4-litre E-Type.

DN WM 22H Series 1½ silver FHC rally car. German LHD.

A 1968 FHC pictured during the 2010 Saxony Classic Rallye. (Copyright Andre Karwath)

DPO 7 3.8 roadster driven by Leslie Fowler, early JDC Chairman. On front cover of *Jaguar Driver*'s *Club* magazine in June 1962 and July 1962.

DQ 046 DA Pale blue with white stripe, series 1 LHD roadster rally car ... Tour Auto.

DTO 87B An early 3.8 FHC with FIA papers, several class wins including 2nd overall at Jabbeke Speed Trials, driven by Steven Elliot

DUD 555C 4.2 FHC track car.

DXC 212B Early modified DHC hill climb car.

DXC 212B, taken at Prescott Hill Climb in April 1967. (Copyright Ted Walker Ferret Fotographics)

E 141 This early racer was formerly campaigned extensively by Brian Spicer; it was later owned by John Quick and Bill De Selincourt under the name of Ember Racing. The car when owned by John Quick was the 'Sister' car to WOO 11. This 1965 DHC ran a 3781cc +30 engine with Weslake head, 45 DCOE9 Webers, Koni shock absorbers and Pearce wheels. E141 was later raced by Reg Woodcock, who had a terrible accident at Silverstone in 1978 when the car crashed, killing two marshalls. The car was later fully rebuilt as a Lightweight replica, and has now begun a new race career in the hands of Nigel Webb, who is a regular competitor at Goodwood, and in 2009 was co-piloted by Desire Wilson.

Brian Spicer in E 141 at Brands Hatch in May 1965. (Copyright Ted Walker Ferret Fotographics)

E 400 Lightweight replica with red coachwork ... not to be confused with EE 400, which is chassis number 18.

E 400 at the Silverstone classic in 2008. (Copyright Ed Callow)

E 1500 Ecurie Ecosse support car.

EAR 100 S1 FHC Brighton speed trials.

EBW 906A Lightweight replica.

EBW 923A Lightweight replica driven by Mike Newman.

ECD 400 Sopwith Factory competition car. Chassis number 850005 is perhaps one of the more famous early racing roadsters, in that it was made so by Graham Hill. ECD 400 along with BUY 1 (the Coombs-entered roadster) made its race debut on 15 April 1961 at Oulton Park. Driven by Graham Hill, it won the race. A full and extensive article on the car and its history appeared in the January 2008 edition of *Jaguar World*. After such a successful start, the car was on the front cover of the Nottingham Sports Car Club Silverstone race meeting programme on 17 June 1961. An interesting advert appeared in *Autosport* October 1967, listing the car for sale at the incredible price of £640. It stated that it was fitted with competition crank, rods, clutch and head, and had straight cut gears, a modified brake servo, koni shock absorbers, an air scoop and R6 tyres (!) on offset wheels. Naturally the car

ECD 400 in the hands of Jack Sears at Crystal Palace in May 1961. (Copyright Ted Walker Ferret Fotographics)

has appeared in numerous books, magazines and even promotions over the years, including those for BP and Lodge sparkplugs.

ECH 707C FHC hill climb car driven by Paul Slade.

EE 400 Equipe Endeavour Factory competition car. Chassis number 850018 (but has been quoted as 850019) is another of the 'Magnificent 7' ZP Factory competition cars. EE 400 was supplied to the Equipe Endeavour team run by Tommy Sopwith. This car was the Equipe Endeavour's sister car to ECD 400 and was also the road car for Mike Parkes, the main driver of the team. The car was also registered 616 AUF and UPM 400.

E-Type UPM 400 seen at Goodwood in 2013. (Copyright Paul Skilleter)

EGF 551B LHD 3.8 FHC rally car.

EGF 551B ... a 1961 LHD FHC seen at the 2016 Le Mans Classic. (Copyright David Merrett)

ELA 67C Jackie Oliver FHC. This 4.2 FHC was driven by Jackie Oliver and Chris Craft in the Guards 1000km race at Brands Hatch on 22 May 1965.

ELA 67C driven by Jackie Oliver at the Guards 1000km. (Copyright Ted Walker Ferret Fotographics)

ELC 791C Heavily modified FHC known as 'Gilda.' More of a modified road car than a racer.

ESV 683 Lightweight replica.

ESV 683 photographed at Donington on 25 May 1992. The 'for sale' sign in the window is asking for "offers around £22,000" ... Isn't hindsight wonderful! (Copyright Peter Griffiths)

EUL 452C FHC hill climb car.

EYY 32B This is the Factory built production Semi-Lightweight E-Type FHC built for Pierre Bardinon. A detailed article on this car appeared in *Jaguar World* magazine in March 1997. Chassis number S890193. French registration was 4465 QC 75.

E-Type FHC of Pierre Bardinon, chassis number S890193. (Copyright Paul Skilleter)

EYY 618B S1 Grey FHC Goodwood racer.

FCO 55E Series 2 Roadster hill climb car driven by Cliff McKinnon.

FJ 3858 See GB 8488.

FNC 1 Used by Fred Cliffe on various cars, including 8448 TJ, the John Cuff car.

FNC 2 Used by Fred Cliffe on various modsports E-Types that he raced.

FNC 2D A Lightweight replica built by Fred Cliffe.

FOY 235D Early FHC sprinted by JDC stalwart Pierre Rohan.

FPH 60B LHD roadster track day car.

FSN 1 See description under the later registered number of SSN 300.

FYX 190 Series 1½ DHC hill climb car.

FYX 190 at Gurston Down Hill Climb in November 1977. (Copyright Ted Walker Ferret Fotographics)

GB 461 See GB 8488.

GB 8488 Owned and driven by Sir Gawaine Baillie. Chassis number 850008 is one of the seven Factory competition cars under 'Project ZP 537/24.' Also registered FJ 3858 and GB 461.

GE 500 018 Swiss S1 roadster Lightweight replica rally car in red.

GER-ET 11H Lightweight replica.

GKP 631D This number was painted on the rear of 7 CXW at one time. It may not be the car's registration, but possibly, could be the tow cars registration?

GNX 513C Series 1 FHC racer.

GPK 93J S2 FHC racer

GSL 156 1962 E-Type competition car seen for sale at the *Autosport* racing car show at the NEC Birmingham on the 12th January 2008 ... but see 936 VPL.

GT- XE 1H Lightweight replica. Distinctive bright blue with red stripes.

GVC 690N V12 FHC Burgess.

GVC 690N V12 FHC seen at Mallory Park in 1975. (Copyright Ted Walker Ferret Fotographics)

V12 E-Type at Mallory Park in 1975. (Copyright Ted Walker Ferret Fotographics)

GYM 280C Sprint and hill climb roadster.

HBF 903C This was an early modsports E-Type driven by Neville Robinson, which was later converted to Lightweight E-Type specification. It has recently been used in foreign rallies.

HBF 903C Lightweight replica photographed at the E-Type Challenge at Silverstone in July 2011. (Copyright Peter Griffiths)

Neville Robinson's E-Type at the JDC test day at Mallory Park. (Copyright Peter Griffiths)

HH- GT 744H Lightweight replica.

HJP 400 Lightweight replica.

HON 140D David Robinson and his roadster HON 140D were regularly featured in the Jaguar magazines in the late 1980s and early 1990s. His car is on the front cover of *Jaguar Driver* magazine in August 1988. In 1987 he was awarded JDC Competition Driver of the Year. In the June 1989 edition of *Thoroughbred and Classic Cars*, he featured in an article covering the BBC *Top Gear* Heritage Team Challenge.

HON 140D lightly modified roadster of David Robinson seen here at Donington in June 1991. (Copyright Peter Griffiths)

HOO 535B Lightweight replica.

HOT 12 Heavily modified FHC driven by Trevor Baines. Instantly recognisable by its unusual rear end styling by Williams and Pritchard.

HOT 12 driven by Trevor Baines at Mallory Park on 3 May 1992. (Copyright Peter Griffiths)

HS 06122 Dark blue with white stripes, FHC S1 rally car.

HTU 942K This is the V12 FHC regularly campaigned by Jaguar stalwart Ron Lea from the early 1980s until a few years ago when the car was sold. During the late 1980s, Ron led the JDC Intermarque team with this car and in 1986 took the JDC team to victory, winning the championship. In 2012, Ron wrote his life story in his book *If at first you don't succeed ...* which includes detailed accounts of this car as well as his other racing E-Types, the ex-Warren Pearce car 310 WK, and the ex-Dave Moore modsports DHC.

HWD 669D Tulip rally car.

HWD 669D driven by Gordon Whiting at the 1967 Tulip Rally. (Copyright Ted Walker Ferret Fotographics)

HX Z1H Lightweight replica. Distinctive, bright blue with blue stripes, and sometimes confused with GT XE 1H.

J 62 White modsports FHC. Guernsey hill climb car.

JAG 038 Australian registration on Bob Jane's Lightweight S850667.

The Lightweight E-Type of Bob Jane raced without a roof! (Copyright Les Hughes)

JFO 534 S1 FHC hill climb/rally car. Maroon with two white stripes. D-Type style wheels.

Series 1 FHC JFO 534 at Brooklands in 2012. (Copyright Ian Hunt)

JL 24 Jack Lambert DHC racer.

JLG 694C The incredible sprint and hill climb roadster of Herbert Shepherd who was still competing in his 70s and managed to accumulate in excess of 350 trophies. The car, an S1 4.2 looked virtually standard but had a well tweaked engine and ran on Minilite wheels.

JLG 694C spotted at Donington on 9 June 1991. (Copyright Peter Griffiths)

JM 71 1961 DHC of EJB (John) Mitchell competed in 1962. Dark blue.

JNU 399C Don and John Oxborough's sister car to 666 DUL. Previously registered 1000 UP. FHC modsports later converted to roadster modsports.

JPD 251C Early Sprint and hill climb car driven by Bob Jennings.

JPD 251C driven by Bob Jennings at the September 1967 Prescott Hill Climb. (Copyright Ted Walker Ferret Fotographics)

JS 11 FHC racer New Zealand.

JTJ 20K This is the monstrous V12 E-Type driven by Will Cole. This 7-litre dry-sumped 500bhp monster was predominantly a sprint and hill climb car. The engine bay with its six side draught Webers was a sight to behold. A regular competitor at Shelsley Walsh, Gurston and Curborough, the car is featured in the book *History of Shelsley Walsh*, *Speedscene* magazine June 1989, and regularly in *Jaguar Driver* magazine.

The thunderous V12 roadster of Will Cole seen here at the Curborough sprint meeting in 1979. (Copyright Ted Walker Ferret Fotographics)

The thunderous V12 roadster of Will Cole, seen here at the Curborough sprint meeting in 1979. (Copyright Ted Walker Ferret Fotographics)

Under bonnet shot of Will Cole's V12 roadster showing six beautiful sidedraught Weber carburettors. (Copyright Peter Griffiths)

KBV 871F 4.2 white FHC race car, heavily modified.

KE VA 8 S1 Roadster rally car. Silver with black stripes.

KGJ 745A Lightweight LDC replica.

KGJ 902A FHC racer.

KGU 899D Lightweight replica. Silver with blue roof.

KLA 885D Series 1 DHC trials and autocross car.

KOM 386E Primrose yellow series 1½ DHC rally car.

Rallycross car. (Copyright Ted Walker Ferret Fotographics)

KO WE 380 H Series 1 roadster, LHD silver German rally car.

KPJ 85C This is the successful modsports FHC raced by Chris Shipton. A photograph of the car appeared on the front cover of *Jaguar Driver* in June 1984. A regular competitor in the Intermarque Challenge series, and part of the JDC winning team in 1986.

KPJ 85C at the Donington meeting in June 1991. (Copyright Peter Griffiths)

KPJ 85C, the FHC of Chris Shipton seen at Donington 9 June 1991. (Copyright Peter Griffiths)

KSK 620 A red series 1 FHC racer/hill climb car. 1962 with FIA papers.

KTW 6J Standard Series 1 DHC.

KYX 308 Pirelli Classic Marathon car.

LAU DT 67 H German LHD V12 FHC rally car in green.

LJA 50F One of Eike Welhausen's several modsports cars.

LID 24B Follow on number for the ex-Jack Lambert car, RL 26. (850016)

LMD 24B Follow on number for the ex-Ropner Semi-Lightweight. (S850817)

LNX 7 Lightweight LDC replica.

LRP 935 Lynx Lightweight LDC replica.

LWJ 100D 1963 Series 1 4.2-litre FHC racer. Originally a standard looking red coupe complete with bumpers, wire wheels and full Webasto sunshine roof. When sold via Bonhams in 2007 it was silver with a blue stripe, no sunshine roof, no bumpers and D-Type style wheels.

LWJ 100D driven by Tony Mather at Mallory Park on 3 May 1992. (Copyright Peter Griffiths)

LWV 498P Lightweight replica.

M BD 38H LHD S1 FHC pale gold rally car.

MCH 627D Initially raced as a standard roadster by Phil Stott complete with bumpers and soft-top, and progressively modified by him for the HSCC historic roadsports race series. It is now a beautifully prepared car driven by Nick Thompson. A full story of this Lightweight style hill climb racer appears in the August 2003 edition of *Jaguar Enthusiast*.

MCH 627D in its early form seen here at Donington in June 1991, and owned by Harvey Cook. (Copyright Peter Griffiths)

MCH 627D seen here in its later form looking more like a Lightweight replica, at Donington, May 1992. (Copyright Peter Griffiths)

MT 111 S1 DHC of Max Trimble. Hill climb car.

NBD 2 One of the original Bryan Wingfield Lightweight replicas in green.

NKT 237F A 1967 4.2 roadster driven by Henry Pearman (owner of Eagle E-Types) and Gordon Cruickshank to 1st place in the 1989 Pirelli Classic Marathon.

E-Type NKT 237F seen at Silverstone 2011. (Copyright Peter Griffiths)

NCC 669 Early racer driven by Henryk Synowiec.

NRW 574F This is the well known and always beautifully presented sprint and hill climb car of Oliver Walker, and later Nigel Pow. This car had silver coachwork with a distinctive bright blue nose. This regularly campaigned, immaculate, all-steel bodied roadster was often seen at Shelsley Walsh and Loton Park during the 1970s. This was the ex-Peter Harris of Bournemouth 4.2 sprint car, often featured in *Jaguar Driver* and other period magazines. Photographs of the car also appear in *E-Type, End of an Era* by Chris Harvey (p173), *Jaguar Sports Cars* by Paul Skilleter (p259), and *The Jaguar Driver's Yearbook* by Paul Skilleter of 1979/80 (p58).

NRW 574F, Oliver Walker's immaculate roadster at the JDC Wiscombe Hill Climb. (Copyright Peter Griffiths)

The beautifully prepared roadster of Nigel Pow seen here at Prescott Hill Climb in May 1973. (Copyright Ted Walker Ferret Fotographics)

Nigel Pow in his immaculate roadster seen here in September 1972. (Copyright Ted Walker Ferret Fotographics)

NW VB62H S1 FHC rally car.

An LHD 1962 FHC series 1 E-Type taking part in the Heidelberg Historic Rally in 2015. (Copyright Radoslaw Drozdzewski)

NXC 997D This 4.2 roadster, an early modsports car of Fred Cliffe was badly damaged at Harewood in the 1970s, and was left untouched for a while until I bought it and began a full rebuild. This project was sold on to John Oxborough who completed the rebuild and used the car for sprints and hill climbs with great success. I then bought back the car, and sprinted with it for two years. It featured on the back cover of the book *Uphill Racers* by Chris Mason, and a photograph also appears in Nigel Thorley's book *The Jaguar E-Type*. The car was later shipped abroad, and is now owned by Jaime I Del Valle, a true Jaguar enthusiast (and official Jaguar dealer) in Puerto Rico.

The author with his modsports racer at the West Malling Airfield Sprint in Kent. (Copyright Peter Griffiths)

NXC 997D makes an impressive start at a sprint meeting spinning its wheels. (Copyright Peter Griffiths)

ONE 858H 4.2 series 2 roadster in red with Minilite wheels. Driven by Tony Bancroft in hill climbs, and later owned by Gerry Marshall and Willie Green.

OSL 828 Incorrect number, seen advertised as such, but should be USL 828.

OWC 4 Lightweight replica, silver.

OWT 477E 4.2, 2+2 FHC hill climb car of Derek Hastings.

PAG 622A Lightweight FHC driven by Martin White, light blue.

PAG 630A Lightweight replica in Briggs Cunningham colours.

PAH 521 Low drag coupe replica, green with gold stripe.

PB 1 Registration number used by Phil Bennett on his Modsports roadster.

PBC 112 John Wilson modsports. See the excellent article in *Jaguar Quarterly* magazine May/June and July/August of 1992. This prolific E-Type race car has had many owners since John Wilson, including Ted Worswick, Mike Franey, Dave Moore, Brian Mills, John Myerscough, Fred Cliffe, Chris Mason and still used today by Hayden Spedding.

Hayden Spedding in the current version of PBC 112. (Copyright Andrew Basterfield)

PBC 112 piloted by John Wilson circa 1967. (Copyright Ted Walker Ferret Fotographics)

PBC 112 John Wilson followed by Warren Pearce at Silverstone in 1968. (Copyright Ted Walker Ferret Fotographics)

John Wilson leading John Cuff at Silverstone. (Copyright Ted Walker Ferret Fotographics)

PEE 22 1970 4.2-litre S2 FHC regularly raced from the late 1970s to the early 1990s by Tim Sisson and Michael Tye.

Tim Sisson in his series 2 FHC seen here at Mallory Park. (Copyright Peter Griffiths)

PFL 478 FHC Lightweight in Cunningham colours.

PLV 40F Standard roadster used for sprinting.

PMB 324H Later registration number for CUT 7 (version 2). In roadster form it was unrecognisable, as it carried a series 3 V12 bonnet!

PMW 336H The author's series 2 FHC Sprint car driven at Brands Hatch, Lydden and Goodwood. At the Goodwood sprint in 1978 the clutch went, due to my over-exuberance whilst changing gear through the chicane.

PMW 336H seen here at Brands Hatch in the 1970s. (Copyright Peter Griffiths)

PMW 336H seen here in the paddock at Lydden Circuit in Kent. (Copyright Peter Griffiths)

PNW 127C Lightweight replica raced by Statham and Shephard.

PPB 155 Modsports 3.8 coupe of Bernie Breeze.

PS 1175 Original Lightweight E-Type raced by Phil Scragg, and still seen today at many Goodwood events. Chassis number S850669. Later registrations include AH 600 and 4 RH.

Lightweight E-Type PS 1175 photographed at the Lynx test day at Goodwood. (Copyright Peter Griffiths)

Lightweight E-Type PS 1175. (Copyright Ramgeis)

PS 1175 at the Goodwood Revival in 2010: a nice overhead shot in the pits. (Copyright Ian Hunt)

PS 1175 at the Goodwood Revival in 2008. (Copyright Ian Hunt)

PUP 66 Lightweight replica in dark blue.

PW 1 Paul Webb number used on several cars.

Paul Webb's E-Type PW 1 seen at Silverstone. (Copyright Laurie Abbott)

PWM 1 Paul Webb Motors (see 6900 WK).

PZC 73 Very early (Nov 1961) series 1 roadster racer in Northern Ireland, only the third E-Type to be sold there. Raced by Michael Smurfit as a fairly standard car complete with soft top.

RA 1 Lightweight replica.

RAC 100 Original number for CUT 8.

RL 26 Jack Lambert, chassis no 850016. Jack Lambert was one of the main private entrants in club racing in the early 1960s. He raced the car extensively from 1961 until 1964, when he finally put it up for sale for the grand sum of £1600. The car always appeared in fairly standard form, yet sported a wide angle head and twin plate clutch, as well as the usual period braking and suspension modifications. The car later carried the registration 12 MY and then LID 24B (possibly LMD 24B). The car, like other early racers, now appears in full Lightweight specification. I understand that Jack drove RL 26, and his wife, Renee, drove JL 24.

Jack Lambert driving his 1961 roadster at the JDC Silverstone meeting in 1961. (Copyright Ted Walker Ferret Fotographics)

A collection of trophies won by
Jack Lambert spotted on eBay.
(Copyright Pablo Raybould)

Jack Lambert's roadster seen
here at the AMOC St John Horsfall
Silverstone meeting in March 1964.
(Copyright Ted Walker Ferret Fotographics)

RO-A17 FHC Lightweight historic rally car.

ROB 2 This is 7 CXW when raced by Rob Schroeder.

RS 2 Number used on the modsports car of Richard Scantlebury. This was the original FHC prepared by Brian Murphy, and later became known as the Ziebart car. (See non-registered cars section.)

E-Type RS 2 of Richard Scantlebury
seen at Valence in 1971.
(Copyright Ted Walker Ferret Fotographics)

RV 7 The original Sutcliffe Lightweight car, chassis number S850666. RV 7 was the private plate of Bob Vincent during his ownership. It also appeared on Lightweight S850669 when Bob owned it.

SCL 900 Early racer. Chassis number 850162 was regularly raced at many JDC race meetings in the 1980s, and has been continually developed into a full recreation of a Lightweight replica.

SCL 900, chassis no 850162, in the early '80s.
(Copyright Ted Walker Ferret Fotographics)

SCL 900 battles it out with 995 FOO.
(Copyright Ted Walker Ferret Fotographics)

SCL 900 leads Lewis at
Mallory Park in June 1967.
(Copyright Ted Walker Ferret Fotographics)

SGR 167 Early FHC chassis 860137, Brighton Speed Trials modsports race car from 1972 to 1977. Later converted back to standard FHC specification.

SKH 712B Very early highly modified series 1 roadster.

SNG 984 Series 1 dark green roadster.

SSK 732 FHC Lightweight.

SSL 368 3.8 FHC.

SSL 368 ... a 1961 FHC seen at the Le Mans classic in 2016. (Copyright David Merret)

SSL 388 3.8 FHC racer.

SSL 388 photographed at the E-Type Challenge at Silverstone in July 2011.
(Copyright Peter Griffiths)

SSN 300 Chassis number 850216 was a 1961 3.8 roadster delivered to Jackie Stewart. This celebrated car, later driven by Mike Wilkinson, appeared in *Jaguar World* magazine in October 1999, and in *Classic Cars* magazine in January 2011. The car was originally registered FSN 1, and appeared in several adverts featuring Pirelli Tyres.

SSN 300 at the
Cholmondeley
Hill Climb in 2009.
(Copyright Ian Hunt)

SST 569 E-Type dragster. An LHD 3.8 green roadster seen at Santa Pod driven by Leigh Morris.

SUE 196 Early racer driven by the Earl of Denbigh.

The Earl of Denbigh in SUE 196 at the 8 Clubs meeting in 1962. (Copyright Ted Walker Ferret Fotographics)

SVJ 345 H Later registration number for CUT 7 (version 2). Sometimes appeared without the H suffix.

SVJ 345: the second version of CUT 7 now in its roadster form. (Copyright Peter Griffiths)

SVM 740 Original Lightweight E-Type first registered YVH 210.

SVM 740, the Lightweight E-Type of Brian Corser at the parade lap for the British Grand Prix in 1970 at Brands Hatch. (Copyright Paul Skilleter)

SWK 581H One of the first V12 FHC racers which was driven by Peter Taylor who was a development engineer for Jaguar. An article on the car after it had won the 1974 Production Sports Championship appeared in *Autocar* magazine on 5 April 1975. To avoid confusion, it is worth noting that the early V12 experimental cars carried very similar registration numbers. EX 102, the six-cylinder S3, ended up with registration SWK 583H. EX 104 had registration SWK 584H.

SWN 518G Series 2 2+2 track day car.

TES 1 Early FHC which specialised in sprints and hill climbs, driven by Tom Sleigh.

TEU 82C See 2 HAO.

TRX 47D White S1 FHC rally car.

TR XX 46 H LHD, FHC rally car. Maroon with white stripes.

TSY 774 Low drag replica 3.8 racer.

TUF 3 FHC Lightweight.

TUF 4 Replica Low Drag Coupe driven by Jon and Jason Minshaw. Silver coachwork.

TUF 4 at the Cholmondeley Hill Climb in 2009. (Copyright Ian Hunt)

TUF 6 Lightweight replica.

TUJ 1 A 1966 FHC ex-Jim Thompson of Guyson Sandblasting, one time record holder of Marque Sportscars at Harewood. Ran with a big valve wide angle head with fuel injection. The car was rebuilt to standard road specification by Glenn Watson.

TWL 66K 'Challenger' Cunningham Lightweight replica.

TWL 66K, whilst not actually an E-Type, gives a very good impression of one as it is a 'Challenger' replica, seen here at Donington on 9 June 1991. (Copyright Peter Griffiths)

TYJ 682 Phil Stott Lightweight replica/E-Type experience.

TYJ 682, a car used in the E-Type experience under Phil Stott Racing. (Copyright Peter Griffiths)

UPM 400 Early DHC ZP car. See EE 400.

USL 828 Chassis number 860182 was the early FHC modsports racer of Nick Crocker and Robin Cardwell. This was later turned into a Low Drag Coupe replica for the new owner, Laurie Abbott.

E-Type USL 828, Low Drag Coupe replica. (Copyright Laurie Abbott)

E-Type USL 828 engine detail. (Copyright Laurie Abbott)

UUT 945H Series 2 FHC racer.

UUT 945H driven by Don Lord at Mallory Park on 3 May 1992. (Copyright Peter Griffiths)

UVG 444 Series 1 FHC, trials and autocross car.

UVG 444 at Croft in 1968.
(Copyright Ted Walker Ferret Fotographics)

UWD 645G See 1 FUE, the Penny Woodley FHC.

UYP 022 Pale blue FHC land speed record/race car of Allen Shephard, Australia.

E-Type of Allen Shephard: the land speed record holder for its class.
(Copyright Les Hughes)

VHT 195H See 2 HAO.

VKV 752 Number issued in 1958 originally on E1A then later on E2A.

E2A at Goodwood during a test day in 2010.
(Copyright Tony Bailey)

VKV 752 (E2A) at Goodwood in 2008.
(Copyright Ian Hunt)

VKV 752 (E2A) seen at the Goodwood revival in 2012. (Copyright Ian Hunt)

VPL 9 4.5-litre Lightweight replica.

VS 70 LHD S2 FHC rally car in red. Russo Baltic Racing Team, historic Monte Carlo rally entrants from Latvia and Russia.

VS 71 LHD S2 FHC rally car in red ... as above.

VS 1968 LHD S2 FHC rally car in red ... as above.

WAG 939 FHC hill climb car driven by Martyn Griffiths.

WAK 1 Later number for 8448 TJ, the John Cuff car when owned by John Walker.

WAP 66 Chassis number 850301 also registered PNW 127C was extensively raced in the 1960s by Mick Jones and later by Fred Cliffe. The car was damaged at Croft in 1970 and was rebuilt by Phil Bennett who raced it in the early 1970s until it was again damaged. It has subsequently been rebuilt as a Lightweight replica.

WAP 66. A 1962 Lightweight replica. (Copyright Rex Gray)

WFY 22 Standard FHC racer driven by Bruce Goddard.

WGG 708 Blue S1 FHC track day car. Featured in *Practical Performance Car* magazine September 2009.

WLK 345G Bryan Wingfield Lightweight replica.

WOO 11 Along with 310 WK run by Warren Pearce, WOO 11, owned and driven by John Quick was equally one of the most successful racing E-Types of the 1960s. *Jaguar Quarterly* magazine in summer 1991 and autumn 1991 ran comprehensive articles on 'A QUICK E.' The car also appeared in *Hot Car* magazine in June 1971.

WOO 11 was an extremely successful racing E-Type because of the team effort of John Quick, Stuart Davey and Eddy Jukes. The sheer number of races entered and results obtained, bears witness not only to the skill of the driver, but the reliability of the car created and maintained by Stuart and Eddy.

The articles in *Jaguar Quarterly* magazine were written by Mike Cotton; who was John Quick's co-driver in the early competition life of WOO 11. Initially, John and Mike drove in international rallies: first, the 1965 Tulip rally, where they finished second in class, and later the Alpine rally, where they recorded only a DNF. John continued his racing career with sprints and hill climbs before progressing to full circuit racing, where he was in his element. The dark metallic green E-Type (some publications have misquoted this as BRG, or even blue) was even mentioned in *The Guinness Book of Records* when it notched up 26 wins during the 1969 season.

WOO 11, a 1962 FHC, chassis number 860675, was a prolific racer from 1964 until the early '70s and competed in around 100 events during that period. (I have included a photograph of race results.) The car was a regular competitor at Jaguar events, and although initially driven to the circuits, was later taken by a trailer pulled by John's S-Type Jaguar, or his company van showing his sponsorship logo 'Electrowares.'

Although John entered the car in prodsports races, it could easily be argued that the car was pushing into the grey area of modsports. It is not disputed that the 'standard' E-Type is no race car, and from as early as 1961 drivers had been modifying their cars. John was no exception. Prodsports allowed certain modifications of course, but where did prodsports end and modsports start?

Mechanical mod aside, WOO 11 had an aluminium bonnet that was later changed to fibreglass. This was not only to save weight, but also to save costs in the event of a prang. Fibreglass doors and rear hatch soon followed. The rear wings (also fibreglass) were slightly wider than standard and had rear brake ducts incorporated to aid the inboard cooling. The standard of the modifications was first class and therefore the fibreglass WOO 11 didn't look like a typical modsports car.

Mechanical modifications included: 3.8 XKE engine with +30 pistons, skimmed block and Westlake head, Iskerderian camshafts, lightened flywheel, and a specially tuned D-Type style exhaust.

Carburettors were Weber 45DCOE3s (not the later 9s everyone uses today) mounted on a D-Type manifold obtained from Peter Sargent.

The diaphragm clutch was from a 4.2, and the rear axle ratio changed to 3.77:1.

The battery (standard heavy type in those days) was moved to the centre of the car for better weight distribution.

John also told me that the engine was tilted on its mounts by 5 degrees in order to straighten the Webers. I have never been sure if this helped performance, or was a 'Quick' quirk for aesthetic perfection.

The car ran with stiffer Koni shock absorbers, and the rear radius arm circular bushes were turned through 90 degrees to stiffen up the rear end.

Standard Metalastik bushes were replaced by phosphor bronze alternatives, and rose joints incorporated wherever possible.

WOO 11 ran with distinctive Brabham alloy wheels, 9x15 on the front and 10x15 on the rear. These 10in rears looked 'normal' under the extended rear wheel arches, but it could be argued we are almost into modsports territory here.

With the longer races, oil was a crucial factor. Besides the necessary oil temperature gauge was an electric oil pump switch that allowed oil to be pumped into the sump from the Duckhams oil can mounted under the bonnet ... a two-way catch tank!

Stuart Davey, John Quick's long-term friend and mechanic, kindly sent me the following words for inclusion in the book:

"Dog owners profess there is only one best dog in their lives, those involved with all things motoring might infer the same sentiment when it comes to cars. WOO 11 is such a car, and the relationship between John Quick, Eddy Jukes and myself survives to this day.

"Those of us involved with motorsport, in particular circuit racing and production cars with a sporting heritage, face a dilemma of problems in achieving a competitive edge when compared to a pure bred race car. The production Jaguar E-Type, even in its much vaunted 'Lightweight' form, could rarely achieve parity with in period pure racing machinery, without some serious modification.

"The production E would not go where it was pointed, would not stop, and ended up facing the opposite direction to the intended, very quickly, even in capable hands, if a sporting mode of driving was employed.

"The two E-Types that took part in

and were accepted as entrants in international competition were those of John Quick and Warren Pearce. I believe the last full international circuit event that the cars were accepted for was the British Grand Prix sports car race in 1967. These two cars that were accepted were modified, and bore little resemblance to the standard production car, and I do not include the later modsports cars in this personal point of view, a sentiment that appears to be lost on those responsible for setting out the regulations for today's events held for the E-Type.

"The success that John and I achieved with WOO11 over my time with the car was a 'team effort,' and in no small way due to Eddy Jukes who for nothing else but for the hell of it put in many hours both in the small workshop we operated from and the circuits, sometimes two meetings in a single weekend. Equipment by today's standards was basic, even the welding equipment came through a hole knocked through the adjoining wall with Tizer, the soft drink manufacturer's vehicle workshop. Happy days."

This race history listing was supplied by Marc Devis, current owner of WOO 11.

	John Quick				
21/04/64:	Tulip Rally, Holland	-	J.Quick	-	4th in class
25/07/64:	Valence School, Sevenoaks MC, Hillclimb	-	J.Quick	-	1st in class
08/64:	Alpine Rally, Coupe des Alpes	-	J.Quick	-	-
25/10/64:	Brands Hatch, MG Car Club, Sprint	-	J.Quick	-	1st in class
29/11/64:	Brands Hatch, East Surrey MC, Sprint	-	J.Quick	-	1st in class
11/64:	RAC Rally of Great Britain	-	J.Quick	-	-
14/03/65:	Blackbushe Aerodrome, Sprint	-	J.Quick	-	1st in class
20/04/65:	Tulip Rally, Holland	-	J.Quick	-	2nd in class
25/04/65:	Brands Hatch, Sprint	#6	J.Quick	-	1st in class
16/05/65:	Lyden Hill, Sprint	-	J.Quick	-	1st in class
22/05/65:	Goodwood, BARC, GT Race	-	J.Quick	2nd	-
29/05/65:	Goodwood, Sprint	-	J.Quick	-	1st in class
08/65:	Alpine Rally, Coupe des Alpes	-	J.Quick	-	-
12/09/65:	Brands Hatch, BARC, GT Race	#76	J.Quick	2nd	-
12/09/65:	Brands Hatch, BARC, Handicap Race	#76	J.Quick	?	started
02/10/65:	Silverstone, Newton Oil Trophy	#244	J.Quick	20th	-
09/10/65:	Silverstone, BARC, Handicap Race	#112	J.Quick	1st	-
10/10/65:	Eelmore Plain, Sprint	-	J.Quick	1st	1st in class
14/11/65:	Brands Hatch, BARC Circle CC, Sprint	-	J.Quick	1st	1st in class
11/65:	RAC Rally of Great Britain	-	J.Quick	-	-
03/04/66:	Brands Hatch, Sprint	#227	J.Quick	1st	1st in class
11/04/66:	Castle Combe, BARC, GT Race	-	J.Quick	1st	1st in class
17/04/66:	Brands Hatch, 750MC, GT Race	#55	J.Quick	2nd	-
24/04/66:	Brands Hatch, BARC, Marque Race	#120	J.Quick	1st	1st in class
24/04/66:	Brands Hatch, BARC, Handicap Race	#120	J.Quick	-	started
07/05/66:	Oulton Park, BARC, GT Race	-	J.Quick	2nd	1st in class
12/06/66:	Croft, BARC Yorkshire, GT Race	-	J.Quick	2nd	-
12/06/66:	Croft, BARC Yorkshire, Handicap	-	J.Quick	Rtd	broken crank
19/06/66:	Silverstone, GT Race	-	J.Quick	4th	-
02/07/66:	Crystal Palace, BARC, GT Race	#74	J.Quick	6th	-
23/07/66:	Valence School, Sevenoaks MC, Hillclimb	-	J.Quick	-	1st in class
29/07/66:	Castle Combe, GT Race	-	J.Quick	Rtd	spun
05/11/66:	Brands Hatch, East Surrey MC, Sprint	-	J.Quick	1st	1st in class
	Warren Pearce Motors Ltd				
19/03/67:	Brands Hatch, Surrey Sporting MC, GT Race	#14	J.Quick	1st	1st in class
01/04/67:	Brands Hatch, MC Car Club, GT Race	-	J.Quick	3rd	-
15/04/67:	Silverstone, BARC, GT Race	#114	J.Quick	1st	1st in class
14/05/67:	Mallory Park, BARC, GT Race	-	J.Quick	1st	1st in class
29/05/67:	Crystal Palace, BRSCC, Anerley Trophy	#75	J.Quick	-	2nd in class
11/06/67:	Blackbushe, Fairthorpe SCC, Slalom Sprint	-	J.Quick	1st	1st in class
02/07/67:	Brands Hatch, BARC, GT Race	-	J.Quick	3rd	-
02/07/67:	Brands Hatch, AMASCO, Sports & GT Race	-	J.Quick	2nd	-
15/07/67:	Silverstone (British GP), Sports & GT Race	#39	J.Quick	9th	-
15/07/67:	Silverstone (British GP), RAC Wills Trophy	#39	J.Quick	14th	-
30/07/67:	Silverstone, BARC, GT Race	#114	J.Quick	1st	1st in class
05/08/67:	Crystal Palace, BARC, Marque Race	#166	J.Quick	?	started
08/08/67:	Crystal Palace, BARC, GT Race	-	J.Quick	2nd	-
13/08/67:	Brands Hatch, Prodsports & GT Race	-	J.Quick	1st	1st in class
20/08/67:	Brands Hatch, BARC, GT Race	-	J.Quick	1st	1st in class
15/10/67:	Brands Hatch, Jaguar DC, GT Race	-	J.Quick	3rd	-

	Warren Pearce Motors Ltd				
17/04/68:	Brands Hatch, Race	-	J.Quick	3rd	-
19/05/68:	Brands Hatch, Sports over 2000cc	-	J.Quick	?	started
26/05/68:	Brands Hatch, BARC, Sports over 2000cc	-	J.Quick	2nd	-
02/06/68:	Brands Hatch, BRSCC, Sports over 2000cc	-	J.Quick	1st	1st in class
03/06/68:	Thruxton, Race	-	J.Quick	1st	1st in class
09/06/68:	Brands Hatch, BARC, Race	-	J.Quick	1st	1st in class
16/06/68:	Snetterton, BARC, Race	-	J.Quick	2nd	-
23/06/68:	Brands Hatch, London MC, Race	-	J.Quick	3rd	-
07/07/68:	Brands Hatch, BRSCC, Race	-	J.Quick	2nd	-
13/07/68:	Castle Combe, BARC, GT Race	#1	J.Quick	1st	1st in class
04/08/68:	Thruxton, BARC, Race	-	J.Quick	Rtd	broken crank
18/08/68:	Brands Hatch, Race	-	J.Quick	1st	1st in class
25/08/68:	Silverstone, Race	-	J.Quick	1st	1st in class
31/08/68:	Silverstone, Albert Powell Trophy	-	J.Quick	Rtd	thrown rod
09/03/69:	Brands Hatch, BRSCC, Race	#102	J.Quick	1st	1st in class
15/03/69:	Oulton Park, Race	-	J.Quick	1st	class lap record
16/03/69:	Thruxton, Race	-	J.Quick	1st	class lap record
22/03/69:	Snetterton, Race	-	J.Quick	1st	class lap record
23/03/69:	Brands Hatch, Race	-	J.Quick	1st	class lap record
07/04/69:	Brands Hatch, BRSCC National Open	-	J.Quick	1st	class lap record
13/04/69:	Silverstone, GT Race	#68	J.Quick	1st	class lap record
27/04/69:	Brands Hatch, Race	-	J.Quick	1st	1st in class
10/05/69:	Castle Combe, Race	-	J.Quick	1st	class lap record
11/05/69:	Brands Hatch, Maidstone & Mid-Kent CC	-	J.Quick	1st	1st in class
18/05/69:	Brands Hatch, Race	-	J.Quick	1st	1st in class
25/05/69:	Brands Hatch Stadium, Mini-Seven Club	-	J.Quick	1st	1st in class
26/05/69:	Thruxton, Race	-	J.Quick	1st	class lap record
15/06/69:	Brands Hatch, Race	-	J.Quick	2nd	-
02/08/69:	Crystal Palace, Race	-	J.Quick	1st	class lap record
17/08/69:	Brands Hatch, Race	-	J.Quick	1st	1st in class
31/08/69:	Thruxton, Race	-	J.Quick	1st	1st in class
01/09/69:	Castle Combe, Race	-	J.Quick	1st	1st in class
13/09/69:	Crystal Palace, MG CC, Group 4/5 Race	#10	J.Quick	10th	-
14/09/69:	Brands Hatch, Maidstone & Mid-Kent CC, Race	-	J.Quick	2nd	-
21/09/69:	Thruxton, BARC, Race	-	J.Quick	2nd	-
12/10/69:	Thruxton, BARC, Race	-	J.Quick	1st	1st in class
09/11/69:	Brands Hatch, Race	-	J.Quick	2nd	-
22/11/69:	Brands Hatch, Race	-	J.Quick	1st	1st in class
02/05/70:	Greenham Common, RAC Sprint	-	J.Quick	3rd	-
03/05/70:	Thruxton, BARC, Race	-	J.Quick	1st	1st in class
25/07/70:	Silverstone, Jaguar DC, Race	#89	J.Quick	?	-

The race history of John Quick's WOO 11. (Copyright Marc Devis)

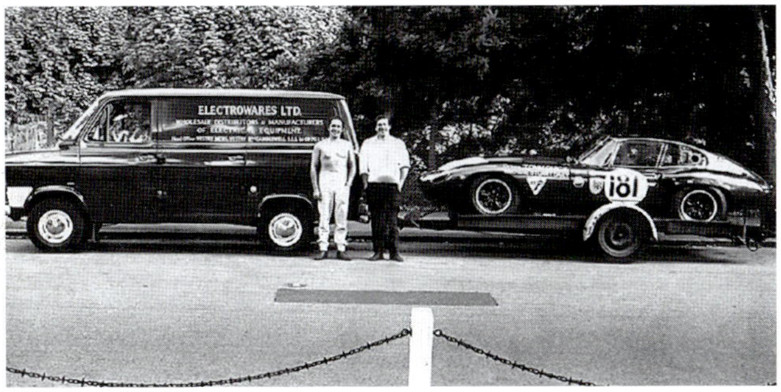

John Quick and mechanic Stuart Davey with their racing setup WOO 11 being pulled by John's company van, Electrowares Ltd. (Copyright Stuart Davey)

John Quick with his winner's trophy at Silverstone in 1969. (Copyright Stuart Davey)

John Quick in WOO 11 at the JDC Silverstone meeting July 25 1970, where he finished first in the modified sports car race. (Copyright Paul Skilleter)

WPN 159 Early Series 1 FHC racer, chassis number 860357. On front cover of *Jaguar Driver* magazine October 1962.

WPV 818A Lightweight replica.

WPV 952A Red roadster with white nose band. An S1 Lightweight replica/tour auto rally car. A full account of this car appeared in *Jaguar World Monthly* in July 2007. The article was entitled 'Birth of an FIA E-Type,' and over three pages featured some stunning photographs.

WSU 723 Lightweight replica, gunmetal grey rally car: the same number later seen on a dark blue racer.

WSU 723 driven by Guy Broad at Donington on 25 May 1992. (Copyright Peter Griffiths)

E-Type WSU 723. (Copyright Laurie Abbott)

WUO 3K Rarely seen sporting its number plate, this is the V12 modsports FHC of Guy Beddington. This famous and highly successful car was fitted with a 6-litre dry-sump engine, with six Weber carburettors. Later owners included Steve O'Rourke, Roy Standley and Dick Soans. The car continued to be modified, and an article entitled 'Monster E-Type' appeared in *Jaguar*

World in October 2008. Eventually, the car went to Australia and is now owned by John Rundell (incidentally, Guy Beddington now lives in Australia).

The ex-Guy Beddington V12 FHC, now in its current home in Australia. (Copyright Les Hughes)

Guy Beddington's V12 E-Type in the Silverstone pit lane awaiting his turn in the 6-hour relay race as part of the JDC team. (Copyright Peter Griffiths)

The ex-Guy Beddington V12 E-Type in its later stage of development, seen here at Donington in June 1991 as part of the E-Type birthday celebrations. (Copyright Peter Griffiths)

A nice engine bay shot of Guy Beddington's V12 FHC, showing the detail of his fuel injection system. (Copyright Peter Griffiths)

WVS 426 Lightweight replica in silver.

XAJ 1 Original Semi-Lightweight, also registered CJX 672C, 166 YHN, BXG 326B, and 1 WW. Chassis number S850817. In the *Jaguar Enthusiast* magazine in July 2009, registration plate XAJ 1 was photographed on a V12 E-Type roadster, which was for sale in North Yorkshire.

XAJ 1, one of the original Semi-Lightweight Factory cars seen here at the JDC Silverstone meeting in 1972. (Copyright Ted Walker Ferret Fotographics)

XAN 555 Lightweight replica in green raced by Chris Scragg.

XAN 555 Lightweight replica photographed at the E-Type Challenge at Silverstone in July 2011. (Copyright Peter Griffiths)

XAS 885 Lightweight replica with blue coachwork driven by Stephen Radcliffe, Diane Osbourne and Desire Wilson.

XVE 1 See 1 VHP.

XYJ 228A Blue 3.8 FHC racer RHD. Distinctive rear Perspex window with air vents, nice tidy looking car. 2014 build, FIA papers.

YLU 470H A beautiful pale blue 1970 Series 2 FHC, which, although appearing fairly standard, does in fact have many racing upgrades. It was a regular competitor from 1988 until 2004, achieving numerous class wins and a 1st overall in the E-Type Challenge series in 1992. Driven with great style by Roger Seymour.

XTV 470J 1971 V12 Race and sprint car.

YOR 20 Dark blue FHC, modified, Minilites, used by the Jaguar E-Type Driving Experience.

YRP 999 Chassis no 850020, early racer, modsports then Lightweight replica. Another car that went through the usual modsports stage in the late 1960s, ending up with full Lightweight spec in the late 1980s. Now a regular competitor at Goodwood.

YRP 999 photographed at the E-Type Challenge at Silverstone in July 2011. (Copyright Peter Griffiths)

YVH 210 Original Lightweight E-Type driven by Peter Sutcliffe. Later registered SVM 740. Chassis number S850666. Also registered RV 7 and BTB 640A.

Lightweight E-Type YVH 210 at Silverstone 2011. (Copyright Peter Griffiths)

Non-registration list – see separate appendix

Naturally any list such as this cannot be exhaustive, but is produced from my records built up over the last 40 years or so. I apologise for any omissions, and of course would welcome information on any racing E-Type. My image usage is limited because, whilst I have a photograph of most of the race E-Types listed here, I do not always own the copyright to the image. This book, therefore, is a collection of not only my own photographs, but also those of Ted Walker (Ferret Fotographics), Paul Skilleter, Tony Bailey, and other enthusiasts who have allowed me to use their resources, and to whom I am extremely grateful.

The list is also predominately UK-registered cars, although certain foreign race cars have been included where they are known to me, perhaps from being registered in the UK before moving abroad, raced in the UK, or simply being well-known outside their country of use.

Appendix B

Cars with no known registration number

Unfortunately, not all race E-Types carry number plates, which often makes for difficult identification. When the cars change hands, new owners sometimes wish to put their own mark on their car, maybe a repaint and possibly body modifications, making it unrecognisable from last season's model.

Most modsports cars began as road cars, which were continually developed, but some were created from parts and never were complete cars. It seemed pointless to pay for heavy metal parts (bonnet and doors), which would be replaced, let alone interiors, glass and a host of mechanical parts that would all be discarded or replaced with more suitable race versions. Items such as the radio, window mechanisms, heaters, etc would all be discarded, and items such as wheels, tyres, brakes, suspension, etc would all be replaced. To go racing, why 'ruin' a perfectly good road car when a damaged, rusty example would probably be a better starting point?

I have listed here some of the more 'famous' cars, with the particular drivers who were arguably the most successful with them as the means of identification. (I have been unable to assign a particular registration to these cars, but it doesn't follow that they never had one.)

John Burbidge

John and his early 3.8 FHC modsports car (chassis 860081) stormed onto the modsports scene in the late 1960s with fellow modsports driver Tony Shaw, when they would often be seen racing together under the sponsorship banner of

John Burbidge in his FHC at Castle Combe in October 1971. (Copyright Ted Walker Ferret Fotographics)

John Burbidge at the 1974 JDC meeting at Silverstone. (Copyright Ted Walker Ferret Fotographics)

Comet-DellTune. John was a regular competitor at JDC events and just about any other modsports races he could find, particularly at Thruxton, his local circuit (Thruxton Racing Services even sponsored his car for a while). The car has been subsequently owned by Bob Kerr, Tom McCallum and Bernie Breeze. Now painted bright yellow, it was reportedly for sale in France in 2016.

Robin Cardwell and Nick Crocker

This 1963 FHC modsports car was originally raced by Robin Cardwell, and later by Nick Crocker. This early car was continually developed with a 4.5-litre engine and was a regular competitor at JDC events in the '70s and '80s. The car was part of the JDC team in the 1976 Intermarque six-hour relay when managed by John Quick. Halfway through its restoration by Fred Cliffe in the '90s, it was purchased by Laurie Abbott and converted into an aluminium Low Drag Coupe replica.

Modsports FHC at the paddock at Silverstone, and raced by Robin Cardwell and Nick Crocker. (Copyright Peter Griffiths)

This is the original modsports car driven by Robin Cardwell and then Nick Crocker seen at Silverstone. It was later converted to a Low Drag Coupe Lightweight replica. (Copyright Peter Griffiths)

Another shot of the Cardwell/Crocker modsports car seen at Silverstone. (Copyright Peter Griffiths)

The Cardwell/Crocker E-Type at Silverstone. (Copyright Laurie Abbott)

Alistair Cowin

Modsports FHC was very successful in the mid 1960s. When the car was put up for sale in June 1968, it boasted successes for the current season of 8x1st, 4x2nd, 2x3rd and 2x4th.

Malcolm Hamilton six-cylinder

Before coming to even greater prominence with his V12 racer (The World's Fastest E-Type), Malcolm successfully raced this six-cylinder FHC Modsports racer which was sponsored by Kearns-Richards Service (KRS) where Malcolm was in charge of restoration and servicing and Rob Beere in charge of engines. Malcolm was part of the successful JDC team with this car which won the Intermarque championship in 1986.

Bernie Breeze next to the ex-Hamilton six-cylinder FHC modsports car seen here pre accident at Brands Hatch in 1990. (Copyright Peter Griffiths)

Bernie Breeze's ex-Hamilton six-cylinder FHC modsports car seen here post accident at Brands Hatch in 1990. (Copyright Peter Griffiths)

The car has been regularly photographed in the *Jaguar Driver* magazine and appeared on the front cover of the *Jaguar Enthusiast* magazine in August 1991. The car had held lap records at the following circuits; Silverstone, Mallory Park, Donington Park, Brands Hatch and Oulton Park. Malcolm put this car up for sale in 1988 (the year he purchased the V12). The car was purchased by Bernie Breeze who raced it in the early 1990s.

Bernie Breeze's ex-Hamilton six-cylinder FHC modsports car seen here post accident at Brands Hatch in 1990 ready for the return journey. (Copyright Peter Griffiths)

Malcolm Hamilton V12

Referred to as 'The Beast,' and the pinnacle of E-Type development. The V12 E-Type earned the title 'The World's Fastest E-Type' in 1997 when it repeatedly attained outright winner status in the highly modified class of the Intermarque Challenge Championship. It was further endorsed in 2001 at the Woodbridge Speed Trial, when it achieved a record at 184mph.

The car has been extensively covered in books and magazine articles since 1988.

See article reprinted in Appendix E.

The World's Fastest E-Type driven by Malcolm Hamilton at Donington Park in 2001. (Copyright Ted Walker Ferret Fotographics)

Les Hughes

This book would not be complete without mentioning Les Hughes, Jaguar stalwart in Australia, editor of *Jaguar Magazine* and E-Type race enthusiast, who has been very helpful in supplying additional photographs. Les still finds time to compete, and a couple of shots of his car are reproduced here.

The series 1 FHC of Les Hughes in Australia. (Copyright Les Hughes)

throughout the world.
The XK 120 sports car was launched in 1948 and presented to the new American market in early 1949. It was a tremendous success. That year Sutton and Lee

PACE

'Lofty' England made the Jaguar cat almost as famous as the British lion.

Les Hughes' FHC makes the Australian press. (Copyright Les Hughes)

James Mehew FHC

James Mehew was a regular competitor during the early 1970s with his modsports FHC. A photograph and race report appears in *Autosport* magazine, 12 August 1971.

James Mehew at Cadwell Park in July 1971. (Copyright Ted Walker Ferret Fotographics)

Minters FHC

The 4.2, S1 FHC highly modified modsports E-Type of Ian Watson and Martin Wheatley was a regular competitor in the early 1980s. In 1985, the car was sponsored by Minters, and became instantly recognisable being painted bright yellow with 'MINTERS' emblazoned on the bonnet and sides. The car later passed to Chris Drake and eventually to Straight Six in the late 1980s, which painted it in American racing colours of white with blue stripes, ready for the Intermarque series. The car appeared on the front cover of *Jaguar Driver* magazine in May 1985.

The modsports FHC of Martin Wheatley and Ian Watson. (Copyright Peter Griffiths)

The Minters FHC modsports car in the good old days, photographed at Silverstone at an early JDC race meeting when it was green with wide steel wheels, before it changed to its yellow coachwork. (Copyright Peter Griffiths)

Moore/Gamble/Lea DHC

This roadster started life as one of Fred Cliffe's modsports creations, and continued to have a long and successful career in the hands of drivers Phil Scragg, Richard Gamble, David Moore, and Ron Lea. The car was not modified too greatly during its career, which made it easier to follow its progress. It maintained its red coachwork throughout, as well as its unique bonnet louvres. The car was written off after an accident at Croft whilst being driven by Ron Lea.

Modsports E-Type raced by Dave Moore seen here in the Silverstone paddock. (Copyright Peter Griffiths)

Brian Murphy FHC

This modsports FHC has had a long and successful racing career in the hands of several drivers, and has changed its appearance and colour scheme at every opportunity, which makes tracking its history more difficult. The car was initially driven by Brian Murphy from 1970 to 1973. During 1974 and 1975 it was raced by Brian Litherland, and in 1976 by Richard Scantlebury, when it became known as the Ziebart car, being repainted white with 'Ziebart' emblazoned across the bonnet. During the early 1990s the car was restored by Fred Cliffe and put up for sale, it was purchased by Tony Kember. Note: not to be confused with the other famous Brian Murphy car, the DHC 310 WK.

The 'Ziebart car,' seen here at Brands Hatch in July 1976 driven by Richard Scantlebury, started life as Brian Murphy's original FHC modsports car. (Copyright Ted Walker Ferret Fotographics)

Richard Scantlebury in the 'Ziebart car' at Mallory Park in March 1976. (Copyright Ted Walker Ferret Fotographics)

Seen here at the Donington anniversary meeting in June 1991, this is the ex-Murphy/Ziebart car, then owned by Tony Kember. (Copyright Peter Griffiths)

John Oxborough

A regular modsports driver in the '70s and '80s, along with his father, Don, which sometimes led to confusion as to whether it was John or Don racing. Their number plate, DJ 44E, was simply used to denote 'Don, John 4.4-litre E-Type.' John had some extremely quick and – perhaps quite wildly – modified cars, all of which he prepared himself. An extremely competent mechanic, he helped in the rebuild of the author's three modsports cars, including the Simon Watney FHC, the Fred Cliffe DHC (one of many Fred cars), and the V12 Hamilton roadster, the World's Fastest E-Type.

John Oxborough in his highly modified modsports car at Mallory Park in March 1976. (Copyright Ted Walker Ferret Fotographics)

Harry Phillips FHC

FHC modsports E-Type raced by Harry Philips in the early 1970s, later driven by Dave Moore and Mike Hill.

Harry Phillips at the 1972 JDC meeting at Silverstone. (Copyright Ted Walker Ferret Fotographics)

Engine bay shot of the modsports FHC raced by Harry Phillips. (Copyright Peter Griffiths)

The modsports FHC of Harry Phillips seen here in the paddock at Silverstone. (Copyright Peter Griffiths)

Saunders/Smith

This very highly modified FHC has had several owners during its life, including Charlie Saunders, John Smith, Fred Cliffe, Will Pringle, Colin Shute, Ian Gorrie and John Green. The car has raced at Silverstone, Oulton Park and Croft, but has mainly been used as a sprint and hill climb car. I first came across the car at Brands Hatch (see photo). It was continually improved, and later changed from its familiar red coachwork to white.

Probably unrecognisable to most, but this is the original form of the Saunders/Smith modsports car first spotted by the author at Brands Hatch. In the true spirit of modsports you can just make out the rear air intakes, which are none other than a 90 degree drainpipe bend. (Copyright Peter Griffiths)

Mike Smith/Brian Mills/Brian Russel FHC

Brian Mills was very successful in the early 1970s in his highly modified modsports E-Type. An article in *Autosport* on 12 April 1973 reports him winning the Blue Circle modified sports car championship round at Oulton Park ahead of Brian Murphy, who came in 3rd. I have reason to believe that the car could have previously belonged to Mike Smith – it looks very similar, having identical bonnet scoops/vents and rear door detailing. Also, in *Autosport* July 4th 1969 there was an advert "Racing E-Type wanted, contact Mills." In *Autosport* July 30th 1970 Mike Smith's modified E-Type was up for sale, the advert read "Modified 3.8 E-Type, big brakes, 4.2 box, triple Webers, racing seat, off-set wheels with new racing tyres. £850 – ring Mike Smith." The car was later owned and raced by Brian Russel. It came up for sale in early 1981, boasting a complete rebuild with a new 330bhp engine ready for next season's racing, with a price tag of £12,000.

The pale yellow FHC of Mike Smith and Brian Russel at Silverstone. (Copyright Peter Griffiths)

Mike Smith's modsports FHC photographed in the paddock at Silverstone. (Copyright Peter Griffiths)

Brian Spicer DHC

Brian Spicer's modsports 3.8 E-Type was a regular competitor during the '60s and early '70s. The first car, a modsports DHC, was later recognisable by its three 'U' shaped cut-outs on the bonnet nose, similar to the Ferrari GTO's. Brian was also the driver of E141. Photographs of Brian's E-Type appeared in *Autosport* magazine 30 September 1966 and 11 June 1970.

Brian Spicer at Snetterton in September 1967. (Copyright Ferret Fotographics)

Simon Watney FHC

Simon bought this very early 3.8 FHC in 1973 from Fred Cliffe who had been using it for hill climbs. It was a typical modsports car with fibreglass bonnet and rear door with all the upholstery, heater and other unnecessary equipment removed. Initially, the engine was fairly standard but had Weber carburettors, D-Type exhaust and a shaved head ... it ran on 10in front wheels and 12in rears, wheels were Minilites to take the slicks and J A Pearce to take the wets. Simon continued to develop and race the car in its dark blue livery with a yellow nose until eventually selling it to Paul Webb in the late 1970s. Paul further developed and raced the car, changed its livery to bright red, and ran with the registration numbers PW1, PWM 1 and 6900WK.

In the late 1980s, the car was sold to Paul Palmer. It then lay dormant for a few years until I bought it in the early 1990s, when I had the bodywork restored to its modsports form. It was then sold again to Paul Webb, who rebuilt the car to FIA/HTP specification.

The ex-Simon Watney FHC modsports car now painted red and driven by Paul Webb, seen here at Mallory Park. (Copyright Peter Griffiths)

The ex-Simon Watney FHC modsports car photographed at the JDC Silverstone meet, the original colour being dark blue. (Copyright Peter Griffiths)

Eike Welhausen

From Germany, but living in Chesterfield, Eike was a prolific modsports racer in the 1970s, before he went on to racing Listers. His cars always seemed to be extensively modified – indeed, one could describe them as 'wacky.' That said, Eike, a brilliant carburettor specialist, always seemed to make his cars go quicker than the opposition. The cars often sported F1 wheels and tyres on the rear!

Because he was an expert with carburettor setup, Eike was regularly called upon by fellow racers to tune the triple Weber or Dellorto carburettors that were often the chosen replacements for the standard triple SUs.

Dick Whittington

This early FHC of Fred Cliffe was transformed into the highly modified two-tone brown monster of Dick Whittington. It sported a rear wing, wide wheels, side skirts and front spoiler. A regular competitor at Brands Hatch (my local circuit at the time) I was often able to photograph the car. *The Jaguar Car Club Journal* described it as "fearsome looking." It was later raced by Martin Barrow, although with a more subtle body image!

The ex-Dick Whittington modsports FHC seen here at Donington on a rather wet race day. (Copyright Peter Griffiths)

The extreme FHC of Dick Whittington seen at Brands Hatch. (Copyright Peter Griffiths)

Land speed record cars

American

An interesting classified advert appeared in the December 1991 issue of *Jaguar Driver* magazine. There was a photo of a series 1 FHC on steel wheels (XJ6 or V12 E-Type) with the following caption: "Jaguar E-Type. 1961 flat floor FHC. Land speed record holder 1977-1988 at Bonneville USA. All complete, loads of history."

Australian

A book by Phil Shephard titled *The World's Fastest E-Type Jaguar – A Quest for the Record* (Motoring Past Vintage Publishing, 2016) tells the story of the attempt to set the land speed record for a production car in an FHC E-Type Jaguar on the Australian salt flats.

The E-Type of Allen Shephard on the Australian salt flats. (Copyright Les Hughes)

American E –Types

Like the Lightweights, the two V12 racers in America have been widely covered in books and magazine articles. In 1974 Bob Tullius entered the Group 44 car in race events on the East Coast, whilst Joe Huffaker had a similar idea on the West Coast. (Both cars had official backing from Jaguar for sales promotion.) The E-Types ended up looking fairly similar – both roadsters had no full windscreens, the Tullius car was white with a full safety roll cage, whilst the Huffaker car was silver with a driver-only roll bar. A good original article appeared in the October 1974 issue of *Jaguar Driver* magazine, entitled 'Jaguar V12 Victory in USA Race Debut.' Another good article (by Philip Porter) appeared in *Jaguar Driver* in February 1995, which also included other early E-Type racers.

The V12 Group 44 E-Type at the British Motor Museum in 2016. (Copyright Karen Roe)

The V12 Group 44 E-Type at Goodwood in 2014. (Copyright Brian Snelson)

Another shot of the V12 Group 44 E-Type at Goodwood in 2014. (Copyright Brian Snelson)

The Group 44 V12 roadster at the Goodwood Festival of Speed in 2011. (Copyright Ian Hunt)

Another American car, sometimes confused with the aforementioned V12s, is the six-cylinder 4.2 1970 roadster raced under the banner of Gran Turismo Jaguar by Fred Baker. Again, with no windscreen it looked similar to the V12s.

For those of you who trawl the internet for E-Type racers, you will have probably come across the beautifully prepared cars of Donovan Motorsports, which, with its silver and green striped roadsters, claims to be "one of the most successful vintage racing teams in the last decade."

Note: In America, where the DHC retains its windscreen and hard top, these are called 'roadsters with hard top.' Where the DHC runs with no windscreen these are known simply as roadsters.

Appendix C

Index of E-Type race drivers

To start with, I apologise for any misspelled names. Many names have been shown differently in various publications, and so I have chosen the more commonly used spellings. I also apologise for anyone I have missed. Each year sees a new batch of drivers, and I have included all those I know of or have read about at the time of going to press.

In several publications I have found that many drivers' names have been confused with others, which has sometimes made tracing the history of a car all the more difficult. For example:

Alistair Cowen raced in the same period as Alistair Crawford.

Jack Lambert raced in the same period as Jack Le Fort. Period race commentary often said just 'Jack.' Then there was Jack Hayden.

Roy Standley raced in the same period as Richard Scantlebury, Rob Schroeder, and don't forget Roy Salvadori and Robin Sturgess. RS 2 was the number carried on Richard's modsports car.

There were many modsports drivers of the '70s called Brian. Brian Murphy, Brian Litherland, Brian Mills, Brian Russel, Brian Spicer, Brian Waddilove, and Brian Redman. If they were in the same race, the reports often just referred to Brian?!

Those that were not Brian, were usually called Peter: Peter Sargent, Peter Lumsden, Peter Sutcliffe, Peter Lindner, Peter Nocker, Peter Archer, Peter Berry, Peter Harris, Peter Taylor, not forgetting Pierre Rohan and Pierre Bardinon.

Those who were not Peter were usually called John: John Wilson, John Cuff, John Lewis, John Burbidge, John Quick, John Filbee, John May, John Harper, John Oxborough, John Young ...

I hope you get the point now.

I have also seen the following error: the genuine Lightweight of Phil Scragg was PS 1175, but I have seen this attributed to Peter Sutcliffe, presumably because of the same initials. Although I've not yet seen it attributed to Peter Sargent!

The alphabetical list of drivers I have compiled here from extensive research is, therefore, accurate to the best of my ability, taking the above into account.

Where a driver is associated with a particular famous car or period, this is mentioned. Most names listed are from the UK, although the more famous and documented names from abroad have been included for completeness.

Richard Abels	
Mike Adams	ABD 799A and LWT replica 245 YUB
Neil Allen (Australia)	
Fred Allenby	Modsports
Anthony Archer	
Peter Archer	Early FHC racer 336 PAR
Gary Arnold	
John Arnold	
P Ashley	
Dave Astle	
Gregoire Audi	Masters
F Avy	
Adam Bagnall	
Sir Gawaine Baillie	Early racer GB 8488 one of the ZP cars
Trevor Baines	Modified FHC racer HOT 12
Fred Baker	4.2 roadster Gran Turismo Jaguar
Ken Baker	Original driver of 7 CXW
Anthony Bamford	
Tony Bancroft	ONE 858H S2 DHC
W Banks	
Marcus Barclay	
Pierre Bardinon	Factory Semi-Lightweight EYY 32B
Mike Barker	
K Barrow	
Martin Barrow	Ex-Dick Willington FHC modsports
Rob Beck	V8 Egal 590 DXR
Guy Beddington	V12 FHC modified racer WUO 3K
Bobby Bell	
Dave Bennet	
Philip Bennet	Early modsports PB 1 and Lightweight replica 95 PJ
P Bennison	
Peter Berry	3 BXV, 4 BXV
A Berstein	
M Billingham	
J Binns	
James Blackhall	129 KVA
Patrick Blakeney-Edwards	
J Bolwell	
Richard Bond	YVH 210 Lightweight/Red Rose Motors
Jamie Boot	E-Type Challenge, Masters
Graham Bovit-White	3.8 FHC Standard
Jack Brabham	
Bernie Breeze	Ex-Hamilton 6cyl PPB 155
Merle Brennan	
John Breslow	
Charles Bridges	4 WPD/Red Rose Motors
Guy Broad	
M Brook	
John Brown	
Rob Brown	
W G Brown	
Martin Brundle	PS 1175 Lightweight
Ollie Bryant	
Grahame Bull	E-Type Challenge 700 FVN
Alex Buncombe	E-Type Challenge
Glenn Bunch	
John Burbidge	Modsports FHC
Rodger Burnett	
Tim Burnett	
John Burton	AFD 250, 4 BXV
John Bussell	Masters
Dave Bye	129 KVA
J Campbell	
John Carden	Ex-Le Mans 49 FXN
Robin Cardwell	Modsports chassis 860182 4.5 FHC
M Carey	
Barry Carpenter	
Paul Castaldini	2164 WK, 924 FXC, 1302 WK
B Cave	
Maurice Charles	Le Mans 503 BBO
Gordon Chippindale	
Martin Chisholm	
Paul Chownes-Dove	
Laki Christoforou	Pre '66 GT FHC
John Churchill	Modsports
C Clark	
E Clark	
John Clark	E-Type Challenge, Masters, RAC
Sam Clarke	
John Cleland	E-Type Challenge

Fred Cliffe	898 BYR, 8448 TJ, WOO 11, 129 KVA, 310 WK, FNC 1, and FNC 2.
Mark Clubb	E-Type Challenge
Will Cole	V12 roadster JTJ 20K, mainly hill climbs
Charles Cook	
Roger Cook	Ex-Tony Shaw car
Harvey Cooke	
John Coombs	
V Cooper	
J Conway	
Roger Cope	E-Type Challenge
Nigel Corner	2 GXO Lightweight
T Costello	
Tony Cotterall	
James Cottingham	492 YUF
J Coundley	Le Mans 503 BBO
Alistair Cowin	Modsports
David Coyne	E-Type Challenge
S Cracknell	
Chris Craft	ELA 76C
V Crapnell	
Alistair Crawford	Modsports, 9 WKJ
Oscar Crespo	
Richard Creswell	
Nick Crocker	Modsports FHC chassis number 860182
Tony Crossingham	
A Crowther	
Henry Crowther	
Gordon Cruickshank	
John Cuff	8448 TJ
Briggs Cunningham	1337 VC (931 PUU), 5116 WK Le Mans
David Cunningham	CUT 7
Neil Cunningham	E-Type Challenge
Peter Curtis	
R Darlington	
A F Davenport	AFD 250
Norman Davidson-Kelly	
Jim Davies	
Mick Davies	
Martin Dawson	V12 prodsports
John Dean	995 FOO
Andrew Dee-Crowne	Lightweight replica 1480 WK, 5104 WK, Masters
M Delingpole	
Jaime I Del Valle	8448 TJ, ex-Cliffe Modsports
Earl Of Denbigh	SUE 196 early racer
Marc Devis	WOO 11
R Dewar	
Gary Dickens	
Anthony Ditheridge	Masters
Graeme Dodd	E-Type Challenge
P Dodd	
Jim Donnelly	
M Drain	
Chris Drake	
Paul Drayson	
E Duthoit	
Alistair Dyson	FHC modified
David Edge	
Debbie Edwards	Rally driver S2 FHC, 2 HAO
W Ellam	
Steven Elliot	DTO 87B
Les Ely	E-Type Challenge
M Faller	
Eric Falce	159 XKK
Robert Farrell	
Paul Farren	
Hon. John Fellowes	
Al Ferguson	
Alain Figaret	
John Filbee	Modsports 4778 LJ
A Firmin	
Mike Fisher	Lightweight
Gregor Fisken	
Justin Fleming	
Joaquin Folch-Rusinol	
Colin Folwell	
Rick Forbes	
Rod Forbes	
John Ford	
John Foster	Semi-Lightweight CJX 672C
Andrew Fordyce	130 HPO

Leslie Fowler	DPO 7
Mike Franey	Modsports ex-John Wilson
Douglas Fraser	
Robert Frouwein	E-Type Challenge
M Fruitnight	
F Gaddie	
Richard Gamble	Modsports ex-Cliffe, Scragg
David Gate	
Robert Gate	E-Type Challenge
Oliver Gavin	
Mark Gibbon	5497 WK
Alan Gibson	
R Gibson	
Ian Giles	Sprint
Roberto Giordanelli	Modsports, 828 WFM
R Gletton	
Bruce Goddard	WFY 22
Bill Goodall	
Read Gomm	E-Type Challenge, Masters
Robbie Gordon	
C Gorman	
W Grabham	
J Graham	
J Grandidier	
Derek Green	138 XKE
Willie Green	Lightweight
Nigel Greensall	
Robert Gregson	
Rod Gretton	V12
A Griffiths	
Martyn Griffiths	WAG 939
Peter Griffiths	PMW 336H, NXC 997D modsports, ex-Cliffe/Hamilton V12
Tony Griffiths	80 FOE
Peter Griggs	Early racer
Stephen Griswold	49 FXN
Trevor Groom	Early racer, E-Type Challenge
Grossmann	5115 WK Le Mans
Dan Gurney	4 WPD
Andrew Haddon	
R Haddon	
Bob Haddow	

Andrew Hall	
David Hall	5497 WK E-Type Challenge
Rob Hall	
Malcolm Hamilton	6-cyl modsports V12 World's Fastest E-Type
A Hammond	
Sam Hancock	
Walt Hansgen	5114 WK Le Mans
Des Harden	
John Harding	Hill climb car BMT 606H
Peter Hardman	
Paul Hargreaves	
Keith Harmer	
John Harper	7 CXW
Andrew Harris	
Chris Harris	
D R Harris	
Peter Harris	NRW 574F (Pow and Walker)
Tom Harris	E-Type Challenge
Tony Harrison	2 GXO Lightweight
Roddy Harvey-Bailey	2164 WK
Derek Hastings	OWT 477E
Roy Hatfield	Lightweight replica 3613 WK
V Hatton	
Jack Hayden	Original FHC racer 995 FOO
J Henley	
J Heppenstall	
Jeff Hickson	Modsports 4270 WK (ALJ 92A)
Joseph Hickson	Modsports 4270 WK (ALJ 92A)
Mike Hill	
Graham Hill	Original racer ECD 400, 4WPD
D Hobbs	
Steve Hodges	E-Type Challenge
Will Hodges	E-Type Challenge
Jools Holland	Lightweight replica
Keith Holland	Modsports, 9 WKJ
J Holt	
A Hopkins	The Scragg Lightweight
David Howard	
D Howe	
Sigi Huber	
Rob Huff	
D Hughes	

Jonathan Hughes	E-Type Challenge
Les Hughes (Australia)	*Jaguar Magazine* Editor
G Humble	858 MY
Bill Hunt	
Martin Hunt	
Anthony Hutton	7 CXW
S Jackson	
Robert (Bob) Jane (Australia)	Original Lightweight
Tony Jardine	E-Type Challenge
A Jenkinson	
Bob Jennings	YVH 210 Lightweight, JPD 251C
D Jesson	
Per Anders Jonsson	BNE 438B, E-Type Challenge, RAC
B Jones	
Mick Jones	Modsports WAP 66
Bernard (Barney) Juchli	3.8 FHC , West Coast USA
Phil Judd	AVT 575A
E W Judge	
Wolfgang Kaufmann	
Andrew Keith-Lucas	Masters
Tony Kember	3 BXV
J Kennerley	
K Kenyon	
Bob Kerr	V8 Egal 590 DXR
Laurence Kinch	Masters
Nathan Kinch	Masters
Najeeb Khan	
Tony Knight	Original racer 9 WKJ
Jack Lambert	Original racer RL 26, JL 24
Colin Lane	Early FHC racer
A Lanfranchi	
Peter Lanfranchi	6182 RW FHC racer, E-Type Challenge
William Langley	Standard V12
Patrick Langlois	
Henry Lawson	
Stuart Lawson	RAC
Ron Lea	V12 FHC HTU 942 K/ex-Pearce 310 WK/ex-Moore
Bill Leech (Australia)	
Alan Leeson	Supercharged modsports 666 DUL
A C (Jack) Le Fort	666 DUL
Jason Len	
Ed Leslie	Qvale Lightweight
John Lewis	Owner 256 DJU (the second Protheroe CUT 7)
E Liddell	
M Lilley	
Chris Lillingstone-Price	
A Lindemann	
Peter Lindner	4868 WK Le Mans 1964
Ludovic Lindsay	
Tim Line	
Brian Litherland	Modsports ex-Murphy FHC
Alan Lloyd	
Allen Lloyd	898 BYR Le Mans, and Lightweight replica
Callum Lockie	
Don Lord	
Loreille	
Oliver Louisoder	E-Type Challenge, Masters
Mike Loveday	Modsports, 9 WKJ
Jim Lowry	
Mick Luck	
N Ludlow	
Peter Lumsden	898 BYR Le Mans, 49 FXN
Shaun Lynn	
J Lyon	
J Lumsden-Taylor	
Roger Mac	256 DJU, CUT 7, 86 PJ Lightweight
Michael Macdowel	YVH 210 Lightweight
Galal Mahmoud	Masters
C Malkin	
E Malkin	
Spencer Martin	Bob Jane Lightweight
Gerry Marshall	CUT 7
Chris Mason	Modsports ex-Wilson
O Mathai	
D L Mather	
Tony Mather	
J Mathias	
John May	2164 WK

Nicholas McCaffrey	Ex-Adams FHC, E-Type Challenge
A McCaig	
Tom McCallum	Ex-John Burbidge FHC
Richard McCann	S1 FHC Sprint car
J McCartney	
Mike McDowall	
B McFall	
Allam McGregor	
S McIntyre	
Colin McKay	E-Type Challenge
Cliff McKinnon	FCO 55E
Bruce McLaren	3 BXV
Campbell McLaren	Lightweight 5114 WK
Paddy McNally	2065 DF
Bob Meacham	
James Mehew	
J Meighan	
Richard Meins	CUT 7
Martin Melling	E-Type Challenge
Michael Merrick	Monte Carlo Rally
Ray Merrick	Monte Carlo Rally
Liz Miles	Modsports, 671 EUT
Mike Miles	Modsports, 671 EUT
Brian Mills	Modsports
Robert Mills	RAC
Chris Milner	
John Milton	
E Minihan	87 GXM
Alan Minshaw	7 CXW
Jason Minshaw	TUF 4, E-Type Challenge
Jon Minshaw	40 FN, TUF 4, Masters, RAC
Ben Mitchell	
E J B (John) Mitchell	JM 71
John Monson	
Carlos Monteverde	E-Type Challenge
Ian Montgomery	RAC
Art Moore	
Dave Moore	Modsports
Michael Moore	
Terry Moore	
Tony Moore	
B Moran	4.2 Sprint
Frank Morrill	Qvale Lightweight
Andy Morris	5104 WK Lightweight replica
Keith Morris	
Leigh Morris	SST 569 E-Type dragster
David Morrison	
Ronnie Morrison	
Steve Morse	
P Mould	Early 3.8 racer
Alan Mountain	CVY 10C
Lee Mueller	V12 Huffaker racer
Brian Murphy	FHC modsports, and ex-Pearce modsports, 310 WK
Jim Murphy	
H V Murray	
J Murray	
T Mustard	
John Myerscough	Modsports, PBC 112
N Napier	
David Neil	V12
E Nelson	CUT 8
Adrian Newey	PS 1175 Lightweight
Matthew Newman	
Mike Newman	EBW 923A
Rodger Newman	
Peter Nocker	4868 WK Le Mans 1964
Georg Nolte	E-Type Challenge
Martin O'Connell	E-Type Challenge, Masters
K Oldham	
Jackie Oliver	ELA 76C
Robert (Bob) Oram	Speed trials FHC modsports, 140 HPO
Steve O'Rourke	WUO 3K
Michael O'Shea	5497 WK E-Type Challenge
Diane Osborne	E-Type Challenge XAS 885
Walter Ovando	
Brian Overy	
M Owen	
Don Oxborough	Modsports JNU 399C and 666 DUL
John Oxborough	Modsports JNU 399C and 666 DUL
Augie Pabst	5114 WK Le Mans
Graham Paddick	
Mark Pangbourne	
Paul Palmer	3 BXV
A Parkes	

D Parkes	
Mike Parkes	Early racer, EE 400
James Patterson	
Derek John Pearce	E-Type Challenge
Warren Pearce	310 WK
Henry Pearman	NKT 237F winner 1989 Pirelli marathon
Gary Pearson	Goodwood, E-Type Challenge, Masters
John Pearson	RL 26, E-Type Challenge, Masters
Harley Pederick (Australia)	
Win Percy	
Harry Phillips	FHC modsports
Roy Pinder	Monte Carlo Rally
Emanuele Pirro	
J A Playford	
D Plumstead	DF 358
Charles Pollard	Monte Carlo Rally
Mark Pollard	
Nigel Pow	Hill climb car NRW 574F
Albert Powell	
Graham Powell	
Peter Preston	888 RYA
Will Pringle	
E R (Dick) Protheroe	CUT 7 (3 cars)
John Pullen	Standard DHC sprint car
P De F C Pyecroft	
John Quick	Modsports WOO 11
J Quinn	
Michael Quinn	E-Type Challenge
Tony Quinn	2014 HZ
Kjell Qvale	5113 WK Lightweight
Stephen Radcliffe	XAS 885
Trevor Raines	
Joy Rainey	S2 FHC
Giovanni Ramponi	LHD S1 FHC
Capt C Ramsay	
Brian Redman	4 WPD
S Reakes	
P Richards	5115 WK Le Mans
G Richardson	
Frank Riches	
M Riddle	3.8 modsports
K Ridgeway	
Mark Ridley	Modified DHC sprint car
Hans Rieters	
Alexander Rittweger	Lightweight YVH 210
G Rimmel	
David Robinson	HON 140D
Neville Robinson	Modsports HBF 903C
R Robinson	
Justin Rockett	5167 KV yellow S1 FHC
Pierre Rohan	FOY 235D
Sir Robert Ropner	1WW Semi-Lightweight
G Rose	
Manfredo Rossi	E-Type Challenge
Hon. Amschel Rothschild	
Ian Rothwell	3.8
Ian Rowley	
Trevor Rowney	
John Rundell (Australia)	WUO 3K
Brian Russel	Modsports
Mark Russell	E-Type Challenge 5167 KV
Peter Rutt	E-Type Challenge
Martin Ryan	
P M Ryan	
Roy Salvadori	4WPD, 5116 WK Le Mans, 86 PJ Lightweight
Christophe Sapet	Monte Carlo Historic
Jules Sapet	Monte Carlo Historic
H Sargent	
Peter Sargent	898 BYR, 49 FXN, both Le Mans
Charlie Saunders	Modsports FHC
Rhea Sautter	
De La Sayette	
Richard Scantlebury	Modsports RS 2
John Scardifield	
R Scarth	
Pino Scarpino	
Hans Schenk	
Rob Schroeder	Modsports, 7 CXW
John Scott-Davies	49 FXN
Harding Scott-Wiseman	504 FOF
Chris Scragg	968 UXY, E-Type Challenge, Masters
Phil Scragg	2 GXO, PS 1175 Both Lightweights

Jack Sears	4 WPD
Susanne Sears	
R W (Bill) De Selincourt	E141, 5292 UR
Roger Seymour	YLU 470H
Stephen Sharp	Modsports, 7 CXW
R Shaw	
Tony Shaw	Modsports BGC 22B
T A Shaw	
Gordon Shedden	
Allen Shephard (Australia)	Land Speed Record S1 FHC
Phil Shephard	*World's Fastest E-Type* book, LSR FHC
Herbert Shepherd	Sprint car JLG 694C
Chris Shipton	Modsports FHC KPJ 85C
Rob Schirle	
Ben Shuckburgh	
E Sibley	
John Simms	2164 WK
R Simpson	
John Sisson	
Tim Sisson	PEE 22
Stephen Skipworth	E-Type Challenge
Tim Slack	
Paul Slade	CWA 740B, ECH 707C
Tom Sleigh	TES 1
John Smith	Modsports FHC
Andrew Smith	Autocross 188 HYT
Miki Smith	Modsports
Robert Smith	
Roderick Smith	E-Type Challenge
Michael Smurfit	PZC 73
Dick Soans	WUO 3K
Hayden Spedding	Modsports, ex-Wilson
Brian Spicer	E 141
Roy Standley	Ex-Pearce modsports, 310 WK, WUO 3K
Eric Stansfield	129 KVA
Bob Staples	Modsports
George Stauffer	
D Stead	
Brian Stevens	WPV 952A
Jackie Stewart	4 WPD, SSN 300
Phil Stott	MCH 627D
Tony Strawson	Modsports roadster
Martin Stretton	Masters 1196 WK
Robin Sturgess	2 BBC
Peter Sugden	E-Type Challenge
Chris Summers	V8 Egal 590 DXR
Peter Sutcliffe	YVH 210 Lightweight
Neville Swales	
Henryk Synowiec	NCC 669
Frank Sytner	Lightweight
Steve Tandy	Masters
Andrew Tart	
Mike Tate	
Simon Tate	RAC
Anthony Taylor	
Dennis Taylor	
Peter Taylor	Prodsports V12 FHC/SWK 581H
Sid Taylor	
James Tester	
Julian Thomas	
Jim Thomson	AAN 389C, TUJ 1
Nick Thompson	MCH 627D
Gordon Tipton	
Roberto Tonetti	
Christian Traber	E-Type Challenge WOO 11
Mark Trenoweth (Australia)	
Max Trimble	MT 111 S1 DHC ex-C & D Driver
John Truelove	
Jenny Tudor-Owen	Modsports
Bob Tullius	Group 44 V12 roadster
C Turnbull	
Mike Tye	PEE 22
Alex Van Tienhovan	
L Vard	
Paul Vesty	256 DJU
Bob Vincent	YVH 210/ RV7 Lightweight
Marcos Graf Von Oeynhausen	E-Type Challenge, Masters
Rainer Vorkoper	E-Type Challenge
Brian Waddilove	Modsports BRW 26, light blue FHC
E Wadsworth	
G Wainwright	
Fredrick Wakeman	
David Wansborough	CUT 7
B Walker	

John Walker	WAK 1 (8448 TJ)
Oliver Walker	NRW 574F
Peter Walker	105 ENX
R Walker	
F Wall	
J Walton	
P Walton	
Tim Wander	AJN 985A
Ross Warburton	
T H Warburton	
Chris Ward	
Richard Ward	Early 3.8 racer
A Warnell	
Roger Warrell	Modsports
Graham Warwick	
Bruce Waters	
Simon Watney	Modsports
Ian Watson	
Sandy Watson	E-Type Challenge, Masters
David Watts	
J Webb	
Nigel Webb	E141, E-Type Challenge
Paul Webb	13th Lightweight 5081 WK, 6900 WK modsports, 7 CXW
Jeremy Welch	E-Type Challenge
Eike Welhausen	Modsports
Max Werner	
W Westlake	
R Weston	
Martin Wheatley	Modsports
Martin White	PAG 622A
Dick Whittington	FHC modsports
George Wicken	1 PKL early racer
Dave Wilding	CUT 7
Bernard Wilhelm	E-Type Challenge
Nick Wilkins	
Mike Wilkinson	AFW 165A, SSN 300, E-Type Challenge
Barrie 'Wizzo' Williams	2 GXO, 590 DXR (V8 Egal) E-Type Challenge
R M Williams	
Desire Wilson	Goodwood, E-Type Challenge
John Wilson	Modsports PBC 112
K Wilson	
Barry Wood	RAC
Chris Wood	3.8
Tony Wood	RAC
J Woodbridge	18 HYO
Reg Woodcock	
Penny Woodley	86 PJ Lightweight, 1 FUE, UWD 645G
Ted Worswick	Modsports, PBC 112, 138 FLY (8448 TJ)
Ronald Wren	3142 BH early 3.8 FHC
Chris Wright	
Frank Wright	
Mark Wright	
Mike Wright	
Mike Wrigley	Masters
Harry Wyndham	E-Type Challenge
Jack Young	
John Young	CUT 7, 3 BXV
E Zeller	
Stefan Ziegler	
Roland Zoomers	E-Type Challenge

Note

Masters: refers to Masters Historic Racing, 'Gentleman Drivers' Pre-1966 GT Cars.

RAC: refers to the Royal Automobile Club, Tourist Trophy for Historic Cars.

Appendix D

Magazines containing racing E-Type articles

Jaguar Enthusiast

Most issues contain a section on 'Club Racing News,' which invariably has an E-Type seen racing that month.

July 1995	FHC 'HOT 12'
December 1997	The World's Fastest E-Type season review
October 1998	The World's Fastest E-Type season review

From 1999 to 2000 many issues carried articles/updates on the club's sponsorship of the two race E-Types of Malcolm Hamilton and Mike Adams.

August 2003	Race Bred E-Type MCH 627D
December 2006	Ron Lea V12
June 2007	Lightweight replica
October 2007	Ron Lea V12
December 2008	Alan Leeson/John Oxborough modsports
August 2009	CUT 7
September 2009	CUT 7 part 2
November 2009	310 WK Warren Pearce
April & May 2010	Maurice Charles 503 BBO Le Mans
Feb 2011 to July 2011	Six articles on the E-Type at 50
June 2011	4868 WK
July 2011	Early racing
August 2011	Modsports racers
May 2012	8448 TJ John Cuff
December 2012	8448 TJ John Cuff
March 2013	The Lightweights including 4 GXO
June 2013	The World's Fastest E-Type, part 1
July 2013	The World's Fastest E-Type, part 2
August 2013	The World's Fastest E-Type, part 3
February 2015	The Lightweights
March 2015	The Lightweights (new and old)
July 2015	The new Lightweights

Jaguar Driver

Most issues contain the sections 'Competition News' and also 'Wide Angle,' which invariably mentions a racing E-Type.

July 1975	Simon Watney modsports
July 1982	4868 WK

March 1986	E-Type in competition
December 1986	Intermarque championship
August 1990 to January 2000	Articles on Debbie Edwards rally E-Type. (See rally section).
July 1996	AFD 250
December 1997	The World's Fastest E-Type
June 1992	310 WK Warren Pearce
June 1993	The Lightweights
October 1994	2 BBC Sturgess
November 1994	The Lightweights
December 1994	The Lightweights
February 1995	V12 racers
January 2002	Le Mans E-Types 898 BYR, 49 FXN

Classic & Sportscar

May 1984	CUT 7
April 1986	The Lightweights and E-Type evolution
June 1987	2 GXO Lightweight
June 1995	YLU 470H S2 FHC racer
August 2006	Lightweight 86 PJ
February 2015	4 WPD
July 2016	CUT 7 and CUT 8

Thoroughbred & Classic Cars

April 1975	Lightweight E-Type
May 1982	Last of the Lightweights
May 1990	256 DJU

Classic Cars

March 1974	CUT 7
January 1999	Lightweights
April 1999	The Qvale Lightweight
Spring 2002	CUT 7
March 2008	Debbie Edwards rally E-Type.
January 2011	Jackie Stewart's E-Type SSN 300
June 2017	Allen Shephard's land speed record FHC

Autosport

Naturally, most issues from April 1961 onwards seem to mention the E-Type. A small selection of different drivers/cars which include photos are listed below.

6 July 1962	Le Mans 898 BYR
14 December 1962	Ken Baker
1 May 1964	David Cunningham
4 December 1964	Dick Protheroe
9 July 1965	Peter Lumsden
15 October 1965	Tony Knight
25 March 1966	Alistair Crawford
22 April 1966	Charles Bridges and George Humble
5 August 1966	Rob Beck Egal
28 July 1967	Bob Vincent and Harding Scott-Wiseman
8 December 1967	Mike Miles
19 April 1968	Jenny Tudor-Owen
7 June 1968	John Quick
28 June 1968	Rob Schroeder
11 October 1968	John Lewis and John Wilson
11 April 1969	John Filbee
30 October 1969	Mike Loveday
13 November 1969	John Burbidge
11 June 1970	Brian Spicer
27 August 1970	Peter Archer
15 October 1970	Tony Shaw
12 August 1971	James Mehew
14 September 1972	Harry Phillips
5 October 1972	John Burbidge and Frank Wright
12 April 1973	Brian Mills and Brian Murphy
2 August 1973	Bob Meacham and Roger Warrell
14 August 1975	13 years of the E-Type in competition by Doug Nye

Motoring News (weekly newspaper)

Many issues will have mention of the E-Type of course. Some examples are:

22 February 1968	Photo: Rob Schroeder at Brands
1 April 1971	The new V12 E-Type and modsports racing photo
12 March 1986	25th anniversary, racing E-Types

Motor Sport

August 1961	Coombs BUY 1
April 1962	Sturgess, 2 BBC and Baker, 7 CXW

January 1967	Warren Pearce and John Quick WOO 11
September 1984	Lightweights

Autocar

28 July 1961	ECD 400 and BUY 1
5 April 1975	Peter Taylor V12 Prodsports

Jaguar Quarterly

Autumn 1990	4868 WK
April/May 1991	E-Type souvenir issue with many cars photographed, eg 7 CXW, CUT 7, 4868 WK, BUY 1, ECD 400, 86 PJ
Spring 1991	The World's Fastest E-Type
Summer 1991	John Quick WOO 11, part 1
Autumn 1991	John Quick WOO 11, part 2
Autumn 1991	30th Anniversary meet at Donington, many race E-Types
May/June 1992	John Wilson PBC 112, part 1
July/August 1992	John Wilson PBC 112, part 2 and The World's Fastest E-Type

Jaguar World/Monthly

March/April 1993	Cunningham's roadster 9023 DU
July/August 1993	Le Mans E-Type 898 BYR
November/December 1993	4 WPD
May/June 1994	Zealia Lightweight
November/December 1995	The World's Fastest E-Type
March/April 1996	Mike Adams E-Type
March/April 1997	Pierre Bardinon FHC Semi-Lightweight
October 1999	Jackie Stewart's E-Type SSN 300
November 1999	Qvale Lightweight
June 2001	CUT 7 LDC
July 2003	E-Types at Le Mans
September 2006	CUT 7 v 49 FXN
July 2007	WPV 952A
January 2008	ECD 400
October 2008	Guy Bedington's V12
October 2010	LDC
December 2010	LWR Lightweight
February 2011	E-Type evolution
September 2011	Gran Turismo E-Type
December 2013	Lightweights
April 2015	The World's Fastest E-Type

Hot Car

January 1969	Rob Schroeder 7 CXW
June 1971	John Quick WOO 11

Supercar Classics

May 1988	The Lightweights

Cars & Car Conversions

August 1976	Brian Murphy modsports 310 WK
January 1994	Forward Engineering's 8-litre E-Type

Motor

24 February 1968	BUY 1. The Sporting Jaguars

Vintage Motorsport

Sept/Oct 2010	5114 WK Lightweight

Sporting Cars

December 1982	Lightweights and Le Mans

Collector's Car

May 1980	Competition history of the E-Type

Motor Racing

October 1961	Bruce McLaren, 3 BXV

EJag

February 1987	Lightweights by Peter Wilson

Octane

August 2012	4 GXO a new Lightweight.
October 2014	The new Lightweight E-Type

Practical Performance Car

September 2009	WGG 708 track day race E-Type

Sports Car Graphic

September 1962	Huffaker/Morrill race E-Type

Appendix E

Magazine articles by the author

The author has written several articles on racing E-Types for *Jaguar Enthusiast* magazine, and some are reproduced here.

JAGUAR E-TYPE FORUM

CO-ORDINATOR: GARETH KEY TEL: 01473 742648 EMAIL: GARETH.KEY@JEC.ORG.UK
BODY & PAINTWORK – KEITH PARRINGTON. EMAIL: KEITH.PARRINGTON@XJRESTORATINS.CO.UK OR TEL: 01323 720009 (EMAIL PREFERRED).
TECHNICAL ADVICE: COLIN FORD. TEL: 0208 304 1221 (AFTER 6.30PM)
TECHNICAL ADVICE: KEN JENKINS EMAIL: UKJAG@HOTMAIL.COM OR TEL: 07836 241101 (UP TO 8PM)

The story of the fastest E-type in the world

Picture taken outside Fred Cliffe's workshop as the car was in its final stages of preparation. Photo by Peter Griffiths.

Having laid dormant for just over ten years the ex-Malcolm Hamilton/Rob Beere V12 race E-type has started its long awaited rebuild. Peter Griffiths tells the story.

In summary, I bought the car from Malcolm Hamilton and Rob Beere four years ago. Now two house moves later I am sufficiently settled to turn my attention to the V12. It has been a difficult four years and the E-type was even put back up for sale for a while when finances dictated. Thankfully I managed to hold onto the car and sold other items instead, including the ex-Alan Leeson/John Oxborough/Dave Moore 6-cylinder modsports E-type. For those of you who may have seen the adverts for the car, it is now in Czechoslovakia where it is back on the track again. A full story of this race E-type appeared in the December 2008 edition of *Jaguar Enthusiast*.

The editor suggested that I write a series of articles for the magazine on the history of the V12 and the current rebuild. As you are probably aware the car has been well documented and photographed over the years and even sponsored by the Club back in the late 90s. Hopefully I will be able to give some further information on the car that you may not have been aware of.

So, where to begin… the late seventies…

The birth of the car was the brainchild of Fred Cliffe. In *Autosport* magazine, 29th September 1977, it was announced that 'two of the best known names in the Jaguar competition and preparation business, Fred Cliffe and Brian Murphy had joined forces. They would "Mount a two car attack in modsports racing using the ex-Murphy car and a new V12 project which Fred has been working on for some time". (Coincidentally, the Murphy car…. The ex-Warren Pearce car…. has also ended up in Czechoslovakia! ….. wonder what's happening over there?).

The Jaguar Drivers' Club made a similar announcement in their January 1978 club magazine and so started the life of the 'fastest E-type in the world!'

The V12 modsports E-type was continually developed by Fred and although very successful did not seem to get the publicity at the time attracted by Guy Beddington's V12 fhc modsports and the 'standard' V12 racer of Peter Taylor.

Malcolm Hamilton, you may recall, was at the time racing his successful 6- cylinder modsports E-type fhc in the usual red, white and blue livery. A widely used picture back in 1986 showed the JDC Intermarque winning team line up of modsports E-types. Malcolm on the far right with the 6-cylinder car next to the red and silver roadster of Dave Moore…. My old car mentioned above.

Following on from his success in the straight six, Malcolm was looking for something even faster and turned his eye to Fred Cliffe's V12 racer. For those who are interested, Malcolm's old 6-cylinder is now in the hands of E-type racer Bernie Breeze. (note to Bernie…. Have you started the rebuild of that one yet ?)

A change of ownership

After many successful races Fred put the V12 up for sale in 1986. The advert in the January *Jaguar Driver* magazine read as follows:-

"Racing V12 E-type roadster…. The ultimate

40 JAGUAR ENTHUSIAST *June 2013*

The V12 story (*Jaguar Enthusiast*, June 2013)

The original sidedraught Weber carburettor configuration on the Broadspeed engine. Photo by Peter Griffiths.

Photographed outside Rob Beere's workshop, when the car was starting to look somewhat like it still does today.

The car when it carried No. 88, with no roof and 'standard' width doors.

racing E-type… 580bhp, Broadspeed engine, sorted suspension and brakes, Broadspeed gearbox …. Successful racing history…. Complete with trailer and spares."

From here, of course, it eventually ended up with Malcolm Hamilton and the car was initially campaigned through Malcolm's engineering business Kearns Richards Service.

The first appearance of the 'new' V12 was in 1988. Malcolm was joined by Rob Beere on the project and further development of the car started immediately. Thankfully they had a good base upon which to start. The V12 engine that Fred had installed was indeed one of the old Broadspeed engines from the XJ Broadspeed Coupes programme, when Jaguar contested the Group 2 European Touring Car Championship back in 1976 and 1977.

At the first outing in 1988 the car ran with the number 88…. Coincidence… yes and no. Apparently, Malcolm and Rob thought their new car was twice as good as the Group 44 race E-type and therefore managed to get the race organisers to allocate No. 88 for their first race season. After the continuing success of the car, it then raced each following year with the year as its number! Ie. A photo of the car with 99 on it, pinpoints it to a race in 1999. The last race shots of it with 01 show the year of its accident in 2001 which sadly saw the end of its 10+ years successful race career.

The car concentrated on the Aston Martin Owners Club Intermarque Championship series of races. Results for the 1988 season ended with seven outright victories, four second places and one third…. Not bad for the opening season.

One of the early races of the season was typical of things to come. Oulton Park, Malcolm's 'home' circuit on the 23rd April 1988. The Cheshire Trophy Race meeting organised by the Oulton Park Racing Club. Practice - 1st with an average speed of 92.38mph. The race – 1st with an average speed of 86.51mph. over half a minute ahead of the next E-type!

Photographs of the car started to appear regularly in the magazines. In the *Jaguar Driver* magazine for example, it was in the June, August, September, October and December issues. It was on the front cover of the September issue.

To balance the story, it was not all roses. At the JDC Mallory Park meeting on the 31st July, the V12 had to retire, in a cloud of steam, when a water hose came lose. This was captured on the 1988 DVDs marketed by vfsvideos of the AMOC Intermarque Challenge. Typical press coverage of the time can be found in the *Jaguar Driver* report on the JDC Silverstone meeting:-

"Having won the Intermarque race in stirring style Malcolm Hamilton and V12E proceeded to stamp his authority on the Modified Jaguar race which included a few non Jaguar runners in the incorporated Modsports race. After two laps peering up Bainbridge's exhaust Hamilton blasted past to win by 3 seconds."

The 1989 season only managed three outright victories and one second place. An early season 'expensive' engine blow up left Malcolm and Rob urgently looking for sponsorship in order to continue the battle with Gerry Marshall and his V8 Aston Martin.

The 88 car had the red, white and blue livery with KRS (Kearns Richards Services) as the lead sponsor. In early 1989 Rob left his position as manager with KRS to establish his own business, Rob Beere Engineering. A news article in the *Jaguar Driver* magazine in May 1989 read as follows:-

"A Jaguar engine specialist workshop has recently opened in Stockport under the direction of Rob Beere. Over the past 12 years Rob has gained comprehensive experience in all aspects of the Jaguar car, with specialist knowledge of engines. As manager of KRS he rebuilt concours engines and did development work. He prepared and will continue to sponsor Malcolm Hamilton's fully modified 7 litre V12 roadster, which during its first season became the only Jaguar to win the fully modified

The perhaps thankfully short-lived blue livery of the car.

class of the Intermarque Championship with 7 outright victories….. and is now considered the world's fastest V12 E-type."

1989 saw a change of colour scheme for the car, now white with grey and black stripes and Rob Beere Engineering on the spoiler replacing KRS.

The 1990 season was better with four outright victories and two seconds. The colour scheme stayed the same so visibly only the No. 90 replaced the 89 to help identify the races.

Gordon Russell, the Intermarque sponsors of 1989, were replaced in 1990 by Proteus Petroleum. Gerry Marshall and the Aston Martin V8 seemed to be the main rival this year… the closely fought race at Silverstone in October records Gerry first (80.93mph) followed closely in second by Malcolm (at 80.23mph).

One high point of the year (in addition to the race wins) was at the July Silverstone meeting when Malcolm set a new lap record of 1.39.84. This will be recorded for posterity as the circuit changed immediately after this event.

For a short while during the 1990 season, the colour scheme of the car was changed to a complete one colour job of light blue. I only have a few pictures of the car in this livery as it soon reverted to the familiar dominant white paintwork in 1991.

The *Jaguar Quarterly* magazine has done two superb articles on the car, one in the spring 1991 edition and the other in the July/August 1992 edition, however, I assume that these were both written in 1990 as all of the pictures of the car show it carrying the No. 90.

The car continued to gain popularity with racegoers during 1990 and a beautiful photograph of it appeared on the front cover of the *Jaguar Driver* magazine in

Taken at a very wet Brands Hatch race meeting, the car with Modsports driver John Oxborough standing behind the car. Photo by Peter Griffiths.

October 1990. In the September 1990 edition of the *Jaguar Driver* magazine Ron Lea wrote in his competition news section:-

"There was an excellent result for the JDC Team in the Intermarque race on the 23rd June at Silverstone during the AMOC St. John Horsfall meeting. Malcolm Hamilton in his fearsome fully modified E-type roadster prepared by Rob Beere Engineering, now with a 7.3 Litre V12 engine, with Cosworth pistons and dry sump system was just 9/10ths of a second off pole but ended being the easy winner of the Intermarque race".

Another superb article on the car appeared in the April 1991 edition of *Jaguar Quarterly* magazine, once again, photographs of the car bearing the No. 90 livery were used and the article mainly covers the excellent bodywork preparation of Martin Robey Sales and Engineering Ltd.

The 1991 season saw another change of Intermarque sponsor, this time to SKF Engineering products. The paintwork of the car changed from the previous white with grey stripes to white with red and blue stripes, and of course bearing the No. 91. Another successful season, this time with five overall victories.

The 1992 season continued with the run of successes with six overall victories and one second place. At the meeting at Pembray on the 5th July 1992, Malcolm succeeded in setting a new lap record.

After five years of continuous hard fought racing, the car was ready for its first major rebuild. The car did not therefore run during the 1993 and 1994 seasons and only returned to the circuit in earnest in 1995.

TO BE CONTINUED………

The final good looking shape of the car, now with downdraught Webers.

42 JAGUAR ENTHUSIAST *June 2013*

JAGUAR E-TYPE FORUM

CO-ORDINATOR: GARETH KEY TEL: 01473 742648 EMAIL: GARETH.KEY@JEC.ORG.UK
BODY & PAINTWORK – KEITH PARRINGTON. EMAIL: KEITH.PARRINGTON@XJRESTORATINS.CO.UK OR TEL: 01323 720009 (EMAIL PREFERRED).
TECHNICAL ADVICE: COLIN FORD. TEL: 0208 304 1221 (AFTER 6.30PM)
TECHNICAL ADVICE: KEN JENKINS EMAIL: UKJAG@HOTMAIL.COM OR TEL: 07836 241101 (UP TO 8PM)

The story of the fastest E-type in the world – Part 2

The Malcolm Hamilton 'Beast" and Mike Adam's 4.2 litre, in the late nineties sponsored by the Jaguar Enthusiasts' Club.

Following on from last month's feature which covered the history of the car from 1988 to 1992, Peter Griffiths now covers the remaining history up until 2001 when the car was involved in an accident at Oulton Park. The car's racing career was temporarily halted until its 2013 rebuild which will be fully covered in the next article.

As mentioned in the previous feature, the car was completely rebuilt during 1993 to 1994 so did not compete.

When the car reappeared in 1995 it had a totally white colour scheme and sported a rear wing to help keep The Beast on the track. The 1995 AMOC Intermarque Championship was sponsored by ERF and Malcolm successfully picked up from where he had left off in 1992

The car in the then 'new' 1995 colour scheme of white with a spoiler.

A new year and a new sponsor for 1996.

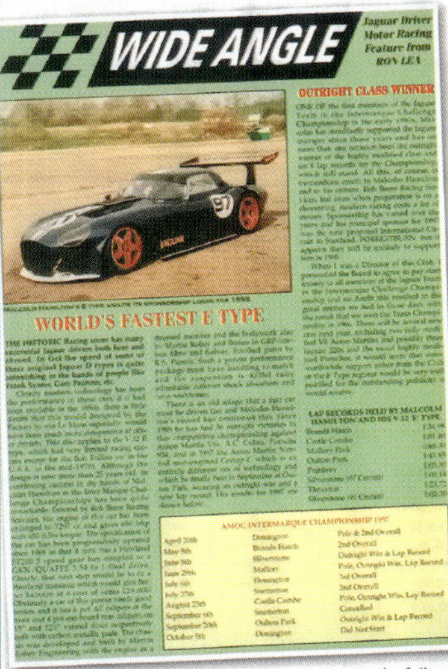

The E-type received excellent coverage of its successes in the 1990s.

finishing the season with 5 outright victories and 3 overall second places.

The press were quick to notice the return of the car and a full report was written in the November/December 1995 edition of *Jaguar World* magazine headed 'Quick off the Marque…Jim Patten hitches a ride in the fastest E-type Racer In the world.'

The 1996 Intermarque season was once again sponsored by ERF and the car now carried the logo of its new sponsor Forrestburn International Circuit, the colour scheme remained predominantly white with red trimmings. The car had mixed fortunes during 1996 with two outright victories, a second, and two third places. However, one interesting fact…the car achieved ten fastest laps during the season, a sign of its continued development. For example, at the Castle Coombe race day on 5th October 1996 Malcolm achieved the fastest lap averaging 100.82mph!

The 1997 season was highlighted by the continual development and race victories (4 outright victories, 3 second places) and again attracted wide press interest. In December both the *Jaguar Driver* and *Jaguar Enthusiast* magazines carried excellent season reviews of the car. The car now with dark blue coachwork was fully established as the world's fastest E-type. In the highly modified Class of the Intermarque series. Malcolm was now the holder of lap records at the following circuits, Brands Hatch, Castle Coombe, Mallory Park, Oulton Park, Pembrey, Thruxton and Silverstone!

A couple of examples of the car's prowess are as follows;

1. At the April BRSCC meeting at Donington Park, Malcolm finished second only 4.5 seconds behind the Aston Martin Nimrod averaging a speed of 96.7 mph.
2. At the August BRSCC meeting at Castle Coombe, Malcolm achieved an outright victory averaging a speed of 107.88 mph.

Racing success continued throughout the 1998 season with 7 outright victories and 2 second places. Again there was wide press coverage including the *Jaguar Driver* magazine (August and September 1998) and in the *Jaguar Enthusiast* magazine (October 1998), where there was an excellent article entitled 'Rob Beere Racing Review'. This presented a glorious two page photograph of the car. On the occasions when Malcolm finished second in a race he was rarely far behind the winner. For example at the AMOC race meeting at Silverstone on 14th June he was only 1.6 seconds behind the winning Porsche GT2… Malcolm's average speed was 98.94mph which earned him the fastest lap award.

A typical Race Report which Rob Beere sent to the sponsors at the time reads as follows;

"AMOC Intermarque meeting at Castle Coombe, Bank Holiday Monday 25 April 1998.

This circuit is not known for its great facilities but the circuit, although quite bumpy, is incredibly fast, with average laps around 110 mph on a minute lap!

Moving on to 1998 and still excellent coverage and yet another colour scheme.

Qualification for the AMOC Intermarque (Race 4 on the day) went well completing 12 laps steadily, as the car is due new tyres and brake pads.

We were, however, concerned about a Jaguar XJ220 and a new Porsche GT2 car. The Jaguar XJ220 had an engine failure but the GT2 car took pole position from us by over 2 seconds and came close to our lap record of 1.01.40 from the 1997 season.

No real changes were made to the car, just a concern about the longevity of the tyres and brakes.

The race started at 2.45pm and surprisingly Malcolm shot into the lead leaving the GT2 Porsche and attaining a 5 second lead by the 5th lap.

Unfortunately he struggled with getting through some back-markers and the Porsche closed the gap to about a second.

2001 colour scheme, picture taken at the Autosport Show that year.

A brief summary of the Beast's racing history

52 Outright Victories
24 Second places
11 Third places.

Declining tyres reduced this even further making the last 2 laps breathtaking with the 2 cars alongside each other right up to the flag-luckily the right man won!...by 8/100ths of a second, gaining a new lap record.

As you can imagine we celebrated this hat trick of victories in style!"

For the 1999 and 2000 seasons the car, resplendent in British Racing Green coachwork and yellow wheels, was sponsored by none other than the Jaguar Enthusiasts' Club. For two years the Club sponsored two racing E-types, the other car being the 4.2 litre fhc of Mike Adams, in a matching colour scheme. The V12 was now transported in a colour co-ordinated Rob Beere lorry and the team looked incredibly professional… naturally the Jaguar Enthusiasts' Club magazine followed the teams exploits in full with very detailed reports in the following magazines; 1999 April, June, August, September, October, November, 2000 January, March, June, August, September, October, November, December 2001 January.

The first article in April 1999 gave a clear indication of the Jaguar Enthusiasts' Club was "Now being the home of Jaguar motorsport" and showing the cars and the transporter in their new livery.

Although outright victories eluded Malcolm in 1999 the car was back in full race order with 6 outright victories in 2000.

A copy of the race report for the AMOC meeting at Silverstone on 24th June 2000 stated that Malcolm finished second by 5.5 seconds behind the Jaguar XJ220 of Win Percy…Malcolm's average speed was 100.48 mph compared with the XJ220 average speed of 101.29 mph.

2001 as we know was the last season for Malcolm because of the disastrous accident at Oulton Park late in the year when a Porsche struck the car quite heavily on the nearside forcing Malcolm to retire. The year had in fact started off

The car in 2000 specification under wind tunnel testing at MIRA.

extremely well and had shown great promise of another superb season with 3 outright victories and 2 second places. The car was now in its new (and perhaps most famous) colours of pure white with 2 blue stripes and bearing the number '01' for the 2001 season. The Team stepped up a gear in 2001 and on 2 occasions went International by attending the meetings at Spa in Belgium.

A big highlight of the year was at the annual Woodbridge Speed Trial day where Malcolm achieved a record speed of 184 mph-thus re-validating the Car as the fastest E-Type in the World! The technical specification of the car is very simply a TWR Group C Le Mans car in E-type clothing. The 7.0 litre V12 engine develops in excess of 700bhp and power to the rear axle is delivered via a special Hewland gearbox. The highly polished alloy wheels are from the XJ220 Le Mans car and the carbon fibre rear spoiler is from an actual TWR Le Mans 'Silk Cut' car.

For those who are interested, there is still a website in existence for the car, http://www.fastjags.org.uk although it is not current. There is also the Pistonheads blog entitled 'Malcolm Hamilton's E-type' which has a lot of information and photographs.

My third article will be a detailed article on the rebuild.

The 2001 car at Oulton Park following the major accident.

JAGUAR E-TYPE FORUM

Co-ordinator: Gareth Key Tel: 01473 742648 Email: gareth.key@jec.org.uk
Body & Paintwork – Keith Parrington. Email: keith.parrington@xjrestoratins.co.uk or Tel: 01323 720009 (email preferred).
Technical Advice: Colin Ford. Tel: 0208 304 1221 (after 6.30pm)
Technical Advice: Ken Jenkins Email: ukjag@hotmail.com or Tel: 07836 241101 (up to 8pm)

The story of the fastest E-type in the world – Part 3

Peter Griffiths continues his story of this well known E-type, this month the repair, refit and the rebuild.

The accident at Oulton Park in 2001 necessitated a complete strip down in order to repair the damaged panels and the car was virtually returned to numerous boxes of its constituent parts.

Twelve years down the road, the jigsaw puzzle of 'what goes where' proved quite difficult. There is no workshop manual for a 100% bespoke race car!

When Rob Beere had the car, I guess he and Carl knew where everything went and I guess they were anticipating building it back up for the next season… obviously that plan didn't quite come off. My understanding is that with the change of Intermarque rules and loss of sponsorship meant that the car was left in Rob's workshop until better times.

The rebuild commences

After dismantling the car, (engine and gearbox out, suspension and brakes out, dry sump oil system out, interior out, etc etc.) they decided that it might be a good time to completely redesign and rebuild a new back end to lighten the car by getting rid of the normal rear cage arrangement. Rob merely started the job…. it took us two months to completely re-fabricate the rear end, beginning with a rear bulkhead and a differential suspended from the rear roll cage extension….. where do you mount the suspension? Where do you mount the petrol tank? Where do you mount the rear wing supports? I think you get the picture!

The passenger door was quite badly damaged in the accident and this was as good a start point as anything. It was disassembled in order to carry out a full repair. Sadly all the paint and sponsor decals were removed in order to accomplish this. The aluminium door was completely rebuilt and primed, hinges repaired, door A and B posts fully repaired and the door re-hung and aligned.

Other panels that were considered far too damaged to be repaired economically were removed and sent to a specialist aluminium fabricator to make duplicates. This included the offside sill including the end panels as well as all louvers within the sill and the bonnet areas. These were exceptionally well made and overall added to the car being 'better' after the accident than before.

The main area of the car that needed the most work was the rear end. As mentioned above, after the accident in 2001 it was decided to completely redesign the rear end. Although this had been started, it was perhaps only 20% complete and a further two months work was necessary to design and build a complete back end.

When I bought the car the rear bodywork was resting on the rear tyres …. Obviously the rear ride height was incorrect… indeed one side was lower than the other. The rear bodywork is one large item not separate wings, boot lid, end panels etc as in a conventional car. This was damaged in the accident and was again completely stripped of its paintwork and decals before repair and primer.

The differential was suspended from the rear roll cage which had been extended through the rear bulkhead. (The rear conventional cage had been done away with in the rear end rethink back in 2001). The suspension whilst still located at the bottom end to the half shafts the top end had no 'cage' to locate into. The top of the shock absorbers were therefore attached to specially made brackets welded to the rear bulkhead. In order to make the ride height even more adjustable, three mounting points were designed into each bracket. The totally adjustable Penske shock absorbers and oversprings could now be adjusted even further.

The rebuilt door.

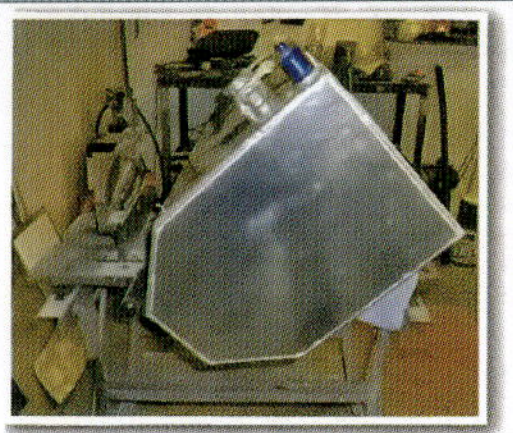

The new petrol tank, a little different to the one normally fitted to E-types!

The massive AP 6-pot brake callipers fitted to Peter's car.

Suspension rebuilt in progress.

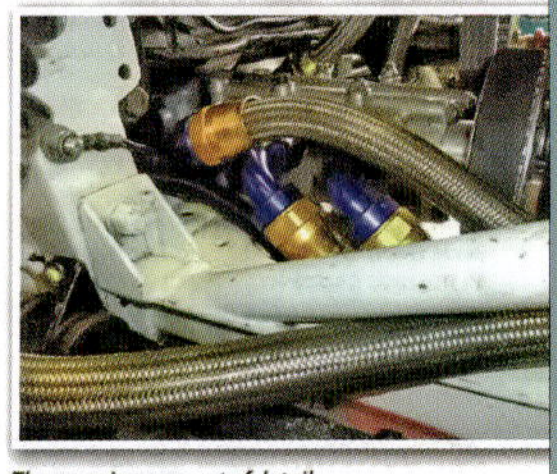

The amazing amount of detail work required on such a car.

An additional strong steel plate was designed and fixed to the underside of the differential. Not only did it provide greater rigidity but it also provided extra frame mounting points and a towing eye.

Using the steel rear bulkhead as the strongest mounting base, a rear space frame was designed and constructed to take a) the petrol tank, b) the rear wing supports, and c) the rear bodywork. With the rear space frame completed we could now design a 'cardboard' petrol tank that fitted into the available space. This along with specific measurements was sent off to the aluminium specialist to create a petrol tank. What came back was truly a work of art….. and it fitted. To meet regulations it was of course foam filled.

Underneath the fibreglass one-piece rear end sat the aluminium diffuser. This was very badly damaged in the accident and could not be saved. The original damaged panels were all straightened and sent off to have identical ones made. Again, a work of aluminium art returned and the rear diffuser, now in place, helped complete and strengthen the rear end bodywork.

The front splitter was also badly damaged in the crash and the only way to repair it was to totally dismantle it, make identical panels and then rebuild it. Thankfully, some of the panels (and there were an awful lot) could be used again, although the plywood splitter itself had to be totally renewed.

The hard top (a very lightweight copy of a standard V12 one) suffered minor damage and this had to be repaired. Like most of the fibreglass repairs this was done using a sort of 'aluminium sandwich' to give strength to the damaged area, rather than just rely on new fibreglass and filler to do the job. These aluminium repairs, neatly riveted into place, were not painted or filled over, but simply left. I thought it looked better that way.

Naturally over the years some parts had gone missing, possibly used elsewhere and these needed sourcing. Thankfully a good spares package came with the car and overall costs were kept within reason.

New regulations

In order to make the car meet current RAC regulations additional roll bars were added. A further bracing strut was added to the rear bulkhead and a passenger door bar was also fitted. Where the roll cage extended into the back end of the car numerous triangular bracing pieces were added to ensure the car was at the pinnacle of safety and rigidity.

As the engine had not run for so long this was naturally treated with a great deal of respect! We had to be sure it would turn over by hand before any real power was forced upon it.

The engine was placed on a stand and tilted a few degrees to one side. Having removed all the plugs etc. very light oil / paraffin mix was drizzled into the engine on the lower side only. We did not want the oil to collect on the top of the dished pistons but merely lubricate the cylinder walls. Otherwise the engine would only smoke unnecessarily after start up until the excess oil had burned off. After a few days the engine was tilted to the other side and the procedure was repeated.

Finally and very thankfully after a week the engine was successfully turned over by hand and all felt fine.

I have done several rebuilds over the years and it never ceases to amaze me how much all those 'little parts' you didn't think about, add up to. For example…. Fibreglass, filler, primer, thinners, paint, abrasives, rivets, nuts, bolts, fasteners, steel plate and tubing, sealant, cylinder repair kits, o rings, welding wire, brake pipes, oil pipes, fuel pipes, etc etc.. Several thousand pounds 'disappears' into the 'sundries' parts list. When you then start to list more major items such as new aluminium body panels, new rear end frame work, new petrol tank, new exhaust, new fire system, new battery, new fuel

The E-type homecoming in 2013.

pumps etc etc you can see the costs start to escalate. Adding the labour element and finally all the race preparation work then I began to realise that running this race winning car is just like a Le Mans Group C car or even an F1 car … ie. A team affair with sponsorship, not a race car for an individual to take out on their own.

The dry sump oil system means that the car sits about 6" lower than a standard car. Consequently the exhausts cannot be routed under the car but have been designed to go through the widened sills on both sides of the car and exit just before the rear wheels. Those of you who have seen the car will know that it is already a good 6" wider than a standard V12 and the squared off sills leave enough space to house suitably large silencers to help maintain the Beast's decibel limit.

A lick of what paint?

As you will have seen from my previous articles the car has had many colour changes and I thought it better to keep the car in its final colour scheme of white with blue stripes … perhaps people would remember it better that way. The repaired panels as mentioned above, lost their decals and with it, I think, a little of the car's identity. I decided therefore to only repaint the repaired areas and leave the rest of the car 'original' with all the race patina left alone. I have written to all the old sponsors to try and get some replacement decals, but to date only Graham Searle at our Club's office has come through with stickers.

Conclusions

Overall the rebuild went well (well over budget as well), although there were the odd hours of panic and the often asked question Why did I start this?". Indeed, why did I buy the car in the first place…"It seemed like a good idea at the time!"

I think that if the car had not been 'rescued' when I purchased it, there may have been a chance that more bits of it may have been used for other projects and its demise may well have been past the point of no return. For example, not long after I bought it I was approached to see if I would sell one set of the spare wheels for an XJ220 project. (I declined, wanting to keep the car together as much as I could). I feel very fortunate therefore that I have played a part in bringing the car back to life so perhaps a new generation of Jaguar enthusiasts (as well as us oldies who saw it the first time around of course) can marvel at the Beast that Rob Beere and his team built and Malcolm Hamilton drove with such success between 1988 and 2001.

As this article had to go to press the car is only 95% finished and final race preparation and sorting still needs to be finished. Above all the car will need an extensive testing programme to assess the new rear end arrangement. I don't, however, foresee any problems in this area as every step of the rebuild has been done with safety and reliability in mind.

Anyone seeking further information on the car is welcome to contact me on griffiths418@btinternet.com

Current specification

- 1971 E-type V12 centre tub carrying almost a TWR Group C spec engine and running gear.
- Overall weight 1275kg.
- Bodywork is a mix of aluminium, fibreglass and carbon fibre.
- The front air dam is ply with titanium skids.
- Engine is a 7.3 litre V12 Jaguar unit developing around 750bhp and around 680ft lbs of torque. Although Rob produced engines ranging from 5.3 litres to 9 litres (!) they settled upon 7.3 litres as being the ideal balance of reliability and Bhp/Torque.

Brief spec:-

- Pistons – Cosworth / RBR.
- Crankshaft – TWR / RBR.
- Cylinder heads – TWR/RBR.
- Camshafts – TWR.
- Compression ratio – 13:1 using race fuel only.
- Carburettors – 6 x twin choke downdraught IDF Webers.
- Bespoke dry sump oil system so the engine sits approx 6" lower and further back than a standard car.
- Aluminium water radiator, oil cooler, dry sump oil tank and oil catch tank.

Electrics:-

- Battery – Varley Red Top with no alternator but with external jump lead for slave battery connected via body mounted Anderson plug.
- Front and rear side lights, brake lights, indicator lights and central diffuser light.
- Plumbed in fire extinguisher system.
- 4 point seat safety harness with Corbeau race seat.
- Removable steering wheel and power assisted steering (you do need it!)

Gearbox:-

- Special Hewland dog box with side by side shaft arrangement with lightweight flywheel and triple plate clutch. Internal slave cylinder and release bearing. This allows for extremely low ground clearance.

Rear wing:-

- Ex Jaguar Silk Cut Le Mans XJR9 made from carbon fibre.

Brakes:-

- Front. 15" AP racing discs with AP 6 pot callipers.
- Rear 13" AP racing discs with AP 4-pot callipers.
- Brake balance adjuster fitted.

Suspension:-

- Penske springs and shock absorbers on modified Jaguar linkages, fully adjustable.
- Wishbones – RBR fabricated and rose jointed specials.
- Anti roll bars – RBR special.
- Wheels – XJ220 Le mans type.
- Tyres – Dunlop 305/650R18.

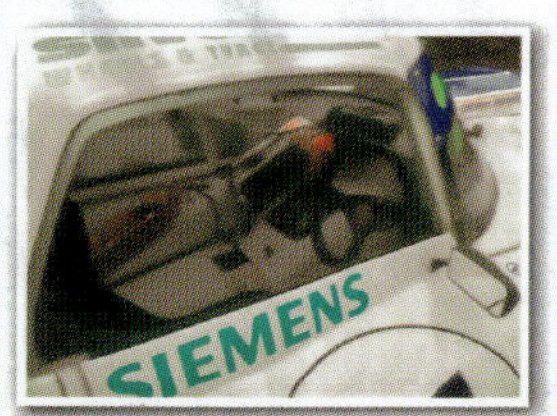

Almost ready to race again.

The rear end rebuild with defuser in place.

24 JAGUAR ENTHUSIAST *August 2013*

Competition E-Type history/originality (*Jaguar Enthusiast*, July 2009)

Competition E-type History/Originality

"I can remember racing E-types commanding around £1000, but now 'aluminium cars with history' can fetch over £300000."

Peter Griffiths discusses aspects of

I have been passionate about the Jaguar E-type and, in particular the competitive models, from the 1960s (which must hint at my age now!). I have been concerned, from time to time, to find that 'original' cars suddenly re-appear, seemingly from nowhere, in pristine condition, complete with 'histories' in order to command high prices when presented at auction.

I would therefore welcome feedback from my articles on members' views as to whether a total rebuild to a totally different specification constitutes 'continuous history' as the court's phrase it, or whether the old crashed cars should die forever. According to the courts ruling (on, for example, the famous Old Number 1 Bentley, several D-types and numerous Ferraris) 'continuous history' seems to imply that it is impossible to totally destroy an old car!! Probably because of this ruling, old 'dead' cars have now started to reappear, and long forgotten E-types have all been resurrected.

It seems a dreadful shame to me that the current trend for every rebuilt racing E-type to look like one of the factory lightweights has detracted from the flair and individualism of the 60s and 70s when every E-type was recognisable by its colour, its wide wheels/ arches, its bonnet design, with Perspex and fibreglass everywhere. Nowadays all the cars look the same, silver/aluminium, peg-drive "D style" wheels, roof and boot vents, sill extensions, etc etc. These are purely clones of the factory originals which were never continuous race winners even in the 60s.

Naming and Shaming

I propose to write about a different car in each article. I will not be too contentious but will leave the reader to consider the points raised and draw their own conclusions as to how 'genuine' the current car/recreation is. My extensive history files on the racing E-types has allowed me to draw on personal photos and information to illustrate my own personal views. I have been taking and collecting photographs of racing E-types since the 60s. Sometimes I don't even recognise a car which I will have photographed a few weeks before, simply because of colour change, or more drastically, complete body style changes.

For example, to give you a taste of things to come…. One of the ex–Dick Protheroe cars was a FHC but is now a roadster! The Peter Preston FHC is now a lightweight replica! The Ziebart sponsored modsports FHC is now a low drag coupe! The list is endless… in an attempt to rebuild the cars to 'original' specification, many old warhorses have been destroyed (literally) and their histories attached to gleaming new replicas. I personally believe these are excellent copies/ replicas, but they are not original. It is no secret that these shiny replicas then turn up at race meetings to 'continue their history': it seems ironic that at the moment there are plenty of race meetings available for this kind of car, (Goodwood being a prime example) but extremely few available for the originals!

I would be extremely happy to hear from anyone with a racing E-type or historical information anyone may have on the racing E-types including photographs. Hopefully this series of articles will put me back in touch with some long lost friends. During the 70s and 80s I was a Director and Treasurer of the Jaguar Drivers' Club. I was Secretary of the JDC E-type register, and often Club Steward at the JDC Silverstone race meetings. ie. I was there at the time! Sadly, E-types disappeared and reappeared then just as now but this trend is perhaps easier to achieve nowadays with so many restoration firms, it is certainly now more financially viable. I can remember racing E-types commanding around £1000, but now 'aluminium cars with history' can fetch over £300000.

If anyone would like to discuss such issues or has suitable information for me, please email: griffths418@btinternet.com ■

July 2009 JAGUAR ENTHUSIAST 29

CUT 7, the ex-Dick Protheroe E-Type (*Jaguar Enthusiast*, August 2009)

JAGUAR E-TYPE FORUM

CO-ORDINATOR: GARETH KEY TEL: 01473 742648
EMAIL: GARETHJKEY@HOTMAIL.COM
TECHNICAL ADVICE: COLIN FORD, 52 PRESTON DR., BEXLEYHEATH, KENT, DA7 4UQ
BODYWORK & PAINTWORK ASSISTANCE: ALAN PROCTOR – TEL: 01909 501660

CUT 7 – The Ex-Dick Protheroe E type

Peter Griffiths throws down the gauntlet over what constitutes an original competition car.

To try and unravel the mystery of the car known as CUT 7 is like trying to unravel the history of just about every other racing E-type from my favourite period of the 60s and 70s. The detailed transformations, change of number plates, even change of body (including change from fixed head to roadster) make the trail of 'continuous history' almost impossible to follow.

So, how many CUT 7s or Ex-DP cars are there? Well you can argue either 3, 4, 5, or 6 depending on your point of view. I shall try to give details of the cars I know, then readers can make up their own minds as to how rare 'the ex-Dick Protheroe car' really is!

Disintangling the Mystery

It is widely acknowledged that the first E-type raced by Dick Protheroe was a FHC chassis number 860004, and registered CUT 7 (or was it?). Being the fourth fixed head this seems fairly accurate! The car started life in opalescent gunmetal grey paint. I have a period photo of the car in grey paint when it also had a pale blue nose band.

Dick was quite competitive with his new car and the successes quoted in his for sale advertisement when he was selling the car said:- *"Only raced in the1962 season – Crystal Palace GT lap record, Crystal Palace race record, Silverstone Club Circuit GT lap record, RAC Tourist Trophy 7th. Present holder Norbury Trophy, AMOC USAAF Trophy, Autosport Championship over 30 00cc award."*

When Dick sold this car in January 1963 the registration number CUT 7 was transferred onto his new E-type (EC 1001), the lightweight low drag coupe.(or was it…see later).

However to continue with this FHC, it was now campaigned by Roger Mac during the 1963 season. (Or was it? – According to Andrew Whyte (Jaguar Sports Racing and Works Competition Cars from 1954). Like most Jaguar enthusiasts, I tend to regard Andrew Whyte's books as 'Jaguar Bibles', but it seems he must be mistaken….. if what he wrote is true, then the identity of other Protheroe cars must be in doubt.

The histories have been pieced together from several sources, but for the sake of completeness the reader should be aware of the following comments…

In Andrew's book he says that Dick Protheroe used to race an XK120 registered CUT 6. Andrew says that DP's first E-type was also CUT 6 and also says that the FHC which Cunningham owned (painted white with blue stripes), was DP's first E-type, (not his second… see later).

Also, author Paul Skilleter in his book Jaguar Sports Cars, states *"DP.. In September 1961 had taken delivery of a FHC E-type….. Registered CUT 6… this car was to have a considerable amount of success in British club racing over the 1962 season".*

The question therefore is – Was the first E-type Dick owned CUT 6 (as stated by Paul in 1975 and Andrew in 1987)? Did they both quote from the same source? Are these respected writers both right, or both wrong?

Martin Buckley in the *Classic Cars* magazine of Spring 2002, seems to have written the definitive article on the history of this car helped by Gerry Marshall who has researched its history.The time scale seems to be that DP raced the car for 15 races in 1962 before putting it up for sale in August 1962. He retained the CUT 7 number to transfer onto his second E-type, and the original E-type was re-registered 636 CJU.

The car was advertised again in January 1963 and finally found a buyer in February 1963… A Mr. Clive Castle from London. Clive was not happy with the car, and it ended up at Universal Salvage at Luton. They sold it to Mike Moore of Broomstick Motors who repaired the somewhat damaged car. He competed in one race, cut the bulkhead to give himself more legroom, and even fitted a sunroof.

This car then "passed through " a couple of owners, (one possibly being John Harper) before being purchased by Ted Walker (Ferret Photographs), who used it as a road car. The car then ended up with John Brown, who turned it back into a race car, did one race before putting the 'Famous race car'

28 JAGUAR ENTHUSIAST *August 2009* www.jec.org.uk

The ex-Protheroe car when owned by Dave Wilding, still at that time with the Perspex rear door and wire wheels. By 1991 the car appeared at Donington with a standard rear door and lightweight E-type wheels, then later that year sported a gold nose and the CUT 7 registration – John Young advertising the car for sale.

into a Coys auction. It sold to Dougie Bell, who didn't use it very much, and this is when Gerry Marshall acquired it. The car is now owned by Nick Whale and Ian Guest.

NB. There seems to be no mention of Dave Wilding, or John Young as owners?

Before the 2002 article the only written history is referred to below but there seems to be a gap of about 10 years after Dick disposed of the car.

The car, then re-registered 636 CJU, appeared in the Jaguar Driver magazine in 1973 and Classic Car magazine in 1974 when Paul Skilleter wrote an in depth article on it. The car now appears as metallic green! By this time the previous features of the large air scoops behind the doors had disappeared (!) as had the complete Perspex rear door.

The car had definitely been rebuilt at least once and later appeared in bright red livery (still registered 636 CJU) owned by Dave Wilding. Jaguar Driver magazine referred to the car as "David Wilding's car definitely claiming to be chassis No.4 as registered to Dick Protheroe in 1962." Another caption in Jaguar Driver says *" Spiritual successor to CUT 7, Dick Protheroe's racing E-type awaits the fray with David Wilding in the hot seat."*

The Plot Thickens

Prior to his book in 1987, Andrew Whyte wrote a lengthy article in *Classic & Sportscar* magazine (May 1984), concerning CUT 7/256 DJU. There is obviously some doubt in Andrew's mind as to how many cars carried the plate CUT 7… he appeared to think only two. The article mentions the often written about 'second E-type', the' Special Coupe' made out of new parts supplied to DP for the purpose of building a 'lightweight' in order for him to be more competitive. It was registered CUT 7 on 22nd March 1963.The log book read… "E SPECIAL COUPE Chassis DP138 D5". Eight days later it was crashed at Silverstone but rebuilt in time for the Easter meeting at Goodwood, where it managed 4th in the Sussex Trophy race. Later, at Silverstone in May he came 3rd at the International.

AUTHOR'S NOTE… According to the website for British International Races 1963, both the above races were entered by CUT 7… EC 1001..ie, the Low Drag Coupe. Is there confusion between the Special Coupe and the one-off low drag coupe?

AWs article mentions the low drag coupe as the second car to bear CUT 7.

The Special Coupe was raced for the last time at Whitsun, so perhaps competed in six or so races in all?

On the 10th June 1963 the logbook stated £5 retention fee paid for CUT 7; 256 DJU issued in place'. The new owner of the Special Coupe was Roger Mac.

According to John Young's "for sale" advert for the above CUT 7, he states "The second car was made from a kit of parts obtained from the factory in an attempt to create a lightweight. It was sold to Roger Mac at the end of the 1963 season... (INCORRECT:: ROGER MAC SOLD IT AT THE END OF THE 1963 SEASON) "...and registered 256 DJU." (confusingly or annoyingly similar to 636 CJU). HOWEVER, contemporary photographs of 256 DJU show it clearly as a FHC with identical air scoops to CUT 7/636 CJU. (Hardly a lightweight spec car?)

Thoroughbred and Classic Cars magazine of May 1990 stated that this car was the second car to carry CUT 7 before the number was given to the low drag coupe. This second car now registered 256 DJU was sold to Roger Mac. After Mac acquired a genuine lightweight for himself, he sold 256 DJU to David Cunningham who painted it white with blue stripes 'a la' Briggs Cunningham! (no relation, still confused?). Paul Vesty (apparently? see below) then bought the car and when this was written off this second FHC was rebuilt as a lightweight replica… yes, a roadster (confused?). Later John Lewis bought the car although he did sell the car only to buy it back a few years later. In John Lewis's hands it was registered SVJ 345 (confused again?) although on the track it still carries the 256 DJU registration number.

A readers letter in T & CC referring to the May 1990 article said:- "The car's early history is correct up to the statement that Paul Vesty bought it. He did not. It was bought by myself and Vestey and driven alternately by myself and Vestey in about 20 races during 1965 and 1966.

The cars original D-type engine destroyed itself at Snetterton whilst being driven by Vestey and it was replaced by a standard 3.8 litre engine from a scrapped saloon. The original aluminium bonnet , which had a different power bulge to those of other E-types, was destroyed at Goodwood, again whilst being driven by Vestey. This was replaced by a glass fibre one. The car was subsequently written off by myself at Silverstone and what was left, which wasn't much, was rebuilt into a new bodyshell. The last time it was driven before being sold to John Lewis was by myself at Silverstone.

To describe the car as it is today as being Dick Protheroe's CUT 7 which then became Roger Macs 256 DJU seems a slight exaggeration. Probably the only original part left is the steering wheel, which I have. Perhaps other readers have some thoughts on rebuilds, and at what point a rebuild becomes a different car". Richard Ward, Cobham, Kent.

What still confuses the author is why did Protheroe sell his first FHC only to replace it with an identical looking one? Why did he not just lighten his first race proven car? If he wanted a lightweight car why did he choose a FHC bodyshell?

Let's Recap – So Far

Car No. 1 – CUT 7…636 CJU
Chasiss No. 860004 bought by Dick Protheroe – September 1961.
Sold – February 1963. (1963 season driven by Roger Mac.)
Sold – October 1963. By Roger Mac (Probably incorrect)
Then uncertain history, but later owned by Castle Moore, John Harper, Ted Waker, Brown, Bell, Dave Wilding, John Young, Whale and Guest.
Colour schemes – Opalescent grey with blue nose, metallic green, bright red, then bright red with gold nose and grey with blue nose.

Car No. 2 (No. 3?) – CUT 7...256 DJU (also registered SVJ 345)
Identical FHC built up from parts. Crashed at Snetterton and rebuilt. Rebodied as 1966 roadster after being written off again.
Raced by Dick Protheroe in 1963.
Sold to Roger Mac.
Sold to Cunningham, Ward, Vestey, Lewis.
Colour schemes – Grey with blue nose, white with blue stripes, dark blue with white stripe.

The Story Continues Next Month ■

CUT 7? Here seen in the hands of John Lewis when registered SVJ 345.

Roger Mac was driving this version of CUT 7 at Donington in 1991. Now the car sports a normal back door and lightweight wheels!

Those old E-Type racers (*Jaguar Enthusiast*, August 2013)

Those old E-type Racers

Peter Griffiths has written before on his investigative exploits into the old E-type race cars and continues with his thoughts this month.

Referring back to my earlier article on the Protheroe cars and all the variants of CUT 7, I am pleased to report that all the cars are still in existence. My subsequent article on 310 WK, the Warren Pearce car, also showed it still exists.

Now moving on and as most of you will know, the construction of our E-types is no different to other cars with a separate body and chassis. The dangers inherent in retaining an old rusty chassis means that many E-types now have replacement chassis (basically the engine support frames), although the body is more easily repaired with many firms now offering after-market repair panels.

So, we are back to my favourite subject of originality. Why, oh why, have so many E-type race cars been rebuilt with everything "new" and turned into Lightweight replicas? I lost track years ago of the number of such replicas but it probably runs into hundreds, if not thousands.

There was a well known E-type that was changed from a successful Modsports fhc into an aluminium Low Drag Coupe (LDC lookalike). The car was a 1962 fhc, chassis No. 860182, which was successfully raced by Nick Crocker and Robin Cardwell in the 1970s and 1980s. Whilst at Fred Cliffe's workshop in the early 1990s for yet another rebuild, it was purchasd in partly restored Modsports form to become the basis of an LDC project.

Simon Dunford was commissioned to replace the fiberglass panels with aluminium ones and replace the fhc roof with an LDC conversion. The beautiful wide racing wheels and tyres were replaced with alloy LWE replicas and the entire car was transformed into an immaculate fast road going car. The resultant light green metallic sports car is fabulous but probably the "history" element and bulkhead are the only "original" parts.

I would like to know what you would prefer, the car that looked like the one that raced or the one that didn't? Also…is it sacrilege to destroy old racers in this way?

I hope you will have enjoyed reading my previous articles on the originality of E-types as particularly applied to the race varieties from the 1960s onwards. The article on the CUT 7 variants brought in a multitude of correspondence and information, including very welcome and much appreciated detail from Pat Wells, who was a mechanic for Dick Protheroe. In fact, I have enough material to produce another couple of articles and I was very pleased to have had such a response, thankfully all positive.

The Nick Crocker, Robin Cardwell 1962 E-type fhc Modsports racer, that ened up as an aluminium LDC.

Although I have extensive files on racing E-types and their drivers, I do wonder what has happened to all the cars and, of course those drivers.

At the E-type 30th anniversary meeting at Donington circuit in 1991, an attempt was made to get many of these cars and drivers back together at the one venue. The list then included John Quick, Warren Pearce, Roger Mac, Jack Lambert, Robin Sturgess, John Oxborough, Tony Shaw, John Lewis, peter Sutcliffe, Herbert Shepherd and many others – what a collection indeed.

Although I do not know the whereabouts of several cars, it would be wonderful to track them all down together again even if only for just one more time (before we all get too old!). Hopefully not all of the cars have been turned into Lightweights and individuality still exists.

The images I supply this month show a selection of cars from the 1960s and 1970s to see if they jog any memories as your input is required please. If you recognize and know the whereabouts of any of these old racers, then please get in touch to let me know. Several members have expressed an interest in getting an E-type race series going again so let's see if we can help.

Peter Griffiths – email: griffiths418@btinternet.com

This pale yellow fhc belonged to Miki Smith and then Brian Russel.

The ex-John Burbridge fhc.

Taken at the Silverstone circuit, this is the Harry Phillips/Dave Moore/Mick Hill fhc.

Back at the Silverstone circuit, this was the well known "Ziebart" fhc.

Taken at Brands Hatch, this is the Extreme fhc of Dick Whittington's.

Taken at Donington in 1991, this was Chris Shipton's fhc.

An E-Type racing history (*Jaguar Enthusiast*, December 2008)

Peter Griffith's Modsports E-type in the early days, here seen in competition with another Club member's car, the V12 belonging to Ron Lea.

An E-type Racing History

by Peter Griffiths

The story of my own car, not a lightweight lookalike recreation (which seems so popular these days), but a faithful rebuild/refurbishment of what it looked like when it last raced in anger. For me, keeping as much as possible of the original car was of paramount importance. Modsports racing cars, from the 60s to 80s era when most E-type racers earned their stripes, were wide wheeled monsters where fibreglass was the order of the day, not aluminium or, dare I say, carbon fibre.

My car started life as a Fixed Head Coupe in the hands of Alan Leeson who supercharged the car in the late 60s and was immediately successful. Philip Porter's book; 'The Jaguar E-type ----The Definitive History', recalls... "The 1970 British club scene saw E-types picking up a prodigious number of firsts in modsports racing, with such pilots as Ted Worswick, John Burbidge, Alan Leeson with a supercharged car, and Tony Shaw well to the fore." Philip Porter also recalls Leeson's results at Brands Hatch as 2nd in a race on the 1st November 1970, and first a week later, also at Brands.

Paul Skilleter's book; 'Jaguar Sports Cars', recalls the home counties racing in the late 60s as well. There is an excellent photograph in Paul's book showing the supercharged engine....."possessed of a great turn of speed down the straight".

Still retaining its supercharger Alan continued to campaign the car until it was sold to John Oxborough in 1974. whom campaigned it until 1977, and took part in some 66 races. In 1975 he came 4th in the BRSCC Midland Motorsport Championship (3 litre); in 1976 he came 2nd in the BRSCC Modsports Championship (3 litre); and finally in 1977 he achieved 1st place in the NSCC Dick Protheroe Modsports Championship (3 litre).

Although John retained the supercharger for a while, in 1975 he decided to change the 3.8 supercharged engine (including special skirt pistons) for a more 'driveable' 4.4 litre Weber carburettor unit. Then, along with so many modsports cars of the time, there was a need to 'save weight' so, in 1976 he cut the roof off the car and turned it into a roadster, adding a fibreglass hardtop and rear wing... quite outrageous, but made it very quick.

During 1976 the car was seen in a new green livery with Viking Engineering as its main sponsor. Then in 1977 the car found a new sponsor in JEB Wheatley and the car was repainted light blue. John campaigned the car at most UK circuits including.. Mallory Park, Aintree, Silverstone, Rufforth, Longridge, Oulton Park, Donington, Cadwell Park, and Croft with some memorable results. In all of his 66 races John only had 2 mechanical failures, and 2 minor accidents. John, from Mansfield, became a local celebrity, and many local papers carried reports of his exploits including the local Observer and Evening Post.

In early 1978 John sold the car to Dave Moore, his team mate in the 1976 Six Hour Relay. David had sold his earlier car to Ron Lea, and knew a good car when he saw one!

David, a garage proprietor from Liverpool, modified the car to his own taste. A new bonnet was put on, and the car sprayed red. He campaigned it at Oulton Park, Mallory Park, Silverstone and Donington, his regular tracks but success was often thwarted by Malcolm Hamilton, with David having to accept 2nd spot on more than one occasion. If you cannot beat them, join them... Final success came in 1986, as part of the JDC Intermarque team, when the team beat the Astons, Porsches and Ferraris, to win the Intermarque Challenge. A photograph of the victorious team (Davids car now

The Leeson car when purchased by Peter.

painted red and silver) appeared in Andrew Whytes book; 'Jaguar, Sports Racing and Works Competition Cars from 1954'. David's two sons, Weston and Stephen have also tried their luck with the car, and as a consequence the car finally ended up repainted again, this time in dark blue.

And that's when I bought it!

I bought the car in 2007 when certain parts were missing (mainly the engine and gearbox), although the car was substantially complete; a rolling chassis and of course I recognised it immediately, and was lucky enough to purchase it from Anthony and Richard Taylor at Autotune, the Jaguar replica builders (and also members of the Club).

As part of my E-type racing memorabilia collection, which includes bonnets, doors, bootlids, wheels etc., I was lucky enough to have acquired the original supercharger, pistons, belts, pulleys and brackets from the E-type when John Oxborough had removed them back in the 70s. At long last the parts could be reunited with the car.

Taking John's advice during the rebuild he had considered a 4.2 litre Weber carbed engine which would have been more sensible, and allow the car to be more usable. But, with the supercharger back with the car to stay, I ask John Oxborough to rebuild the car for me in 2007 and ideally he was the best man for the job.

Amazingly, although the front bonnet support frame had to be replaced following a minor accident with its previous owner, the main chassis frames on the car were still the originals. They still carry the extra support bar for the supercharger, as originally fitted by Alan Leeson. Because of their age, the frames were removed during the refurbishment, shotblasted, repaired and strengthened as required and refitted to the car.

John gave the car a 100% refurbishment, with every last nut and bolt removed, then repaired or replaced. The brief specification of the car is now:-

Bodywork: The main tub has been welded where necessary and the original roll-over cage checked. This is an integral part of the tub giving immense strength. The rear end of the car is moulded from the 'Warren Pearce' body mould in common with many racers from that period, allowing the huge 14" rear wheels plenty of room.

The E-type engine as built today with triple Webers.

The bonnet that came with the car has a large air dam/front spoiler which, although typical of the period, does not allow the bonnet to be opened without removing it fully. I decided to replace this with a more standard looking bonnet with just flared arches to cover the 12" front wheels. Doors are merely skins, with fabricated door catches and even the original door check straps have been retained.... these are spare lengths of supercharger belt!

Engine and gearbox..... 'a la period.'. a fairly standard rebuilt big valve 4.2 litre, mated to a 3.8 Moss gearbox for period feel. (it was what everyone wanted then.) It is fitted with new 45 DCOE Weber carburettors, which were set up by respected E-type and Lister racer Eike Welhausen of Chesterfield. The 'over the frame' exhaust which travels through and then exits out of the nearside sill is from the highly successful Mike Adams FHC which the Club sponsored along with the Hamilton car in the late 90s.

Suspension... the car has been lowered by the usual system of altering the front picture frame 'ears' upwards, and lowering the rear shock absorber mounting points on the half-shafts. The shock absorbers are adjustable Konis, and standard torsion bars are retained. The emphasis has been on reliability/driveability, which is a hallmark of John's long term success.

Wheels/tyres.... 14" rears and 12" fronts on slick tyres.

Inside... An 'almost standard' dash with (for history's sake) the supercharger pressure dial to remind the driver of the car's provenance. Drivers racing seat with 3-point full race harness. It has a built in battery box, and plumbed in fire extinguisher plus internal and external battery and fire extinguisher pulls.

Brakes... The front have V12 ventilated discs with new 4 pot callipers, the rears are standard discs with new XJS calipers.

The story changes direction

Just when I thought I had purchased, restored and planned to keep, probably the last remaining original race E-type and hopefully to race it, settle down and be happy... along comes another one to throw a spanner in the works.

During one of my many 'memorabilia searches,' I discovered that the Rob Beere/Malcolm Hamilton V12 (aka The Beast) could be bought. Absolute terror... what would the bank manager say, let alone my wife? This car, as everyone knows, must be the pinnacle of racing E-types.

I just had to have it. Unfortunately, the car was damaged in its last race in 2001 and needs a lot of work....but that's another story for another day.

The worst news is that this new project will need so much work that I have now decided to sell the Leeson car in order to fund the rebuild. Anyone out there interested? Give me a call.

The E-type as it is today, refurbished, back on the road and ready to race.

24 JAGUAR ENTHUSIAST DECEMBER 2008 www.jec.org.uk

Warren Pearce 310WK (*Jaguar Enthusiast*, November 2009)

JAGUAR E-TYPE FORUM

CO-ORDINATOR: GARETH KEY TEL: 01473 742648
EMAIL: GARETHJKEY@HOTMAIL.COM
TECHNICAL ADVICE: COLIN FORD, 52 PRESTON DR., BEXLEYHEATH, KENT, DA7 4UQ
BODYWORK & PAINTWORK ASSISTANCE: ALAN PROCTOR – TEL: 01909 501660

Peter Griffiths continues his controversial articles about historic E-types, this month he turns the spotlight on the Warren Pearce car – 310 WK.

Background

The 'Warren Pearce' E-type is probably one of the better known modsports cars from the sixties and seventies. The continual development of this particular car made it one of the fastest and most 'outrageous' cars from this period. Unless you have followed its career you will hardly be able to recognise it from one year to the next. Ever changing body design, colour schemes, and many owner changes have made it extremely difficult to keep up with 'the Warren Pearce' car.

The dark blue standard looking roadster of Warren Pearce is the same car as the bright yellow/blue striped car of Brian Murphy, which is the same car as the yellow ochre highly developed car of Fred Cliffe (the supremo of all things modsports E), which is also the same car as the pale blue/dark blue car of Ron Lea..... (which after its last accident, rebuilt in the style of the original Warren Pearce car with its dark blue paintwork!!). Certainly a clear case of full circle!

Warren (of Warren Pearce Motors), Cadogan Lane, London, SW1, specialised in Jaguar performance conversions. His adverts read of gas flowed cylinder heads, triple carburettor manifold conversions for all Jaguar models, brake and suspension modifications for competition work, etc. The complete one piece fibreglass rear end of most modsports roadsters became known as the 'Warren Pearce' back end. The original modsports 'styling' can in most cases be traced back to Warren for the roadsters, and to John Quick for the fixed heads. These were the two most successful drivers of this period.

Warren's successful escapades are well documented in *Autosport* magazines of the mid-sixties.

The early days

Warren's dark blue car (310 WK) originally ran on wire wheels, with bumpers and even a soft top! Paul Skilleters book, The Jaguar E-type, a Collector's Guide, has a great picture of Warren chasing 86 PJ (the ex-Tommy Atkins Lightweight E) during the Guards 1000 miles race at Brands Hatch in May 1965. A very 'standard' looking roadster.

By April 1966 an Autosport article shows the car had acquired a factory hard top, although the body still looked standard and still showed front quarter bumpers. This Mallory Park meeting reported in *Autosport* (29th April1966) gives Warren 1st place in the marque sportscars over 3,000cc as well as the fastest lap. A photo in *Autosport* at the end of the 1966 season reporting on the Snetterton meeting (21st October,1966) clearly shows how 310 WK had 'grown'. The wide rear end had appeared and was accompanied by a vented boot lid, similar to the Lightweights..... the modsports era had begun.

In the January 1967 issue of *Motor Sport* magazine there is an excellent article in which Warren's car is track tested. It reports on the excellent 1966 season recording 17 outright victories in 35 starts, 6 further Class wins, and 4 second places. The article gives an insight into Warren's racing history starting in 1952 and progressing to Jaguars (an XK120) in 1955 which made him catch the Jaguar bug. 310 WK came along in 1964.... 'a secondhand E-type which had been badly repaired after an accident'.

A brief synopsis of the initial modifications to the car reads as follows.....
Dunlop R6 racing tyres, on 6" rims at the front, and 6.5" rims at the rear. (later changed to splined Minilites with Goodyear tyres).
Substituting a 3.54 axle ratio for 2.9. (later changed to 3.77).
Koni shock absorbers fitted and the rear suspension lowered.
Special anti-roll bars.
Larger disc brakes from a Mark IX Jaguar.
Engine bored to 3.9 litres, gas flowed cylinder head with larger valves.
D-type camshafts and triple Weber carburettors.
Special inlet and exhaust manifold.
An aluminium bonnet was fitted, works fibreglass hardtop, and Perspex windows. Full roll cage added.

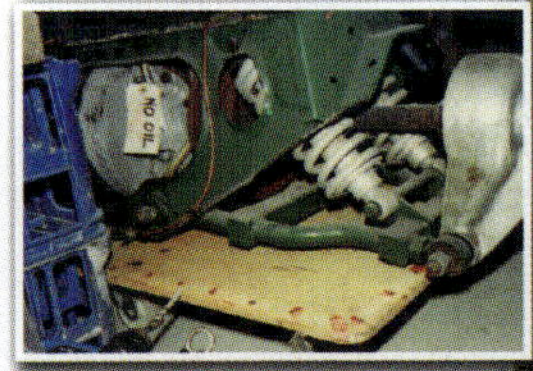

Special rose-jointed rear suspension, a Warren Pearce trade-mark, as fitted to this particular car during his ownership.

28 JAGUAR ENTHUSIAST November 2009 www.jec.org.uk

The 1970s

The car was briefly owned by Frank Wright in the early 1970s with limited development and after competing for several more years, in 1974 the car ended up with Brian Murphy from Liverpool, and the car was shown to the world via *'Cars and Car Conversions'* magazine in August 1976. The bright yellow car with blue stripes and revised bodywork looked nothing like the original 310 WK.

Brian had previously raced an E-type fhc which he sold to Richard Scantlebury, and this roadster would later be sold to Roy Standley. Both having RS as initials is yet another problem I seem to encounter in tracing histories!

310 WK as now modified, started to show the full extent of modsports styling during the 1970s. Wider wheels and wider wheelarches made for truly 'mean' looking cars. Brian's car now had beautiful Gotti split rim wheels, 10"x15 on the front and 12"x15 on the rear.

Brian pays tribute in the article to the Warren Pearce rear suspension set up; part of the whole package that gave him the edge over other racing Jags.

The 1975 season saw Brian winning the 3,000cc Class of the BRSCC Modsports Championship. According to the article the car 'was built for the 1975 season using a brand new, un-used monocoque, straight from the factory". (is this a new car?)

A synopsis of the car at this point is as follows....

Body... fibreglass bonnet, (ultra thin, moulded from John Quick's aluminium bonnet) with air dam. Fibreglass aftermarket (Lenham) lightweight hardtop, fibreglass doors with Perspex windows and one piece fibreglass rear end, even a fibreglass seat.

Brakes... CanAm ventilated discs, four pot callipers on the front, standard on the rear.

Suspension...Front... standard with rose jointed anti-roll bar. (this actual one now fitted on my car incidentally!) Spax shock absorbers. Rear... Modified Warren Pearce set up. Fully rose jointed and fabricated rear wishbones. Koni shock absorbers with modified coil springs.

Engine... 4.3 litre using +60 pistons. Triple Webers. D-type inlet manifold, home fabricated exhaust.

The magazine article gives the power at this stage as 340bhp.

310 WK in later years when at the time it was owned by Fred Cliffe.

Notice when the car was in Fred's ownership there was no front radiator, only a small oil cooler present!

The car re-appears later, now in the hands of Club member Ron Lea, here depicted at Mallory Park. Does anyone recognise the E-types behind. The photo is a little fuzzy but the registration number of the car on the left (dark blue coupe) appears to be something like FXD 830?. The number of the car in the centre is too fuzzy to read but the E-type on the far right seems to have a registration number GTW 377C?

The Cliffe era

The car was then campaigned by Roy Standley in its present form until it was eventually sold to Fred (Mr. Modsports) Cliffe. He was probably the most prolific E-type racer from the 1970s through to the 1990s. Most, if not all, modsports E-types have been built, repaired or modified at some time in their life by Fred. The Warren Pearce car is certainly no exception.

Fred set about a total rebuild of the car to his own demanding high standards. The most obvious modification was the decision to put the water radiator in the boot to aid weight distribution... well I think that was the theory. This involved the addition of huge air intakes just behind the doors which added to the cars already outrageous styling.

This picture was taken in 1992 and shows Fred Cliffe on the left with his "new" aluminium fhc and, on the right 310 WK, after a recent rebuild by John Oxborough (sitting on the car).

The wheels were now split rim Solar Mambas, 12's and 14's, making the appearance of the widest E type ever. The extra water needed to fill the pipe work to the rear radiator did unfortunately add extra weight but the overall balance of the car was improved.

Fred's high standards of preparation included chromed front frames, highly polished wishbones and suspension components, polished brass header tank etc, all giving a more concours appearance than a 70s racer. The car was painted in deep yellow ochre, with no sponsorship decals unlike earlier or later recreations.

Fred campaigned the car extensively and even entered the very last race at Rufforth in 1977, where he won his Class and achieved the fastest lap.

The Lea era

In 1982 the car passed into the hands of Ron Lea. At this point the car was repainted light blue/dark blue, Ron's company colours and sponsors. Unfortunately after only two races Ron crashed the car at Aintree in June 1982, and the car was locked away while Ron concentrated on racing his V12 E-type and replica D-type.

After 10 years, Ron decided on a rebuild of the car back to the original Warren Pearce specification of the 1960s. John Oxborough, a successful modsport builder and racer in his own right was commissioned to carry out the rebuild. A short story of the car along with the rebuilt car was shown in the Jaguar Driver magazine in June 1992.

Here again... is this a new car?

The car was exhibited at the Jaguar meeting at Donington that year, alongside Fred Cliffe's latest project, the aluminium fixed head.

This is 310 WK after rebuild in 1992. It is, at this stage, built to what it would have looked like in 1966/67.

The 310 WK number plate is missing and no hint of the heritage is shown; that is until the number plate re-appears in the early 90s on Ron Lea's rebuilt car.

Where is it now?

Believe it or not, since 1996 the car has resided in a sports car museum in Lany Czechoslovakia. If you are interested the car can be seen with current photos on the museum's website... auto-muzeum.cz.

From this website it seems as if the car may have been modified yet again to comply with current European standards in order to race again... we certainly hope so.

So, quite a long racing career... continual development, body and mechanical changes galore. To refer back to my first article on E-type recreations, is the above truly one car? I think so, because the history is continuous and complete. Probably the only original parts are the rebuilt Warren Pearce modified suspension bits which give an important link to the car's heritage.

My own modsports E-type memorabilia collection includes several items from the car - possibly enough for a replica? Certainly but perhaps not!

As stated before, members comments welcomed along with any further information on the cars I cover in these articles. ■

The front cover of Cars and Car Conversions magazine dating from August 1976 where 310 WK featured, the car then owned by Bryan Murphy.)

Appendix F

Racing E-Type toys and models

I am sure there are hundreds of Jaguar enthusiasts who collect models of their favourite cars. The E-Type in particular has been made in a wide variety of scales, from 1/64th up to the impressive 1/8th scale Monogram model. I think you would find it virtually impossible to collect one of every E-Type model ever made, and even collecting racing models has proved difficult. Just when I thought I was doing quite well, Paragon brought out a series of 1/18th scale Lightweight models at over £100 each – potentially, the collecting never ends.

Shown here are photographs of my collection – some code 3 examples, some made-up kits, but most straight out of the box.

The 1/18th scale Burago models have always intrigued me ... I have no idea where their registration numbers came from!

CUT 7 and 5114 WK look as accurate as can be, but why is the FHC race number 10 registered 5113 WK ... Do they know something we don't?!

The green roadster 004 WD ... I assume this could be 7004 WD, the Monte Carlo rally car.

The other Burago number plate seen on several models is 265 WK. I guess this could be a 'tribute' to just about any Lightweight.

The 'Best' dark blue FHC model, number 14, is presumably Dick Protheroe's CUT 7, but perhaps the makers didn't see the number plate clearly, as it is shown on the model as CUT Z.

I find it very annoying that the model makers have concentrated on standard cars, when presumably they can make several different cars/colours from the same mould. Models of 5115 WK, ECD 400, 1337 VC, and the Le Mans cars, for example, are readily available, yet I cannot find a model of WOO 11, 310 WK or *any* modsports E-Type. The only model I have found is a bespoke example of the Malcolm Hamilton V12, from Gary Oxley Models.

Burago 1/18 models.

Lightweight models.

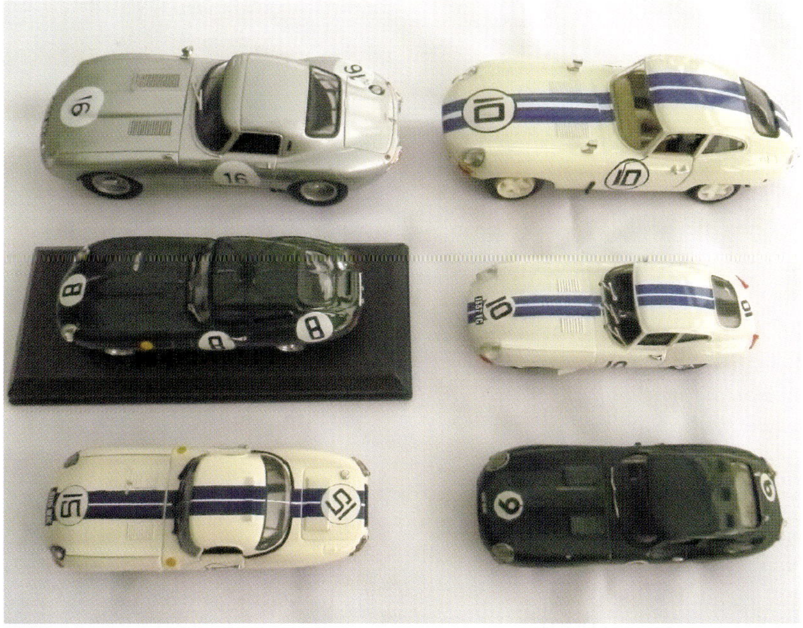

Le Mans models.

Early racers.

Malcolm Hamilton V12.

Rally models.

Odds and ends.

Appendix G

Suggested reading

The Jaguar E-Type – A Collector's Guide, by Paul Skilleter. Published by Motor Racing Publications Ltd. (Contains a great chapter on the E-Type in competition with a large number of period photographs covering many racing E-Types, also a chapter devoted purely to the 12 Lightweights.)

Jaguar Sports Cars by Paul Skilleter. Published by Haynes Publishing Group. (Contains many black and white original and period racing E-Type photographs. Excellent coverage of early racing and E-Type competition and development.)

Jaguar The Sporting Heritage, by Paul Skilleter in association with The Jaguar Daimler Heritage Trust. Published by Virgin Publishing Ltd. (Chapter on 'Spirit of the '60s' with excellent large photographs.)

All About The Jaguar E-Type by Paul Skilleter. Published by Paul Skilleter Books. (Chapters on Lightweights and modsports.)

The Jaguar Driver's Year Books by Paul Skilleter. Published by The Magpie Publishing Company. (Series of three books that detail club events – with photographs – of the late 1970s.)

Norman Dewis of Jaguar – Developing the Legend, by Paul Skilleter with Norman Dewis. Published by PJ Publishing Ltd. (Large comprehensive book with a chapter on developing the E-Type, including early racing and Le Mans.)

Jaguar – C-Type, D-Type & Lightweight E-Type Register by Terry Larson, Penny Woodley, Den Carlow and Paul Skilleter. Published by Anglo Danish Publications ApS. (A detailed description of each car chassis by chassis – not only the Lightweights, but Semi-Lightweights, ZP cars and other early racers.)

Jaguar XK – Forty Years on, by Andrew Whyte. Published by Aston Publications Ltd. (Many previously unseen photographs of the Lightweights and early racers.)

Jaguar Sports Racing and Works Competition Cars from 1954, by Andrew Whyte. Published by Haynes Publishing Group. (A bible for all Jaguar competition cars, including enormous amounts of information on the privateers' cars.)

Ultimate E-Type – The Competition Cars, by Philip Porter. Published by Porter Press International Ltd. (The definitive work on the 12 Factory Lightweights and special competition cars including E2A, the two Semi-Lightweights, and the Protheroe Low Drag Coupe. Also a chapter on the early racing by the Factory and privateers.)

Jaguar, Lightweight E-Type – The Autobiography of 4 WPD by Philip Porter. Published by Porter Press International. (320 pages devoted to the first Lightweight E-Type. The definitive work on this one car.)

Jaguar Sports Racing Cars, C-Type, D-Type, XKSS, Lightweight E-Type, by Philip Porter. Published by Bay View books Ltd. (Detailed descriptions including an appendix of chassis numbers.)

Jaguar E-Type The Definitive History, by Philip Porter. Published by Haynes Publishing Group. (Covers all E-Types with several chapters on the competition cars, also an excellent appendix on the E-Type's competition results from 1961 to 1970.)

The Iconic E type – Celebrating 50 years of the E-Type Jaguar, by Philip Porter. Published by the Jaguar E-Type Club and Porter Press International. (Includes some fabulous motor racing photographs.)

Jaguar – History of a Classic Marque, by Philip Porter. Published by Tiger Books International. (Contains some nice photos of the Lightweights.)

E-Type – End of an Era, by Chris Harvey. Published by The Oxford Illustrated Press Ltd. (This original 1977 version has a chapter on the racing E-Types with many excellent early photographs.)

E-Type – End of an Era, by Chris Harvey. Published by The Oxford Illustrated Press. (This new 1985 edition has a wonderful additional chapter with lots of previously unpublished racing E-Type photographs.)

Jaguars in Competition, by Chris Harvey. Published by Osprey Publishing Ltd. (Includes a fabulous chapter on the Factory and private race E-Types, concentrating mainly on the early racers.)

Great Marques – Jaguar. By Chris Harvey. Published by Tiger Books International. (Includes some great large photos and a section on racing E-Types.)

Jaguar E-Type – A Celebration of the World's Favourite '60s Icon, by Nigel Thorley. Published by Haynes Publishing. (The second edition published in 2011 contains a few extra racing E-Type photographs to the already extensive photo collection of the original 2001 edition.) Now published by Veloce Publishing.

If At First You Don't Succeed ... The Life Story of Ron Lea, by Ron Lea. Published by Melrose Books. (Contains many colour photographs of his three racing E-Types, excellent pictures.)

Cat out of the Bag – Jaguar, The Competition Department 1961-1966, by Peter Wilson. Published by Bookmarque Publishing. (A uniquely authentic account of the Lightweight E-Type development and production by Peter Wilson, who worked there at the time.)

Those Were the Days ... The Brighton National Speed Trials in the 1960s, 1970s & 1980s, by Tony Gardiner. Published by Veloce Publishing. (Includes photographs of E-Types that took part in the trials over those years.)

50 years of the Jaguar E-Type from the makers of *Classics Monthly* magazine. (A 200-page collector's edition on various E-Type articles, including Derek Bell testing CUT 7, the LDC, at Goodwood.)

Jaguar – The Legend, by Jonathan Wood. (Great photos of CUT 7, E2A, 5114 WK, 5115 WK and Pierre Bardinon FHC.)

Jaguar E-Type – Celebrating the World's most Famous Classic Sports Car, a *Jaguar World Monthly* compilation. (Excellent articles including E-Types at Le Mans, and a history of John Filbee's racer.)

Historic Car Racing 3 – Jaguar/Grand Prix de Lausanne, by Rob de la Rive Box. Published in 1983 by Motorstory. (Many racing E-Type photos, especially of 256 DJU.)

Appendix H

Useful websites

E-Type database	http://www.xkedata.com
Lightweights	www.coventryracers.com
Cars and Drivers	http://www.racingsportscars.com
Lightweight E-Types	http://www.wsrp.cz/chassis/chassis_jaguar.html
Worlds Fastest E-Type	http://www.fastjags.org.uk/start.htm
Re Dick Protheroe	http://www.myitshere.co.uk
American racers	http://donovanmotorcars.com
E-Type photos	http://www.paulskilleterarchive.co.uk
E–Type photos	http://www.flickr.com
E-Type photos/models	http://www.jagweb.com

E –Type books	http://www.paulskilleterbooks.co.uk http://www.veloce.co.uk
Racing parts/ engineering	http://www.rob-beere-racing.co.uk
Racing parts/ engineering	http://www.mandcwilkinson.com/racing

As well as specific websites there are numerous 'threads' on all manner of forums – Pistonheads and 10-tenths, for example. One such forum on modsports driver John Burbidge is:

http://www.network54.com/Forum/612068/thread/1215342188/John+Burbidge+1935+-+2008

Plus, there are of course hundreds of photos if you perform a Google image search for racing E-Types.

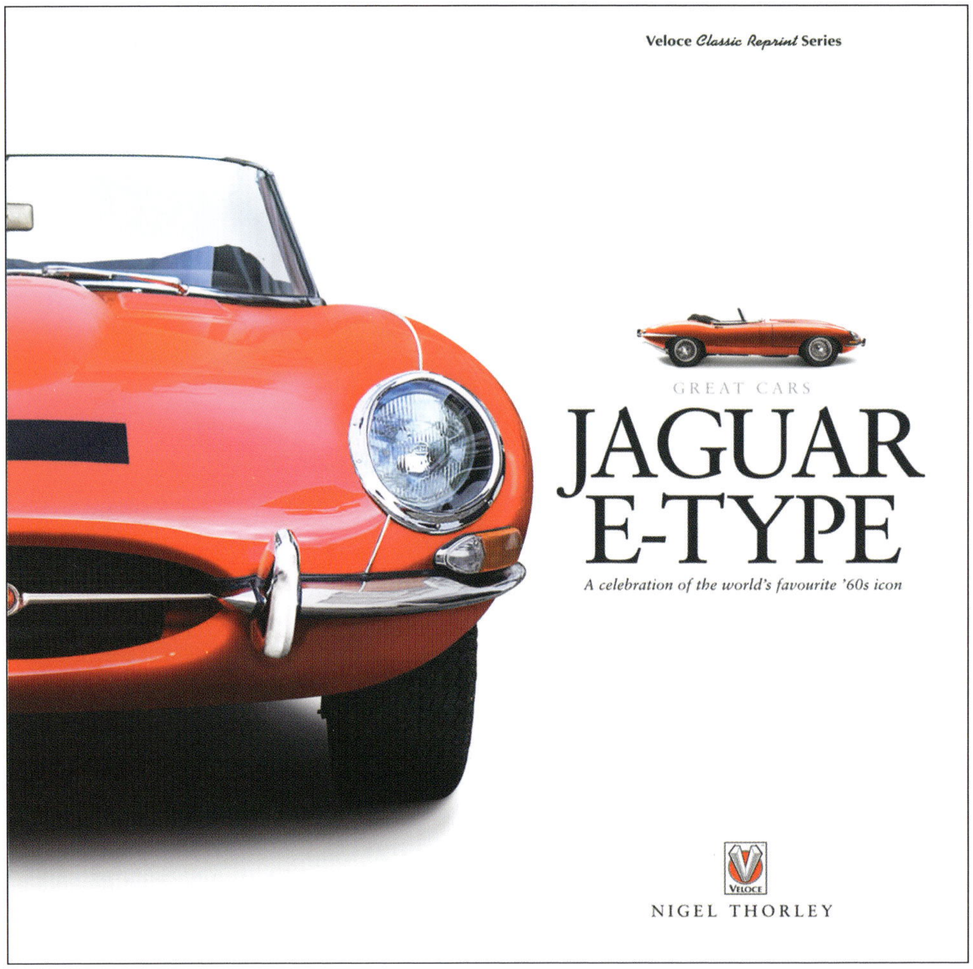

A fascinating look into the background, development and features of Jaguar's iconic E-Type in both historic and modern day terms, beautifully illustrated with superb archive images and modern studio photography.

ISBN: 978-1-787110-25-0
Hardback • 25x25cm • 184 pages • 264 pictures

For more information and price details, visit our website at www.veloce.co.uk
• email: info@veloce.co.uk • Tel: +44(0)1305 260068

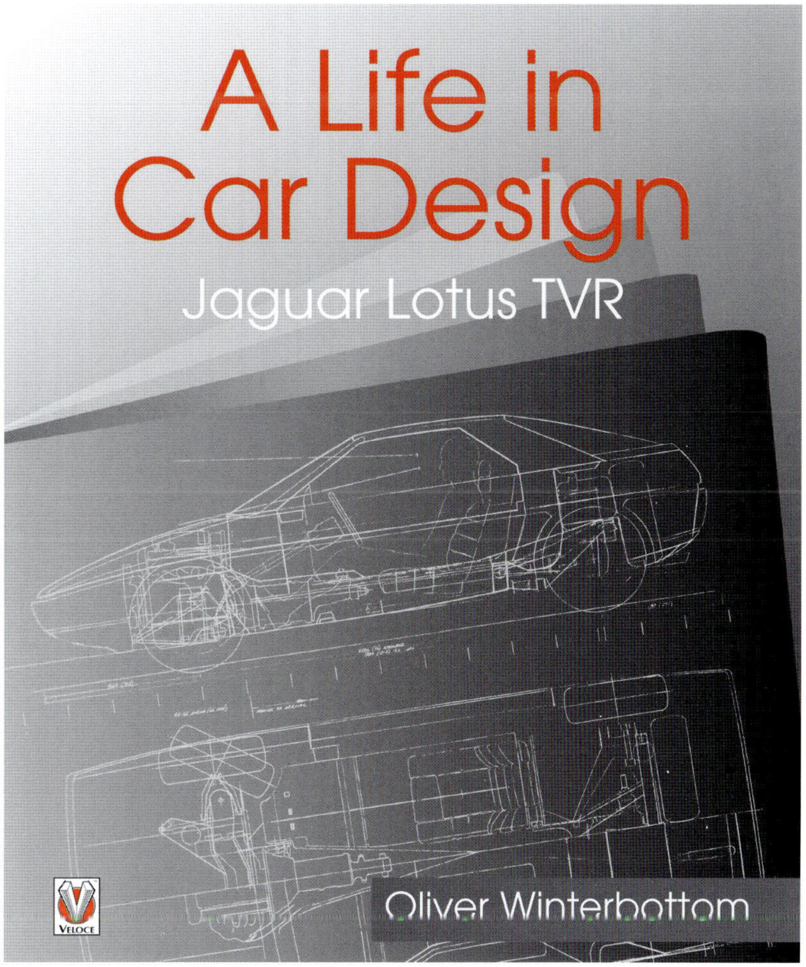

This book gives a unique insight into design and project work for a number of companies in the motor industry. It is aimed at both automobile enthusiasts and to encourage upcoming generations to consider a career in the creative field.
Written in historical order, it traces the changes in the car design process over nearly 50 years.

ISBN: 978-1-787110-35-9
Hardback • 25x20.7cm • 176 pages • 200 pictures

For more information and price details, visit our website at www.veloce.co.uk
• email: info@veloce.co.uk • Tel: +44(0)1305 260068

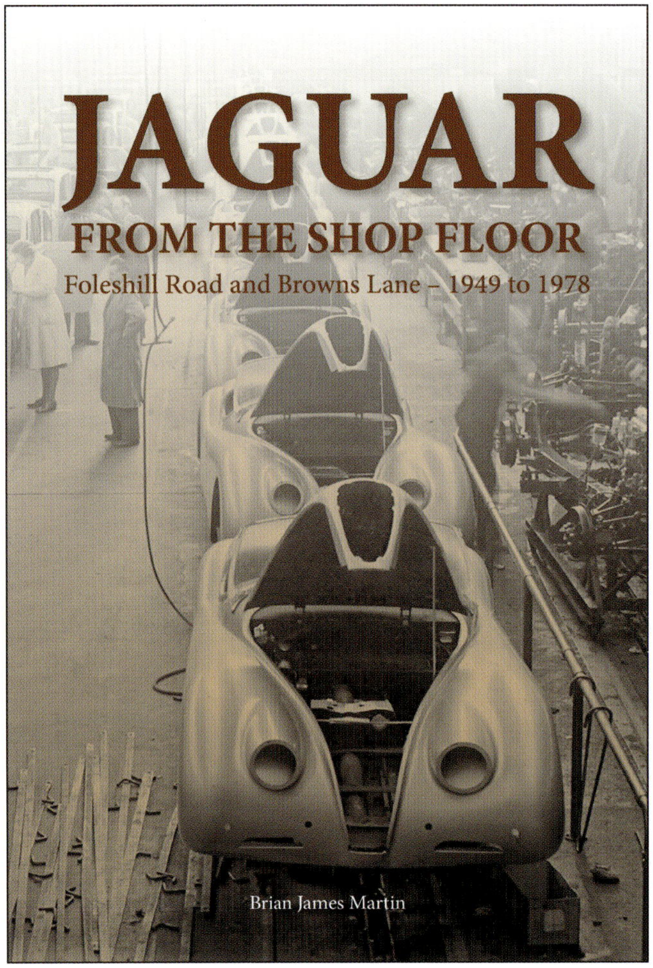

Part auto-biographical, and part historical, this book details life at the Jaguar company from the perspective of a long-time employee and enthusiast. Brian Martin's story tells of his experiences both on the production line and in the elite experimental department.

ISBN: 978-1-787112-79-7
Hardback • 23.2x15.5cm • 192 pages • 99 colour and b&w pictures

For more information and price details, visit our website at www.veloce.co.uk
• email: info@veloce.co.uk • Tel: +44(0)1305 260068